MESSY EUROPE

EASA Series

Published in Association with the European Association of Social Anthropologists (EASA). Series Editor: Aleksandar Bošković, University of Belgrade

Social anthropology in Europe is growing, and the variety of work being done is expanding. This series is intended to present the best of the work produced by members of the EASA, both in monographs and in edited collections. The studies in this series describe societies, processes and institutions around the world and are intended for both scholarly and student readership.

For a full volume listing, please see back matter

Messy Europe

Crisis, Race, and Nation-State in a
Postcolonial World

Edited by
Kristín Loftsdóttir, Andrea L. Smith,
and Brigitte Hipfl

berghahn
NEW YORK · OXFORD
www.berghahnbooks.com

First published in 2018 by

Berghahn Books

www.berghahnbooks.com

© 2018, 2021 Kristín Loftsdóttir, Andrea L. Smith, and Brigitte Hipfl
First paperback edition published in 2021

All rights reserved. Except for the quotation of short passages for the purposes of criticism and review, no part of this book may be reproduced in any form or by any means, electronic or mechanical, including photocopying, recording, or any information storage and retrieval system now known or to be invented, without written permission of the publisher.

Library of Congress Cataloging-in-Publication Data
A C.I.P. cataloging record is available from the Library of Congress

British Library Cataloguing in Publication Data
A catalogue record for this book is available from the British Library

ISBN 978-1-78533-796-3 hardback
ISBN 978-1-80073-207-0 paperback
ISBN 978-1-78533-797-0 ebook

Contents

List of Illustrations	vii
Introduction *Kristín Loftsdóttir, Andrea L. Smith, and Brigitte Hipfl*	1
1. Wise Viking Daughters: Equality and Whiteness in Economic Crisis *Kristín Loftsdóttir and Helga Björnsdóttir*	31
2. "Latvians do not understand the Greek people": Europeanness and Complicit Becoming in the Midst of Financial Crisis *Dace Dzenovska*	53
3. Fairness and Entitlement in Neoliberal England, 2005–2015 *Steve Garner*	77
4. Debating Refugee Deservingness in Post-Celtic Tiger Ireland *Shay Cannedy*	102
5. What Is a Life? On Poverty and Race in Humanitarian Italy *Andrea Muehlebach*	126
6. Policing Crisis in Austrian Crime Fiction *Brigitte Hipfl*	148
7. Crisis France: Covert Racialization and the Gens du Voyage *Andrea L. Smith*	171

8. Navigating the Mediterranean Refugee "Crisis": 196
   Alter-Globalization Activism and the Sediments of
   History on Lampedusa
   Antonio Sorge

9. Epilogue: Declining Europe 220
   Thomas Hylland Eriksen

Index 233

Illustrations

5.1. "They have robbed me of my future but no-one hears me. In Italy, 1 in 3 children are at risk of poverty."   127

5.2. Save the Children campaign "Every One," Italy 2009.   132

8.1. Cave at Cala Madonna, a purported sacred site presided over by a syncretic recluse in the early seventeenth century.   202

8.2. Seized migrant vessels deposited in the "boat graveyard" or eventual disposal.   204

8.3. Interpretive dance at opening ceremonies of LampedusaInFestival.   206

Introduction

Kristín Loftsdóttir, Andrea L. Smith, and Brigitte Hipfl

The economic crisis in Europe at the launch of the new millennium has coincided with a wider sense of crisis in other dimensions of social life. Economic perturbations have affected European countries in radically different ways, generating a growing sense of a future disrupted. They have also raised sharp debates about the relationships between European countries and their membership in the category "Europe"—debates that have intersected with past inequalities and racisms, both within and outside the continent.

In this book, we use the economic crisis as a starting point to look at wider issues of race, gender, and national understandings of self and other in contemporary Europe. We critically examine imaginings of Europe within and in the aftermath of economic crisis, highlighting Europe's historical association with whiteness and modern civilization, and explore how these are re-envisioned or contested within an era that increasingly seems to be characterized by crises of different kinds (Loftsdóttir and Jensen 2014). We invited scholars to link their own research and analysis with the key questions posed here in order to provide case studies from different national contexts on crisis and European racialized identities and subject positions.

While economic crises are often theorized as purely economic issues or—within European contexts—problems related especially to social welfare questions, this book offers a different perspective, one based on a longstanding tradition in anthropology and critical theory in which the economy is seen as an intrinsic part of society and thus as embedded in a larger nexus of social interactions and history (Schwegler 2009; Peebles 2010; Schneider 2002). As Stuart Hall stresses, "No crisis is only economic" (Hall and Massey 2012: 57). Crises—economic or otherwise—are moments of potential change, but they can also be implicated in the reproduction of social relations or prevailing power struggles (Gluckman 1954; Hall and Masssey 2012). In fact, economic crisis can create opportunities for multinational corporations and institutions to move social power further towards neoliberal goals, thus creating new prospects for some but not all, as Klein (2007) has shown. However, crisis also has potential to serve as a platform for radical change or as an avenue for creating different forms of resistance (Boyer 2013).

In this introductory chapter, we situate the central question of the book—the entanglement of crisis with whiteness and race—within theoretical frameworks that have critically evaluated postcolonial engagements of the present. The collection constitutes a contribution to critical research on race and European identities by providing a nuanced sense of how racialized identities in contemporary Europe are played out in the crisis context. We explore and unpack what we term "crisis talk," examining how such discourse motivates public feelings and affects, ultimately shaping bodies, boundaries and communities. We approach these questions from different disciplinary perspectives spanning the humanities and social sciences. While the book's main perspectives come from anthropology, we also draw insights from sociology and media studies. We situate this book within critical perspectives acknowledging the world as postcolonial—a perspective that has long been part of anthropological insights without necessarily being labeled as such (Loomba et al. 2005: 30). In contrast to scholars who claim that postcolonial perspectives are unable to grasp the changing power structures of the present (Hardt and Negri 2000), we share with Ponzanesi and Colpani (2016) the conviction that we need to investigate the "after-effects of colonialism" and how they are shaping current articulations of power.

Debates about Europe's predicament and future often mobilize or touch upon reified conceptions of "Europe," imagined as a fixed location inhabited by certain kinds of people. In this book we approach Europe differently, as a contested space and fluid construction with plural histories (Ponzanesi and Blaagaard 2011). This is made especially clear through empirically grounded case studies that elucidate specific understandings of self and other at specific times and circumstances. Coloniality is deeply saturated in our present, as Escobar (2007) and others have argued, serving as an "underlying logic" (Lee, Hongling, and Mignolo 2015: 187). These contributions emphasize how the articulation of this past and the salience of difference take shape in different European contexts within a time of turmoil. We ask how discourses and sentiments related to Europe and crisis draw upon past forms of categorization and evaluation while articulating with differences across the European continent. The title of the book, *Messy Europe*, is meant not only to emphasize Europe's economic crisis, but to draw attention to these messy identities and subjectivities that are in tension while they continuously shift, intersect and contradict one another.

Crisis Talk, Crisis Europe

The term "crisis" has its origins in the Greek verb *krinō*, to separate, choose, or judge (Koselleck 2006: 358). It developed distinct meanings in Greek legal, theological, and medical usages, but "at all times the concept is applied to life-deciding alternatives meant to answer questions about what is just or unjust, what contributes to salvation or damnation, what furthers health or brings death" (ibid., 361).[1] As German historian Reinhart Koselleck writes, the very ambiguity of the term turned it into a key concept, and from the 1770s on it became a "structural signature of modernity" (ibid.: 374). It has certainly become an organizing metaphor in the twenty-first century, comparable to the salience of the term "risk" in the 1990s. For Mary Douglas the appeal of "risk" comes from its "universalizing terminology, its abstractness, its power of condensation, its scientificity, its connection with objective analysis" (2003/1992: 15). Similarly, crisis texts are a "veritable industry" today (Roitman 2014: 3). Crisis is used to qualify the nature of any number of events, from "the humanitarian crisis" to "the energy crisis." As Roitman (ibid.: 3) observes, "through the term 'crisis,' the singularity of events is abstracted by a generic logic, making crisis a term that seems self-explanatory" (see also Kosmatopoulos 2014; Loftsdóttir and Jensen 2014).

Article and book titles signaling that a place called "Europe" is facing or has faced a "crisis" proliferate daily.[2] Texts as diverse as newspaper headlines and works in scholarly journals reveal a sense of foreboding and concern that wider forces are hampering the potential and promise of European countries and indeed others farther afield. Authors refer to "*the* economic crisis," "*the* refugee crisis," "*the* Eurozone crisis," "*the* subprime mortgage crisis," as if the referent was obvious to all. Yet accounts of these vary widely in location, timing, cause, and scale. Here we reflect more deeply on what it means to evoke crisis in this way.

In her work *Anti-Crisis* (2014: 3), Roitman explores what "crisis" *does* in social theory and in the construction of narrative forms. She underscores the way the "crisis" concept relates to historical consciousness and the ways events are narrated and understood. A declaration that something is "a crisis" or "in crisis" entails a kind of retrospective analysis, a claim that something has gone wrong, and thus carries an implicit or explicit judgment or critique. As Roitman argues, imagining a "crisis state" is possible only in "counter-distinction to imagined alternative societies" (Roitman 2014: 15), an exercise with a specific genealogy.

According to Koselleck, imagining a time of "crisis" became possible only after a shift in historical consciousness in the late eighteenth century. As a temporal division between future and past emerged, this shift was accompanied by a sense that the future should be different and, more precisely, *better* than the present.[3] This new historical consciousness is key to our understanding of the crisis concept and our analysis of "crisis Europe." When a moment is deemed to be one of "crisis," this crisis designation carries with it an implicit critique of the prevailing social order,[4] which is imagined in contrast to how it *should* be. Accounts of crisis, or crisis talk as we term them here, often contain attempts to diagnose the failure, to explain "what went wrong." The mere labeling of a period of time or a particular place or economy as one "in crisis" brings comparisons into the discussion: a "crisis moment" is understood as such only in contrast to some other era, some better past, present, or imagined future. When applied to the European context, this crisis talk brings to mind both the utopian promise of the EU, in contrast to the present moment, as well as idealized notions of Europeanness developed in previous, often colonial times. How do these past or promised social imaginaries compare with those of the present era? How do earlier ideas of European or national exceptionalisms, subjectivities, and talents enter into the equation when a time and place is labeled as one in crisis?

Crisis talk is thus not only descriptive but also performative, and in this book we ask what work the crisis label achieves. Claiming a period of time as one of crisis leads to the elaboration of certain questions and the silencing of others (Roitman 2014: 41). As Roitman reminds us, even the mainstream media are aware that declaring a crisis situation in extra-large font can actually generate the proverbial bank run (ibid.: 116). Which topics become foregrounded by conjuring up crisis, and which are kept to the side? Which kinds of answers and explanations are offered, and which kinds of sentiments are evoked? In her work on the Icelandic economic crisis, Loftsdóttir (2014: 3) similarly stresses the necessity of exploring "what 'crisis' does," pointing to crisis as an "exercise of power" where crisis and the idea of crisis produce different affects.

Roitman's (2014) analysis of "a dizzying array of crisis narratives" found in discussions of the 2007–2009 financial crisis suggests such an exercise of power and indicates how crisis talk can have lasting consequences. As she writes, these narratives "search for origins, sources, roots causes, reasons…none waver in their faith in crisis" (ibid.: 11). These works carry assumptions about how institutions like "the market" or "finance" should function, and thus try to explain how they deviated from some norm or ideal (ibid.: 41). In doing so, they fall into certain predictable patterns with lasting effects: "We should also ask what narratives are *precluded* by the crisis narrative, or the post hoc judgment of deviation, of failure. What are at stake are not only possible stories about the world, but also worlds" (ibid.: 41, emphasis added).

Crisis talk is a constantly shifting field. Indeed, when we first envisioned this volume, we had in mind the specific economic crisis facing so many European polities in the first decade of the twenty-first century. Yet once we focused exclusively on that economic crisis, we found that accounts vary widely in location, timing, and cause. In many works "Europe" is used as shorthand for the European Union, where the phrase "economic crisis" inevitably leads back to the monetary union and the survival of the Eurozone. Extensive discussions of the Eurozone in crisis in European settings raise concerns about the future of the EU, of relations between EU member states, of the Schengen agreement,[5] of the monetary union. Moreover, Europe-based crisis talk has shifted quickly from economic to social concerns as discussions of people migrating to Europe seeking asylum or work become entangled with concerns about the health and economic welfare of the society as a whole. Here, Western media depictions tend to perpetuate an "us/them" binary that is highly racialized. Theorization of Europe in crisis, therefore, cannot be explored without a serious look at the European Union in connection to wider political and economic frameworks. No longer simply a continent or an idea associated with the civilizing mission of the colonial era, "Europe" has become a remarkable social and political experiment, itself challenged by a rapid series of crises (Dervis and Mistral 2014: 7; Dobrescu and Durach 2014). The UK vote to depart from the European Union in June 2016 (Brexit) further stimulates the sense that the EU project is in crisis and the future is insecure and fragile (Coates 2017). Besides uncertainty about what Brexit really means for economic and trade relations, Brexit induces fears that anti-EU sentiment will spread. Parliamentary elections in the Netherlands (2017) and presidential elections in Austria (2016) and France (2017) are all examples in which the leading rival candidates are defined as either for or against the European Union. The British vote for Brexit revealed tendencies toward polarization within the European collective (Balibar 2016), with a part of the population of Europe characterized by an entanglement of anti-European, nationalist, and anti-immigrant sentiments that offer disadvantaged social groups a way to express their anger about their own miserable situation (Braidotti 2016) by scapegoating others.

However, talk of "crisis Europe" extends beyond EU boundaries to involve such countries as Switzerland and Norway, which are not members of the European Union but are connected to the regional and global economy, and Denmark, Sweden, and the United Kingdom (at the time of writing), which all are EU members but not participants in the monetary union. Further, a much wider, global optic comes into view in discussions of refugees, asylum seekers, and the suspension of the Schengen agreement. And debates about the fate of nations, whether within or outside the EU, as well as the fate of the EU itself, often mobilize or touch upon reified conceptions of "Europe," as we develop further here.

Finally, given the shifting focus of European crisis talk, agreement on a definitive beginning and end to the crisis is elusive indeed. In fact, new "crises" seem to emerge repeatedly in the wake of the previous ones; only the labels change. This is exemplified by the shifts in public discourse from "the" economic crisis, to worries that the fiscal crisis in Greece would affect all of Europe, to the EU's so-called "refugee crisis," to Brexit. This constant shifting of focus from one crisis to another clearly reflects the dominance of the crisis trope and indicates a need to further elucidate how crisis talk informs people's understanding and experience of the contemporary world. Like Roitman (2014: 94), we will not argue that all of these European crisis narratives are "false," or that they are "mere representations." Rather, crisis talk itself matters as an object to be analyzed and disassembled. As Roitman (2014: 3) writes, and as several chapters here demonstrate, crisis is mobilized to mark out or designate a "moment of truth," often defined as a "turning point in history" when decisions are taken and events decided. What kinds of decisions are being proposed in contemporary European societies in relation to dire economic indicators? How might nationalist understandings be mobilized as "meaningful and affective constructions" (Loftsdóttir 2014: 21) during moments deemed out of the ordinary, moments of apparent crisis? How might declaring a situation to be one of crisis allow for the resurrection of antiquated or suppressed racist ideologies?

In sum, there is clearly a sense of a place in flux on the European continent, often designated as a place in crisis. In this book we explore how "crisis Europe" is being experienced on the ground, the work to which crisis talk contributes, and the ways in which this experience intersects with, reinforces, or exacerbates contemporary and historical understandings of regional, racial, and gender hierarchies. If the different levels and forces that come together and fuse as crisis are dismantled, crisis can be approached as a "conjuncture," as suggested by Hall and Massey (2012: 55): "a period when different social, political, economic, and ideological contradictions that are at work in society and have given it a specific and distinctive shape come together." Detailed analysis of various linkages that are made, and of associations and identifications that are re-activated, result in deep insights into the complex entanglements that constitute crisis in different national contexts.

Race, Gender, Nation

Pervasive or punctuated periods of budget-tightening measures have led people to evaluate how the diminishing resources are distributed—who gets what and why. Such questions are often associated with the emergence and mobilization of racist ideologies. As we have seen again and again across the world, times of economic growth can be associated with expansive outlooks towards others, while times of trouble can lead to scapegoating and worse as resources shrink (Hilton 1979; Braidotti 2016). What effects has crisis talk had on people living in different European national contexts? Is the generalized anxiety unearthing ugly sentiments or accelerating the rise of integralism, outlined so effectively by Holmes (2000)? The 2015 escalation of refugees and asylum seekers in Europe—often labeled as the most serious refugee crisis since World War II—is accompanied by bifurcated compassionate reactions and anti-immigrant populists' racist claims. As Zizek (2015: 4) points out, an "anti-immigrant wave ... thrives all around Europe." In refugee crisis talk, the concepts of refugee, asylum seeker, and immigrant slide into each other in public discourse. As legal categories that both assign rights to particular groups and exclude others, the concepts "refugee" and "asylum seeker" have increasingly been contested for their narrowness. The colonial reverberations in anti-immigrant public discourses challenge Europe to confront both its colonial past and persistent racism (Hipfl and Gronold 2011: 29).

Tensions over resources typically foster increased racialization, or the re-racialization of populations who had been integrated into the national body. We see this in the cases presented, although in these settings bluntly racist ideologies are muted, for the most part. It appears to be untenable in wider circles to suggest that resources be divided up according to phenotype or ancestry (Desmond and Emirbayer 2009). Clearly a shift has occurred in the past half-century, at least in the contexts studied here, in that the rationale for the hierarchization of peoples is decidedly not due to purported biological inferiority, even if these hierarchies may map neatly onto colonial-era hierarchies. At the same time racism, far from disappearing, is often expressed in indirect language—covertly, as linguists often note (Hill 2008; Modan 2007). One of the key insights of recent race research is the acknowledgement that racism not only takes multiple forms in contemporary societies (Balibar 1991b), but also attaches itself to other features such as religion and culture, and in the process makes these phenomena difficult to untangle. The use of culture in this regard has been extensively demonstrated: "culture" becomes an explanation for the marginalized positions of certain groups, objectifying and homogenizing masses of people in ways reminiscent of past racializing practices. Racism in this sense is often embedded in the language of nationalism and ethnicity, and sometimes referred to as a "new" racism or "cultural racism" (Balibar 1991b; Abu-Lughod 2002; Bunzl 2005; Harrison 2002: 150). Hierarchies emerge and are reinforced, with people being ranked due to essentialist logic, purported behavioral traits, and moral worth, "even when the language of race is not mobilized" (Thomas and Clarke 2013: 307). The current crisis-talk about migration, coupled with increased economic insecurity, has created fertile ground for populist parties across Europe that feed into racialized nationalistic sentiments. Brexit can be seen as responding to and amplifying growing nationalist tensions in northwest Europe (Gingrich 2016), where the scapegoat becomes racialized minorities, refugees, and migrants (Açiksöz 2016).

The fact that racism "is not a single, static ideology" (Miles and Brown 1989/2003, 107) but situational and fluid has made it hard to define what racism is, and what it is not. Grosfoguel, Oso, and Christou (2014: 636) emphasize that racism is a "global hierarchy of human superiority and inferiority" that is produced culturally, politically, and economically so that racism can be marked by multiple variables such as phenotype, ethnicity, and language. As Desmond and Emirbayer point out, context matters: different racial classification schemes will be relevant in different societies, or in the same society in different eras. Moreover, race can be understood only in relation to gender, ethnicity, class, and nationality. As interrelated symbolic categories, they are mutually reinforcing and thus have to be understood in context and in relation to each other (Desmond and Emirbayer 2009: 339).

With the shift in focus away from race as revolving around an "other," toward understandings of racialization as intrinsic to the construction of the European and Western subject, studies of whiteness have become a vital component of contemporary research on racial identity (Hartigan 1997: 498). What makes whiteness particularly challenging as a research topic is that whiteness is not usually consciously reflected upon by those classified in this way, who have white privilege (Hartigan 1997). The power of being identified as "white" hides largely in its invisibility: "white" skin color has become normalized and self-evident in the Global North (Nakayama and Krizek 1995; Puwar 2004). Whiteness, as a relational category, is the "standard" others are judged by (Ware in Blaagaard 2011: 156). However, because whiteness, like other forms of racialization, structures a system of meaning comprised of multiple variables (class, gender, etc.), it too is context-specific.

Scholars stress the need to develop a more nuanced sense of whiteness in the European context (Garner 2006; Ware in Blaagard 2011), and better delineate how it contrasts with whiteness developed elsewhere. American understandings of racism are often seen as too dominating a frame for research on racism elsewhere, constituting the universalizing of particularism, as seen by Bourdieu and Wacquant (1999).[6] Essed and Trienekens suggest that whiteness be understood as a "floating concept" in the European context, and call for further analysis of how it is encoded within such notions as national identity, Western superiority, and civilization (2008: 68). In this book, we consider how notions of whiteness are implied in social discourses that associate Europe and Europeanness with civilization, modernity, equality, and democracy—concepts that have historically been quite important on a continental scale (Lewis 2006; Ponzanesi and Blaagaard 2011)—and ask how these notions are triggered by or even central to crisis talk. Positionality matters: several authors productively discuss "whiteness" as part of their own subjectivity as well as the object of permanent critical reflections. Several of the chapters here address the benefits and challenges of such a subject position for scholars of colonial and postcolonial racisms.

A focus on contemporary racism and whiteness requires an understanding of the ways in which elements of the colonial imaginary are reproduced in the present (Swarz 2005: 231). Quijano (2000) draws attention to the coloniality of power, emphasizing how current structures of power and discourses are informed and structured around ideologies that go back to the formation of the world during the era of imperialism and colonialism. How do these ideologies build upon or reinforce ideas of gender and intersect with ideas of class and sexual orientation?

Colonial formulations about "Europeanness," themselves complex, were articulated differently across the continent. Europe is rich in distinctions, with shifting center and peripheral regions: discussions of Southern Europe's compatibility with the rest of Europe following the massive economic collapse vividly reflect discourses of "more" or "less" European places and peoples (Bickes, Otten, and Weymann 2014). As elucidated by Daniel Knight (2013: 150), Greece was routinely described as corrupt and lazy in wider European discourses. While remaining careful not to reify the distinction between post-socialist and socialist Europe (Gilbert 2006), one should recall that Europe's socialist past and Cold War legacies have to be remembered as consequential in shaping European dynamics as well (Tulbure 2009). Idealized versions of Europe were important as objects of desire in the East, and the recent EU enlargement to Eastern Europe has in turn been characterized by some as a kind of colonization (ibid.). Significantly, the category "Eastern European" has long been racialized in the sense of not representing fully European populations (Buchowski 2006). How do such regional constructions ("southern" vs. "northern" Europe, East vs. West) stem from, reinforce, or challenge prior racist and colonial hegemonies? What kinds of "new" racisms are emerging based on different technologies of power? How do notions of crisis influence how whiteness is imagined and constructed within different localities in Europe, and how does the sense of crisis intensify and change older historical constructions? We consider these questions in multiple national contexts, noting how ideas of national exceptionalism, sovereignty, and relationship to the "Europe" construct are engaged as well.

The chapters in this book demonstrate how crisis talk can frustrate long-standing distinctions between self and other, sometimes mobilizing colonial-era notions of Europeanness, race, and cultural difference, and revealing the contours of whiteness. Brigitte Hipfl discusses how a popular Austrian TV police series locates crisis elsewhere—in Eastern European countries characterized by economic chaos and patriarchy—indirectly associating Austria with stability, the norm. Andrea Muehlebach analyzes the racial politics of humanitarianism, with its differential characterization of black and white orphans in ad campaigns that help distribute compassion unequally while calling up colonial-era tropes. Race is a specter in Andrea L. Smith's discussion as well. While officially France's republican universalist ideals should result in equal treatment of all citizens under the law, the eviction of Roma calls attention to differential degrees of Frenchness recognized by official policy, in which "Gens du voyage," a subgroup of French nationals, have been subject to a distinct regulatory regime due to their distinct placemaking practices and thereby identified as a vehicle bringing crisis to the French social body. As crisis rhetoric ramped up in conjunction with moral panic about an influx of Roma from Eastern countries, the Roma, constructed as fundamentally outside European ideals, were expelled from the national body altogether.

Crisis is also strongly gendered: women often carry the burden of austerity measures, as reduced public services often hit women especially hard (Enloe 2013: 102–104). In the Icelandic chapter in this volume, we see how gender is deployed to inform ethnic/national distinctions and thus is intimately connected to local understandings of whiteness and a specific understanding of Europeanness. Hipfl's chapter also demonstrates the gendered embodiment of crisis in Austrian fictional television through stereotypical TV images of racialized, aggressive male bodies and victimized female bodies. Similarly, "real Europeans" are understood as those societies demonstrating (or at least valuing) gender equality, as we see here in the examples of Austria and Iceland, where understandings of national worthiness intersect with a sense of moral superiority along gender-equality lines. Looking at European countries within the wider globe, Italian children are viewed as deserving of a future, while others deserve to just live (see Muehlebach here).

In several contexts, crisis triggers questions of difference through the frame of "deservingness," as Shay Cannedy trenchantly puts it in her chapter. States are responsible for dividing up rights, responsibilities, and resources, as Steve Garner emphasizes in his chapter. As economic crisis leads to budgetary restrictions and the shrinking of resources, the question arises as to which groups are deserving; apparent in many such discussions is an implicit or covert racialization. In the Irish example (see Cannedy here), for instance, we see asylum seekers bluntly sorted—not by skin tone, but through a language of deservingness that deems some asylum seekers "bogus."

Questions of moral worth circulate and extend beyond national boundaries. Recent critical analysis of humanitarian concerns can be seen as constituting another important avenue for understanding the subtle contemporary processes of racialization in which whiteness operates through an array of discourses that are not in themselves about race. In particular, concerns about global poverty and calls for the intervention of international organizations or well-intentioned people in the Global North help define the "West's place in the world" (Roy 2010: 12). Actions conducted on behalf of a "universal humanity" have provided powerful justification for particular governing technologies that support the superior position of the West (Feldman and Ticktin 2010: 6). In this way, international development helps create the European or Western subject (Escobar 1995; Ferguson 2006). Stoler's (2004: 6) work in the colonial archives of the Dutch East Indies demonstrates that such concerns predate international development, with humanitarian social reforms serving as an important driving force in the colonial empire. It is particularly urgent to analyze how this subjectivity links to racialization and racism. As Cannedy and Muehlebach so effectively argue here, humanitarian impulses work with and reinforce a sense of a hierarchy of humanity (Fassin 2011) in which some people deserve more, and some behave better, than others.

The links between the humanitarian subject, race, and whiteness become especially charged when the humanitarian logic turns inward to tackle need at home, for today's (white) European humanitarian subject is often called on to assist Europeans: we are in a situation in which Europe itself is understood as in crisis and in need of humanitarian support. Muehlebach shows us what happens when the humanitarian logic is turned back onto the nation itself as Italian children are viewed through this lens. Scarcity leads to a sense that nationals are more deserving than "others," whether these others are located internally or overseas. In Garner's analysis here, we see how such ideas are secured while other segments of the population are excluded by reframing discourses on the distribution of basic rights. His chapter elaborates how the idea of "fairness" has become positioned against what is seen as "equality" government policy, characterized as diverting resources to minority ethnic groups and immigrants. In the process he describes how the intersection of Britishness and whiteness becomes intensified during crisis, indicating the importance of locating whiteness within a political economic perspective.

From the "fairness" rhetoric in England that provides a hidden way to challenge the "equality" rhetoric associated with multiculturalism (and thus to justify shifting resources to those who deserve them), to the use of a rhetoric of deservingness against asylum seekers in Ireland, to a sense that others from the East (in Austria), undocumented migrants and refugees (in Lampedusa), or nomads (in France) are arriving with alien values, crisis talk helps create new distinctions between peoples and unearth ancient ones, with some populations, usually those belonging to the hegemonic (white) ethnicity of the nation-state in question (see Eriksen 2002: 98), seen as more deserving than all the others.

Nation-States and the EU

When we first formulated this research agenda, we imagined that notions of "Europeanness" would be front and center in our analysis, and that crisis talk would resurrect colonial-era ideologies about *European* civilization and *European* superiority. The colonial past certainly resonates with EU border control policies. Through border control, the EU racializes bodies based on established histories of European immigration control that in turn were shaped by colonial-era practices and distinctions, while guided by various new technologies of power (M'Charek, Schramm, and Skinner 2014: 473). By keeping certain groups of people out and allowing others to engage with the cosmopolitan present, these border controls offer a powerful statement about which kinds of bodies and subjectivities belong in European space, and which bodies are perceived as *not* belonging. As Steve Garner (2007: 69) has pointed out, the categories of mobility on which Schengen is based overlap with distinctions of geography and class, in addition to being racialized in the sense of clearly distinguishing rights along predominantly European white and Third World nonwhite lines. As elaborated through various studies on migration and borders, those defined as external are also increasingly criminalized through various discourses of illegality. Discourses on the legality of bodies within Europe's borders are extended toward internal populations, where migration and migrant populations are increasingly monitored (M'Chareck, Schramm and Skinner 2014: 479), as are even nomadic populations, as we see in Smith's chapter in this volume.

Notions of "Europeanness" and otherness emerge in several of the empirical studies developed here, but what is noteworthy is the ways the anxieties generated by crisis talk are most often attached to concerns about the *nation* rather than the EU or some imaginary "Europe." Despite regular (and often wishful) assertions to the contrary (Balibar 1991a; Castells 2010; Mann 1993; Morris 1997), the nation and nationalism live on. This finding reinforces what others have written about the European Union and the ways its citizens still tend to think along national rather than pan-national or post-national lines (Eder 2014: 220). Citizens of EU member-states see the origins of the crisis as intimately tied to their country's connection to the EU through the single currency and the Schengen agreement, and the most highly visible attempts to address the interrelated economic and migration challenges politically are playing out at this level. Yet when we attend to how the crisis is experienced, discussed, and worked through on the ground, we hear concerns about the *national* unit, the effects of crisis on the nation's identity, and the future of the citizens of this or that nation-state. Though we do encounter discussions about the future or viability of the EU, identity concerns are more closely related to that of the *nation*: this crisis is being framed as one that challenges the future of the French, or mobilizes principles of Latvian or Icelandic identity, and so on. Whereas some may argue that this is because of certain failings within the EU, such as the lack of real democracy and the need to create a single polity out of the EU member states (see Eder 2014: 229), our findings raise significant questions about the gulf between the sense of belonging to the nation and the salience or resonance of EU membership. Concerns about a nation under threat, moreover, touch on not-unrelated anxieties about state sovereignty, as we discuss further.

Anderson's (1983) work offers insight into why the nation-state continues to carry such lasting force in this era of the EU. In *Imagined Communities*, he famously asked what it is about this form of political organization that encourages people to sacrifice their lives for a community of people, only a fraction of whom they will meet over the course of their lives, exploring what Eriksen (2002: 100) has called the "emotional power" of nationalism. Not only have print capitalism and the creation of standardized languages played a role in uniting members of nation-states, but whole ideological apparatuses have been involved as well: the reproduction of specific histories or "invented traditions" (Hobsbawm and Ranger 1983), the consolidation of an authentic national culture, the deployment of key symbols, the "banal nationalism" associated with everyday practices: coins, stamps, turns of phrase, weather reports that depict the national map, and the generation of a sense of solidarity across the classes (Eriksen 2002: 100–101). In the process, nationalism "can instill passions and profound emotions" (ibid.: 106, citing Kapferer 1988).

The chapters here demonstrate the enduring power of affective associations with nation-states, while emotional connection to the wider super-national EU frame seems less developed. One may ask why this is so. Has the symbolic work foundered (Shore 2004)? Is this related to an absence of "dichotomization" (Eriksen 2002: 28), that is, the need to create sharper conceptual distinctions with an other—a relational concern foregrounded early on by Barth (1969)? Is "EU-ness" only visible in contrast to non-EU spaces and polities? Or is this a question of democratizing the EU, creating a true EU demos, as some suggest (Eder 2014)? As Eriksen (2002: 74) has explained, the EU began in the late 1950s as a "coordinating organ, an economic marketplace and alliance between independant states," and only in the late 1980s did the focus shift to emphasize attachment to the EU itself. This involved the strategic creation of symbols of shared Europeaness, usually associated with nations: logo, flag, anthem (Shore 2004). Shore (2004: 31) demonstrates that the aim was not necessarily so much to generate EU support but to invent the category of the "European public."

However, as the need to navigate the array of national and local traditions in the various EU meetings and commissions illustrates, attempts to implant Europeanness among the member states have been fraught with tensions. One of the (unintended) effects of such efforts is that the differentiation between "more" and "less developed" European subjects is often intensified rather than diminished (Graham 2009). Yet utopian proponents of the EU suggest that the current "crisis talk" might itself be embraced as a way to help further such a project. As Eder asks, "Why not venture the idea that the crisis of Europe opens another path of European integration in which the people no longer appear as the sum of individuals living in Europe, but as people linked to each other as bearers of conflicting interests and ideas?" (2014: 221).

Although EU-ness appears elusive in our case-studies, a sense of "Europeanness" does appear in relation to national, gender, or racial distinctions in several of the chapters. This is especially the case when Europe is viewed from the margins, where various conflicts and differentiations can be more clearly teased out (Loftsdóttir 2012). The ambivalence that can occur (as well as insights we can draw) from the margins is here explored in chapters about Lampedusa, Ireland, Iceland, and Latvia. Three of these chapters concern relatively smaller countries located on the geographic periphery of Europe that have a history of being dominated by others. This past, whether we define it as colonial or not, enters into and helps shape the local response to crisis, whether in arguments for or against asylum seekers or in hardship due to the economic crash in

Ireland, or in Latvian and Icelandic articulations of moral superiority that demonstrate mastery of the requisite cultural markers exemplary of Europeanness.

These chapters reflect ongoing anxieties around securing one's position within the imagined European community, the question of belonging, and how membership is affirmed through various social and political discourses. In spite of strikingly different historical trajectories, national discussions within these three countries similarly reflect the ambiguity of Europeaness. In an atmosphere of crisis, these designations have reverberating ramifications. Kristín Loftsdóttir and Helga Björnsdóttir's chapter on post-crash discussions about gender in Iceland finds public discourse on gender equality to be a way of demonstrating Iceland's place among the more stable and affluent northern European countries. However, essentialized ideas of Icelandic women as key symbols of economic development and "order" reproduce persistent nationalistic ideas of Iceland and reveal racialized hierarchies within Europe itself. Shay Cannedy's chapter demonstrates how Ireland's historical association with racialized others plays out in relation to present-day refugees and asylum seekers in either an emphasis on solidarity or a distancing that sees these groups as a threat to the nation. Both Cannedy's and Loftsdóttir and Björnsdóttir's chapters reflect the shifting dynamics of whiteness as historically constituted, and as something never fully given (Jacobson 1998).

The Italian island Lampedusa, located on the borders of the European continent and discussed here by Antonio Sorge, also shows the ambiguity of borders while elucidating the struggles to give them meaning. After 2011, as extensive numbers of migrants came to the island due to its proximity to North Africa, Lampedusa became a hub for cosmopolitan activists who do not view the island in the same way the locals do. Sorge casts this against the precarious economic and political positions of the local Lampedusans. Dace Dzenovska's essay also speaks to economic marginality within Europe, demonstrating that from the perspective of the European center, Latvia's harsh austerity policies are viewed as exemplary, even though they ironically forced many Latvians to leave in order to survive. Her chapter also demonstrates an imagined hierarchy of Europeanness, founded in this case on purported fiscal responsibility

Anderson's (1983) work on nations as imagined communities demonstrates how nation-states are often founded on an understanding of a shared past and common future. As elucidated by Eriksen

(2002: 61, 68), ethnic classifications and boundary maintainance in general can be seen as creating an order in a social sphere where there is a continuity between past and present. As we discussed earlier, citing Roitman's (2014) work, engaging in crisis talk means critiquing the contemporary moment, which is understood as proceeding differently from how it should: the present is contrasted with an imagined future and assumed past (see also Loftsdóttir 2014). Several chapters in this book explore these temporal dimensions of crisis talk as they take place in the context of the nation. In Hipfl's chapter, crisis is located elsewhere, in populations deemed "backward" through a denial of coevalness (Fabian 1983), and it gets transported into Austria through migration and trafficking. Smith's contribution discusses the challenges that emerged when unsettling continuities between past and present were exposed during Sarkozy's expulsion of Roma in the summer of 2010.

Crisis and the State

Crisis affects the nation-state in two ways that may seem opposite but actually are interrelated. As discussed above, crisis is primarily experienced and dealt with in a national context, calling the state to action and thus implicitly strengthening the role of the state as well as the bond of the population to the nation. At the same time, since each nation-state is inserted into a globalizing world (Clarke 2012: 46), the crisis that emerges is never just a domestic crisis. This makes it very difficult for the state to adequately deal with the problem at hand; crisis can erode the sovereignty of nation-states or at least initiate fear of such erosion. Debates about the role of the state are thus increasingly entangled with questions of sovereignty (Sharma and Gupta 2006: 2). Bauman and Bordoni, in their book *State of Crisis* (2014: 22), address the nation-state's diminishing power and capacity to cope with globally produced problems, calling this a "crisis of agency" and a "crisis of territorial sovereignty." To consider why the contemporary moment should be viewed as one of diminished state power, they contrast the present era with the Great Depression. At that time, states across the developed world adopted "Keynesian solutions" by investing in public works and employing labor when there was no work (ibid.: 2). Citizens knew where to turn: the state. But the current crisis is different in that countries are far too indebted: "All they can do is make random cuts," exacerbating the recession rather than mitigating its impacts (ibid.). Today the state no longer has the power it once had, and much of their work sets out to understand why.

Globalization partly explains this trend. When economic expansion ground to a halt in the 1970s, there was a "growing inability of states to deliver on their promise of providing for their citizens to mitigate the vagaries of fate" (ibid.: 8–9). The idea of the state, in fact, was downgraded at this time, as states became viewed as "obnoxious annoying obstacles to economic progress" (ibid.: 9). Public trust was instead granted to the "invisible hand" of the market, and state functions were increasingly contracted out (ibid.: 10). This has led to "statism without a state," and "governance" has taken the place of a functional government (ibid.: 13). The state has been "expropriated by supra-state global forces": "Finances, investment capitals, labour markets and circulation of commodities are beyond the remit and the reach of the only political agencies currently available to do the job of supervision and regulation" (ibid.: 11–12).

As a result of the state's loss of power to manage its affairs, the local-level political systems in charge of states are unable to tackle the problems that face the state from afar. In this view, states face pressure from two sources: the electors who can put a government in or out of office, and globalized forces—economic shifts, migration, climate change—that "float" in a "space of flows" and can render the decisions taken by the government null and void (ibid.: 19).[7] Neoliberal moves should be viewed in this light:

> Seriously drained of powers and continuing to weaken, state governments are compelled to cede, one by one, the functions once considered a natural and inalienable monopoly of the political organs of the state to deregulated market forces. (Bauman and Bordoni 2014: 20)

Former social functions of the state are now subject to economic calculation, and "viability criteria" are introduced to public services, regulating such areas as education, health, social security, scientific research, and public safety. This is, then, a crisis not only of the state, but of state sovereignty, as state agencies must seek local solutions to globally generated problems, when the industrial worker no longer plays the same role. Balibar (2015: 4) notes that whereas class struggle and social politics secured a certain living standard in the past, today "we witness a double movement … in the name of competitiveness and the control of public debt. One must diminish the real wages of labour and render it precarious in order to make it more 'competitive,' while continuing to develop mass consumption, drawing on the purchasing power of the wage earners or rather on their capacity for debt." As a result, the "proletariat" has become the "precariat," marked by the uncertainty of employment (Bauman and Bordoni 2014: 115).

Within the European context, any discussion of the loss of state powers necessarily circles back to the EU. Balibar (2015: 4) has recently described this supranational project as oriented to a "quasi-constitutional neoliberalism," with competition becoming a key force that intensifies disparities. Some even argue that the crisis demands a rethinking of the entire EU project (Guillén 2012 64). The economist Guillén (ibd: 62) writes that the monetary policy was misguided at the start, for the euro, in contrast to the strong currencies of developed countries (dollar, pound, yen), "has no regional productive system, much less a state, behind it". Postwar economies of advanced capitalist countries were national economies, organized around national systems of production and by countries, through domestic polity (ibid.: 62–63). In his view, the 1970s oil crisis led to a dismantling and reconstruction of these national productive systems, pushing free trade and breaking down barriers to international capital. In this new global neoliberal order, no "global productive system" exists; instead there are "dismantled national productive systems and globalized agents, alongside weak national governments, and insufficient, uncoordinated supranational authorities that operate along their fringes" (ibid.: 63–64). This is the heart of the European crisis, he believes: "a genuine crisis within the global crisis," for the EU is not a "regional productive system," but represents the integration of national productive systems; for this reason "there cannot be a European currency worthy of the name" (ibid.: 64) as the entire project was established on an unstable foundation.

Once neoliberalism became the dominant discourse and practice, and the "real" power of state governments was decreased (Bauman and Bordoni 2014: 18), the names of today's "games" are indecision, prevarication and procrastination. The double bind that governments find themselves in by being constantly exposed to the contradictory pressures of the electorate and global forces often ends up in compromises that are unsatisfying for both sides.

These dilemmas are evident in several of the essays presented here. From Sarkozy's attempts to tackle an immediate crisis by shifting the public's attention to Roma populations, to Latvians' submission to austerity measures so onerous that a significant portion of the population had to leave altogether to survive, to England with its myriad, seemingly endless austerity cuts, we see case after case involving national leaders trying to find some way to tackle the economic crisis of the moment, while presenting a plausible explanation to placate the electorate.

The loss of state power paradoxically encourages state aggression. Under conditions of crisis, there is often a sense among citizens that governments are failing to enforce order, a duty perceived as one of a government's primary roles (Bauman and Bordoni 2014: 21, 46). States often respond, providing a sense of direction by offering more repressive measures of control in a drift toward a "law-and-order society," as Hall et al. (1978) demonstrated in their illuminating study *Policing the Crisis: Mugging, the State, Law and Order* in the case of Great Britain in the 1970s. They analyzed how the moral panic around "mugging" in Great Britain in the early 1970s became the key ideological form in which a historical moment was "experienced and fought out" (ibid.: 221). Mugging obscured the global crisis of capitalism and the crisis of hegemony in Britain at that time, and black underprivileged youth were blamed for an increase of crime, thus preparing the ground for institutional responses to (re)instill law and order. In this way, the state defended and protected the majority against the groups that became the scapegoat for the crisis: criminalized young black males. Smith's chapter addresses a similar case in which *Gens du voyage* in France become the objects of repression.

Ironically, then, a weakened state can become an aggressive state. Neoliberal policies do not depend on abolishing the state, as neoliberal advocates commonly assert; rather, the state takes a "very active role in creating, maintaining and protecting the preconditions of market self regulation" (Connolly 2013: 21). This means that neoliberalism needs an "active state to promote, project and expand market processes" (ibid.: 21). Furthermore, whereas market liberalism advocated that the state should not interfere with "natural" market processes, neoliberalism organizes other parts of civil society in accordance to "neoliberal principles of being" (ibid.: 22).

Fuchs (2013) regards the current situation in Europe as resembling the processes Hall and his coauthors ascertained in Britain in the 1970s. Using Germany as an example, he states that contemporary moral panics vary their objects, drifting from the unemployed to "immigrants, European bureaucracy, an alleged laziness of Southern Europeans, the claim that Southern Europeans … overspend money, do not know how to run a state and the economy and the claim that left-wing parties and movements bring chaos" (ibid.: 3). Here again racist discourses are at work, preventing confrontation of the root causes of crises—global capitalism, neoliberalism and geopolitical decisions by major global players gone awry. Positioning one's own nation against what are labeled the "black sheep" in the European Union while adhering to EU regulations is one way of strengthening the respective nation-states. Another strategy can be found in recent elections across Europe, where the articulation of moral panics regarding racialized others by conservative and right-wing parties pays off with increased votes.

The different analyses of Europe's many crises have produced radically different prognoses. It is partly for this reason that we cannot pinpoint a clear-cut trajectory, periodicity, or geographical boundary in our narration, for to do so brings a whole explanatory apparatus in through the back door: some date "the" crisis to the period immediately following the subprime mortgage crisis at the end of 2007, but others argue it commenced with the implementation of the euro, or with political economic shifts a previous generation of leaders took in response to the oil crisis of the 1970s. Others argue that its roots lie in the devastation of World War II. Though we cannot pinpoint a particular starting point, this latest crisis period has settled into a more generalized state, and we endeavor here to delineate some of the ways it shapes everyday life in diverse locales across the continent.

The case studies presented in this book reflect not only the value of interdisciplinary work and conversations, but also anthropology's methodological flexibility, critically adjusting its methods to changing social realities and thus reflecting, in a way, the "messiness" of both everyday life and the anthropological method. Anthropology has resisted the urge to box in its methods as either quantitative or qualitative (LeCompte 1999: 54), and highly valuing "experience" as a source of insights (Okely 1992) and using different approaches to doing research for deeper understandings (Walcott 1999). As Gabriella Modan (2016) has argued, rapidly changing ways of communicating raise methodological challenges for anthropology and also influence the ways in which anthropologists can engage with their subjects during and after research through various social media. Various communication technologies make it easier to "stay in touch" as local media discussions go global. The chapters reflect this fluidity of methods. Hipfl's and Garner's chapters reflect the methodologies used in their respective disciplines (media and cultural studies, sociology), while the remaining chapters are all written by anthropologists with extensive fieldwork experience in the social settings they discuss. The essays by Cannedy and Sorge convey the results of the classic ethnographic research that has been the hallmark of anthropological methods. The chapters by Muehlebach, Loftsdóttir and Björnsdóttir, Dzenovska, and Smith reflect continued engagement with their ethnographic fieldwork site and base their insights on earlier or continuous fieldwork while also making extensive use of diverse materials, including media articles, images, blogs, and archival sources. Anthropology's commitment to flexibility in its embrace of different methods and materials for analysis makes for particularly effective analyses of the fluid landscape and discursive sites that have characterized Europe in crisis.

In Conclusion: Crisis as a Structure of Feeling

Raymond Williams (1977: 131), in his search for a deeper understanding of cultural and historical specificities, used the term "structures of feeling" to designate "a particular quality of social experience and relationship, historically distinct from other particular qualities, which gives the sense of a ... period." Structures of feeling designate what it feels like to be in a particular situation—the sense of how lives are lived and experienced, which includes the affective practices and emotions circulating in society. They include the role of "imagination" in our current interconnected reality and its workings as a "social fact," as captured by Appadurai's (1996: 5–7) work on globalization. The chapters in this book illuminate what it is like to live under conditions of crisis in different national contexts, and also offer insights into the ways in which crisis talk evokes affective reactions, not least to legitimize state policies and interventions. Crisis talk can be one approach to win social consent and build or reactivate a certain common sense, as the examples of Iceland and Latvia with their respective national identity constructions demonstrate clearly.

How would we describe the structures of feeling of the contemporary conjuncture? It is fair to say that the present atmosphere is characterized by a sense of precariousness: many feel deprived of the past promise of a predictable future, a sentiment shared even by those critical of this future (Muehlebach 2013: 297). As Hipfl lucidly demonstrates here, the media are involved: TV crime fiction, with its continuous repetition of scenarios of crisis, both reflects and provides an education in living with precarity: not only does it reflect the "structure of feeling" of the contemporary moment, but it instructs its audience on how to live with persistent anxiety and uncertainty. The continent is experiencing waves of crisis that roll from one end to the other, a situation narrated in the language of germ theory as an ailment spreading from one country to the next like a contagious epidemic.

When it comes to Europe's current crises, there seems to be a growing sense that the crises will not disappear, and that we have to learn how to live with them (Bauman and Bordoni 2014; Balibar 2010). The volume as a whole clearly reflects this sentiment, as well as the public feelings that emerge with crisis talk. The case studies illustrate how specific emotions are mobilized and analyze the work they do, effecting different bodies differently and opening or foreclosing a possible future and sociality. Although some have argued, perhaps hopefully, that crisis can be generative of positive change (Eder 2014), the mood is quite different in the cases presented here. The issue of increased distribution of wealth to a few in the face of growing class binaries (Harvey 2005) intersects with the increased sense of precariousness and loss of a future. As phrased by anthropologist James Clifford (2012: 422), there is a lingering sense that "it is impossible to say with certainty what comes next", which indicates the sense of loss of a vision for the future, or at least a predictable one (Muehlebach 2013: 297).

Referring back to the title of this volume, *Messy Europe*: within contemporary narratives the concept "messy" often has a negative meaning of something disorganized, untidy, disorderly, confusing, or even dirty. With the title of the book, we emphasize the ambiguity of the term messy, drawing attention to discourses that describe Europe as a "mess" due to its financial crisis, exemplified by crisis talk, while at the same time stressing that messiness is a positive, intrinsic, and undervalued aspect of human life. Europe's messiness is also constituted in its overlapping subjectivities and identities, which, despite efforts to reduce them into discrete national, ethnic, or racist categories, resist such simplification. The crisis talk in the aftermath of the financial crisis makes it all too clear that identities in Europe are messy in the positive sense of being plural—the results of intersecting categories and histories that have never fitted neatly into the boxes created in attempts to organize a confusing social world. As part of the chaos that is humanity, Europe itself has never had clear boundaries, meaning, or origins.

Kristín Loftsdóttir is a Professor at the University of Iceland. She directs the research project "Creating Europe Through Racialized Mobilities" Her research interests include crisis, whiteness, postcolonial Europe, gender, mobility and racism. Her publications include *Crisis and Coloniality at Europe's Margins: Creating Exotic*

Iceland (2019) and the co-edited of *Crisis in the Nordic Nations and Beyond* (2014) with Lars Jensen.

Brigitte Hipfl is a retired Ao. Professor in the Department of Media and Communication Studies at the University of Klagenfurt, Austria. She works on media and gender, subject formations, the affective labor of media, and postcolonial Europe, and is currently exploring migration in Austrian cinema and TV. Her publications include *Teaching "Race" with a Gendered Edge* (2012) co-edited with Kristín Loftsdóttir and *Wir und die Anderen. Visuelle Kultur zwischen Aneignung und Ausgrenzung. (We and the Other. Issues of Appropriation and Exclusion in Visual Culture)* Herbert von Halem Verlag, 2021 (co-edited with Anna Schober).

Andrea L. Smith is Professor of Anthropology at the Department of Anthropology and Sociology at Lafayette College, Easton, PA (USA). Her research interests include postcolonial European social memory and silencing; French settler colonialism in Algeria; and race, ethnicity and place-making. Publications include the edited volume *Europe's Invisible Migrants* (2003) and the co-authored work *Rebuilding Shattered Worlds: Creating Community by Voicing the Past* (2016).

Notes

This volume was facilitated by a generous grant from RANNÍS (Icelandic Center for Research) for the project "Icelandic Identity in Crisis" (number 130426-051).

1. Koselleck (2006) offers a thorough review of the term "crisis," its entry into different European national languages, its expansion in the nineteenth century, and usage in the present.
2. For outsiders to the European context, a basic account of the recent crisis starts with the economic crisis that arrived almost without warning immediately following the subprime mortage crisis that began in the United States in 2007 (Guillén 2012: 42). Following worldwide recession, it reached Europe with Iceland's collapse, spreading into Greece, Ireland, Spain, and the United Kingdom by 2009 and on to Portugal, Belgium, Italy, and later France (ibid.: 54). With a bailout plan involving the International Monetary Fund (IMF), countries across the Eurozone began implementing austerity or structural-adjustment policies that eroded welfare states constructed over decades (ibid.: 55).
3. Koselleck dates the current meaning of the crisis concept to eighteenth-century Europe and the emergence of a new historical consciousness

involving a shift away from a Christian understanding of time (2006; see Roitman 2014: 18). Before this shift, it was widely imagined that the future would bring nothing new and sinful humans would not change until the expected end of the world. After the emergence of a new understanding of time, philosophers argued that the future would be different from the past, and in fact *should* be different. Koselleck explored how the political utopianism of the era involved a new "moral demand for a difference between the past and the future" (Koselleck 1988: 98–137, 2002: 110–44, in Roitman 2014: 28). This shift is intimately related to the idea of "progress," intrinsic to the idea of modernity (Roitman 2014; Norgaard 1994: 49).
4. "Crisis" and "critique" are cognates, an important point underscored by Koselleck (1988, 2002, in Roitman 2014).
5. Schengen is the European agreement on mobility that abolishes border checks between European countries that are part of the agreement; meanwhile external border control continues to exist.
6. Scholarship in the United States is ever evolving. While acknowledging the primary importance of the black/white binary, recent research asks for more nuanced analysis of the interplay of race and ethnicity (Hartigen 1997; Smith and Eisenstein 2013).
7. As Bauman and Bordoni (2014: 29) write, the separation of power and politics is lethal to a democratic state: the constitution promises that citizens will be involved in making common decisions, but these are now made by bodies of people who are appointed non-democratically.

References

Abu-Lughod, L. 2002. "Do Muslim Women Really Need Saving? Anthropological Reflections on Cultural Relativism and Its Others." *American Anthropologist* 104(3): 783–790.

Açiksöz, Can. 2016. Beyond the 'Lesser Evil': Critical Engagement with Brexit. Brexit Referrendum First Reactions from Anthropology." *Social Anthropology* 24(4): 487–488.

Anderson, B. 1983. *Imagined Communities: Reflections on the Origin and Spread of Nationalism.* New York: Verso.

Appadurai, A. 1996. *Modernity at Large: Cultural Dimensions of Globalisation.* Minneapolis, MI: University of Minnesota Press.

Balibar, E. 1991a. "Es Gibt Keinen Staat in Europa: Racism and Politics in Europe Today." *New Left Review* 186(1): 5–19.

———. 1991b. "Class Racism," in *Race, Nation and Class: Ambiguous Identities*, ed. E. Balibar and I. Wallerstein, 204–216. London: Verso.

———. 2010. "Europe: Final Crisis? Some Theses," *Theory & Event* 13(2).

———. 2015. "A New Impulse—but for Which Europe?" *Eurozine*. Retrieved 22 November 2015 from http://www.eurozine.com/articles/2015-02-11-balibar-en.html.

———. 2016. "Brexit, the Anti-Grexit." First published in *Libération*, trans. David Broder, retrieved 20 May 2017 from *Verso Blog*, http://www.versobooks.com/blogs/2735-brexit-the-anti-grexit.

Barth, F. 1969. "Introduction," in *Ethnic Groups and Boundaries: The Social Organization of Culture Difference*, ed. F. Barth, 9–38. Bergen and Oslo: Universitetsforlaget.

Bauman, Z., and C. Bordoni. 2014. *State of Crisis*. London: Polity Press.

Bickes, H., T. Otten, and L. C. Weymann. 2014. "The Financial Crisis in the German and English Press: Metaphorical Structures in the Media Coverage on Greece, Spain and Italy." *Discourse and Society* 25(4): 424–445.

Blaagaard, B. 2011. "Workings of Whiteness: Interview with Vron Ware." *Social Identities* 17(1): 153–161.

Bourdieu, P., and L. Wacquant. 1999. "On the Cunning of Imperialist Reason," *Theory, Culture and Society* 16(1): 41–58.

Boyer, D. 2013. "Simply the Best: Parody and Political Sincerity in Iceland." *American Ethnologist* 40(2): 276–287.

Braidotti, R. 2016. "Don't Agonize, Organize." Retrieved 20 May 2017 from e-flux conversations, https://conversations.e-flux.com/t/rosi-braidotti-don-t-agonize-organize/5294.

Buchowski, Michał. 2006. 'From Exotic Other to Stigmatized Brother." *Anthropological Quarterly* 79(3): 463–482.

Bunzl, M. 2005. "Between Anti-Semitism and Islamophobia: Some Thoughts on the New Europe." *American Ethnologist* 32(4): 499–508.

Castells, M. 2010. *End of Millennium*, 2nd ed. Oxford: Wiley-Blackwell.

Clarke, J. 2012. "'What crisis is this?'" in *The Neoliberal Crisis*, ed. J. Rutherford and S. Davison, 44–54. London: Lawrence & Wishart.

Clifford, J. 2012. "Feeling Historical." *Cultural Anthropology* 27(3): 417–426.

Coates, Jamie. 2017. "'Edgy' Politics and European Anthropology in 2016." *Social Anthropology* 25(2): 234–247.

Connolly, W. 2013. *The Fragility of Things: Self-Organizing Processes, Neoliberal Fantasies, and Democratic Activism*. Durham, NC: Duke University Press.

Dervis, K., and J. Mistral, eds. 2014. *Europe's Crisis, Europe's Future*. Washington, DC: Brookings Institution.

Desmond, M., and M. Emirbayer. 2009. "What is Racial Domination?" *Du Bois Review* 6(2): 335–355.

Dobrescu, P., and F. Durach. 2014. "Euroscepticism: A Sign of a Europe in Distress." *Revista Românăde Comunicare si relatii publice* 16(1): 25–40.

Douglas, M. 2003/1992. *Risk and Blame*. Abingdon: Routledge.

Eder, K. 2014. "The EU in Search of Its People: The Birth of a Society out of the Crisis of Europe." *European Journal of Social Theory* 17(3): 219–237.
Enloe, C. 2013. *Seriously! Investigating Crashes and Crisis as if Women Mattered.* Oakland, CA: University of California Press.
Eriksen, T. 2002. *Ethnicity and Nationalism: Anthropological Perspectives,* 2nd ed. London: Pluto Press.
Escobar, Arturo. 2007. "Worlds and Knowledges Otherwise: The Latin American Modernity/Coloniality Research Program." *Cultural Studies* 21(2–3): 179–210.
———. 1995. *Encountering Development: The Making and Unmaking of the Third World.* Princeton, NJ: Princeton University Press.
Essed, P., and S. Trienekens. 2008. "Who Wants to Feel White? Race, Dutch Culture and Contested Identities." *Ethnic and Racial Studies* 31(1): 52–72.
Fabian, J. 1983. *Time and the Other: How Anthropology Makes its Object.* New York: Columbia University Press.
Fassin, D. 2011. "Policing Borders, Producing Boundaries: The Governmentality of Immigration in Dark Times." *Annual Review of Anthropology* 40: 213–226.
Feldman, I., and Ticktin, M. 2010. "Introduction: Government and Humanity," in *In the Name of Humanity: The Government of Threat and Care,* ed. I. Feldman and M. Ticktin, 1–26. Durham, NC: Duke University Press.
Ferguson, J. 2006. *Global Shadows: Africa in the Neoliberal World Order.* Durham, NC: Duke University Press.
Fuchs, C. 2013. "How Ideology is Policing the Crisis of European Capitalism." *Unified Theory of Information Research Group*, 25 March. Retrieved 22 November from http://fuchs.uti.at/860/.
Garner, S. 2006. "The Uses of Whiteness: What Sociologists Working on Europe Can Draw from US Research on Whiteness." *Sociology* 40(2): 257–275.
———. 2007. "The European Union and the Racialization of Immigration, 1985–2006." *Race/Ethnicity: Multidisciplinary Global Contexts* 1(1): 61–87.
Gilbert, A. 2006. "The Past in Parenthesis: (Non) Post-Socialism in Post-War Bosnia-Herzegovina." *Anthropology Today* 22(4): 14–19.
Gingrich, Andre. 2016. "Scholarship Will Suffer while National Sentiments Are Stoked: Critical Engagement with Brexit; Brexit Referendum First Reactions from Anthropology." *Social Anthropology* 24(4): 485–486.
Gluckman, M. 1954. *Rituals of Rebellion.* Manchester: Manchester University Press.
Graham, M. 2009. "LGBT Rights in the European Union, a Queer Affair?," in *Out in the Public: Reinventing Lesbian/Gay Anthropology in a Globalizing World,* ed. E. Lewin and W. Leap, 29–30. New York: Wiley-Blackwell.

Grosfoguel, R., L. Oso, and A. Christou. 2014. "'Racism,' Intersectionality and Migration Studies: Framing Some Theoretical Reflections." *Identities: Global Studies in Culture and Power* 22(6): 635–652.

Guillén, A. 2012. "Europe: The Crisis Within a Crisis." *International Journal of Political Economy* 41(3): 41–68.

Hall, S., et al. 1978. *Policing the Crisis: Mugging, the State and Law and Order.* London: Palgrave Macmillan.

Hall, S., and D. Massey. 2012. "Interpreting the Crisis. Doreen Massey and Stuart Hall Discuss Ways of Understanding the Current Crisis," in *The Neoliberal Crisis*, ed. J. Rutherford and S. Davison (eds), 55–69. London: Lawrence and Wishart.

Hardt, M., and A. Negri. 2000. *Empire.* Boston, MA: Harvard University Press.

Harrison, F. 2002. "Unraveling 'Race' for the Twentieth-First Century," in *Exotic No More: Anthropology on the Front Lines*, ed. J. MacClancy, 145–166. Chicago, IL: University of Chicago Press.

Hartigan, J. 1997. "Establishing the Fact of Whiteness." *American Anthropologist* 99(3): 495–505.

Harvey, D. 2005. *A Brief History of Neoliberalism.* Oxford: Oxford University Press.

Hill, J. 2008. *The Everyday Language of White Racism.* Chichester: Wiley-Blackwell.

Hilton, M. 1979. "The Split Labor Market and Chinese Immigration, 1848–1882." *Journal of Ethnic Studies* 6: 99–108.

Hipfl, B., and D. Gronold. 2011. "Asylum Seekers as Austria's Other." *Social Identities* 17(1): 27–40.

Hobsbawm, E., and T. Ranger, eds. 1983. *The Invention of Tradition.* Cambridge: Cambridge University Press.

Holmes, D. 2000. *Integral Europe: Fast-Capitalism, Multiculturalism, Neofascism.* Princeton, NJ: Princeton University Press.

Jacobson, M. 1998. *Whiteness of a Different Color: European Immigrants and the Alchemy of Race.* Cambridge, MA: Harvard University Press.

Kapferer, B. 1988. *Legends of People, Myths of State Violence: Intolerance and Political Culture in Sri Lanka and Australia.* Washington, DC: Smithsonian Institute Press.

Klein, N. 2007. *The Shock Doctrine: The Rise of Disaster Capitalism.* Toronto: Knopf Canada.

Knight, Daniel M. 2013. "The Greek Economic Crisis as Trope." *Focaal—Journal of Global and Historical Anthropology* 63: 147–159.

Koselleck, R. 2006. "Crisis." *Journal of the History of Ideas* 67(2): 357–400.

Kosmatopoulos, N. 2014. "Crisis Works." *Social Anthropology* 22(4): 479–486.

LeCompte, Margaret Diana. 1999. *Ethnographer's Toolkit: Designing and Conducting Ethnographic Research.* Lanham, MD: AltaMira Press.

Lee, V.P.Y., L. Hongling, and W. D. Mignolo. 2015. "Global Coloniality and the Asian Century." *Cultural Dynamics* 27(2): 185–190.

Lewis, G. 2006. "Imaginaries of Europe: Technologies of Gender, Economies of Power." *European Journal of Women's Studies* 13(2): 87–102.

Loftsdóttir, K. 2012. "Colonialism at the Margins: Politics of Difference in Europe as Seen through Two Icelandic Crises." *Identities: Global Studies in Culture and Power* 19(5): 597–615.

_____. 2014. "Building on Iceland's 'Good Reputation': Icesave, Crisis and Affective National Identities." *Ethnos*, 81(2): 338–363.

Loftsdóttir, K., and L. Jensen. 2014. "Introduction," in *Crisis in the Nordic Nations and Beyond*, ed. K. Loftsdóttir and L. Jensen, 1–8. Surrey: Ashgate.

Loomba, A; S. Kaul, M. Bunzl, A. Burton and J. Esty. 2005. "Beyond What? An Introduction," in A. Loomba, S. Kaul, M. Bunzl, A. Burton and J. Esty (eds) *Postcolonial Studies and Beyond*, 1–38. Durham, NC: Duke University Press.

Mann, M. 1993. "Nation-States in Europe and Other Continents: Diversifying, Developing, Not-Dying." *Daedalus* 122(3): 115–140.

M'charek, A., K. Schramm and D. Skinner. 2014. "Topologies of Race: Doing Territory, Population and Identity in Europe." *Science, Technology and Human Values* 39(4): 468–487.

Miles, R., and M. Brown. 1989/2003. *Racism*, 2nd edition. London: Routledge.

Modan, G. 2016. "Writing the Relationship: Ethnographer-Informant Interactions in the New Media." *Journal of Linguistic Anthropology* 26(1): 98–107.

_____. 2007. *Turf Wars: Discourse, Diversity and the Politics of Place*. Malden, MA: Blackwell.

Morris, L. 1997. "Globalisation, Migration, and the Nation-State: The Path to a Post-National Europe?" *British Journal of Sociology* 48(2): 192–209.

Muehlebach, A. 2013. "On Precariousness and the Ethical Imagination: The Year 2012 in Sociocultural Anthropology." *American Anthropologist* 115(2): 297–311.

Nakayama, T., and R. Krizek. 1995. "Whiteness: A Strategic Rhetoric." *Quarterly Journal of Speech* 81(3): 291–309.

Norgaard, R. 1994. *Development Betrayed: The End of Progress and a Coevolutionary Revisioning of the Future*. London: Routledge.

Okely, Judith. 1992. "Anthropology and Autobiography: Participatory Experience and Embodied Knowledge" in *Anthropology and Autobiography*, ed. J. Okely and H. Callaway, 1–28. New York: Routledge.

Peebles, G. 2010. "The Anthropology of Credit and Debt." *Annual Review of Anthropology* 39: 225–240.

Ponzanesi, S., and B. Blaagaard. 2011. "Introduction: In the Name of Europe." *Social Identities* 17(1): 1–10.

Ponzanesi, S., and G. Colpani, eds. 2016. *Postcolonial Transitions in Europe*. Lanham, MD: Rowman & Littlefield.

Puwar, N. 2004. *Space Invaders: Race, Gender and Bodies Out of Place.* Oxford: Berg.
Quijano, A. 2000. "Coloniality of power and Eurocentrism in Latin America." *International Sociology*, 15(2), 215–232.
Roitman, J. 2014. *Anti-Crisis.* Durham, NC: Duke University Press.
Roy, A. 2010. *Poverty Capital: Microfinance and the Making of Development.* New York: Routledge.
Schneider, J. 2002. "World Markets: Anthropological Perspectives," in *Exotic no More: Anthropology on the Front Lines*, ed. J. MacClancy, 64–85. Chicago, IL: Chicago University Press.
Schwarz, B. 2005. "Afterword: 'Strolling Spectators' and 'Practical Londoners': Remembering the Imperial Past," in *The Politics of Heritage, the Legacies of Race*, ed. J. Littler and R. Naidoo, 216–235. New York: Routledge.
Schwegler, T. 2009. "The Global Crisis of Economic Meaning." *Anthropology News* 50(7): 9–12.
Sharma, A., and A. Gupta. 2006. "Introduction: Rethinking Theories of the State in an Age of Globalisation," in *The Anthropology of the State: A Reader*, ed. A. Sharma and A. Gupta, 1–41. Malden, MA: Blackwell.
Shore, C. 2004. "Whither European Citizenship? Eros and Civilization Revisited." *European Journal of Social Theory* 7(1): 27–44.
Smith, A., and A. Eisenstein. 2013. "Thoroughly Mixed Yet Thoroughly Ethnic: Indexing Class with Ethnonyms." *Journal of Linguistic Anthropology* 23(2): E1–22.
Stoler, A. 2004. "Affective States," in *A Companion to the Anthropology of Politics*, ed. David Nugent and Joan Vincent, 5–20. Malden, MA: Blackwell.
Thomas, D., and M. Clarke. 2013. "Globalisation and Race: Structures of Inequality, New Sovereignties, and Citizenship in a Neoliberal Era." *Annual Review of Anthropology* 42: 305–325.
Tulbure, N. 2009. "Introduction to Special Issue: Global Socialism and Postsocialism." *Anthropology of East Europe Review* 27(2): 1–18.
Walcott, Harry F. 1999. *Ethnography: A Way of Seeing.* Lanham, MD: AltaMira Press.
Williams, R. 1977. *Marxism and Literature.* Oxford: Oxford University Press.
Zizek, S. 2015. "We Can't Address the EU Refugee Crisis without Confronting Global Capitalism." *In These Times*, 9 September. Retrieved 22 November 2015 from http://inthesetimes.com/article/18385/slavoj-zizek-european-refugee-crisis-and-global-capitalism.

1

Wise Viking Daughters

Equality and Whiteness in Economic Crisis

Kristín Loftsdóttir and Helga Björnsdóttir

Introduction

In 2011, three years after Iceland underwent massive economic meltdown, the *Guardian* published an article about Iceland under a headline asking, "Is Iceland the best country for women?" Not long before, *Newsweek* magazine had declared Iceland to be the "best place" in the world for women (Cochrane 2011). Iceland was the first European country to experience a severe economic crash in October 2008. The country was technically bankrupt, and the copious international media discussions of Iceland's "fall" induced a widespread sense of humiliation (Chartier 2010) and consequently an urgent desire to repair the country's reputation (Loftsdóttir 2014a). This feeling of humiliation engaged with historical anxieties revolving around Iceland's past position as a colony, pushing Icelandic intellectuals to stress Iceland's belonging as fully European (Loftsdóttir 2012).

In this chapter, we show that at times when national identity has suffered a serious blow, proclamations of "gender equality" can be an important means of re-establishing a respected European subject position. In Iceland, as we point out, reified notions of gender became one part of the nation's re-establishment as a fully legitimate *European* nation. Furthermore, gender ideologies engaged with the plight of "other" women in the "post-conflict" or "developing" world have underscored Iceland's belonging in modern Europe for the past decade. The sense of being European has to be understood as enmeshed with colonialism's "imperial ruins," to use Stoler's (2013: x) terminology, where we seek to capture the "deeply saturated, less spectacular forms in which colonialism leaves it marks." At the same time, the sense of being in "crisis" evokes the past and visions of the future by producing particular affects and spaces of engagement (Loftsdóttir 2014a: 13; see also introduction). However, this past is never passively brought into the present; rather, it selectively serves the needs of the present (Popular Memory Group 1982).

Our discussion draws attention to the reification of gender at times of crisis while also highlighting the interplay of gender and racialization. The above-mentioned *Guardian* article that refers to Iceland as the "best country in the world for women" can be located among persistent notions of the Nordic as marked strongly by gender equality (Holli, Magnusson, and Rönnblom 2005; Holter 2003; Holter, Svare, and Engeland 2009; Gullestad 2002) and also intersects with wider conceptions of the Nordic countries as exempt from imperialistic and colonial history (Loftsdóttir and Jensen 2012; Keskinen et al. 2009). This positioning of the Nordic as existing outside colonial history remains salient even though some Nordic countries, such as Denmark and Sweden, have been empires at particular times in history (Naum and Nordin 2013), and all the Nordic countries have in one way or another engaged with colonialism and the racism that was part of colonial and imperial thinking (Loftsdóttir 2013). The relatively recent research situating the Nordic countries within wider networks of colonial power and racism (see Gullestad 2002; Keskinen et al. 2009; Loftsdóttir 2013; McIntosh 2015), it firmly seeks to draw attention to Nordic subjects as part of a world that continues to be deeply racialized. Such a focus emphasizes Nordic identities as shaped by transnational processes that are embedded in the colonial encounter, while trying to understand how these links with the past are reanimated or contested in the present.

Our discussion also intersects with another discursive realm, one in which racism has been curiously absent. Globalized discourses of international development often seem to forget that the Enlightenment's goals of modernization were embedded in violent colonial encounters between people from different parts of the world (Escobar 2007). This means that the "ruins" of colonialism (Stoler 2008) and the persistence of racism are seldom addressed in relation to international development (Goudge 2003). Development discourses are a part of the creation of subjects—and not only those targeted for assistance—and actively shape notions of what it means to be a European and Western subject (Escobar 1995; Ferguson 2006). Care by white European "strangers" often factors heavily into the popularization of the "suffering" of others that features so predominantly in the current media-saturated world (Bornstein and Redfield 2010: 3–4), suffering that is generally constructed as existing outside history or contemporary politics (Ferguson 2006). Whereas feminists have noted that humanitarian discourses on women in war-torn countries are often used to conceal Western countries' brutal pursuit of their own political and economic interests (Moran 2010; Otto 2006), our discussion emphasizes that these discourses also contribute to creating a particular kind of subject "back home." Racialization thus plays a part in a global construction of a particular people, for the most part socially categorized as "white," as having a role in "helping" others, without concomitant acknowledgment of the entangled histories of colonialism and racism.

Socially categorized as white, Icelandic anthropologists working in the West, we are aware of our part in this global imaginary and classification of peoples and places through history, and therefore of the need to take a critical stance toward our own history, culture, and society. That is what we have attempted to do in our research on Icelandic society, of which this chapter is a part. Besides deconstructing the rigid construction of home and field that historically attached higher value to fieldwork in remote places (Gupta and Ferguson 1997), anthropologists have also critically engaged with the term "native" anthropologists, pointing out its consequential intersections with other cultural identifications like race, gender and class (Narayan 1993). While we recognize these important contributions, we also stress, as others have, that anthropology "at home" can be part of "decolonizing anthropology" (Jacobs-Huey 2002), which works to dislodge cultural difference as a key principle in the ethnographic project (Bunzl 2004: 439, 440). In line with the need to further decolonize the discipline and the recognition that "whiteness" often gains it power by its invisibility (Hartigan 1997), we find it important, as "white" anthropologists, to take a stand by deconstructing the way ideas of whiteness in Iceland engage with larger racial geographies. In the Icelandic context, the intersection of whiteness and gender becomes particularly salient in constructing the Icelandic body, perceived in its wider construction as a Nordic body. The data directly referred to here come from media analysis and form a part of a larger research project based on ethnographic fieldwork, participant observation, and interviews with immigrants and workers in the Icelandic financial and banking sector. For native anthropologists such as ourselves, the boundaries between participant observation and the everyday life that we share with those who are the focus of our research can be blurred and complicated. We also base our analysis on our previous anthropological research. Helga Björnsdóttir has studied ideas of masculinity and militarization in relation to peacekeeping in Iceland, and Kristín Loftsdóttir has done work on the historical formation of race and national identity in Iceland.

We start by focusing on Iceland's historical contextualization of gender and its strong desire for recognition as a civilized, sovereign country in the early twentieth century. The discussion then relates this past deeply embedded in postcolonial anxieties to current interpretations of Iceland's position within a globalized world, and to essentialized notions of Icelandic women that arose after the crash. The last section of the chapter explains how concern about gender equality became a way to rehabilitate Iceland as an important European player and thus preserved Iceland's status as a "white," privileged European country.

Historical Ideas of Gender and National Identity in Iceland

Iceland's position as a Danish colony was instrumental in shaping Icelandic national identity and the country's relationship with the outside world. The nationalistic movement, claiming independence from Denmark, emphasized Iceland's medieval literature and language as signifying factors in the nation's distinct identity (Sigurðsson 1996: 42) and considered the commonwealth period—more than a thousand years ago—to be Iceland's golden age. After that, the story goes, Iceland's subjection to Norwegian rule in 1262 and then Danish rule in 1380 led the country into a long period of decay (Hálfdánarson 2000). Inspired by romantic notions of Iceland's past, Icelandic men of the upper classes saw themselves as leading Iceland's transformation from one of Europe's poorest countries into a state of modernity, and thus rehabilitating the country's reputation (Matthíasdóttir 2004; Rastrick 2013). As is the case in nationalistic imaginings, Icelandic women were perceived as representing the country's timeless traditions (Matthíasdóttir 2004; see also Björnsdóttir 1997).

European travel writing about Iceland historically described Iceland as wild and semi-savage, a depiction that has raised vehement objections from Icelandic intellectuals through the ages (Durrenberger and

Pálsson 1989). This early stereotype clearly shows the importance of seeing whiteness as a historically and socially constituted and unstable category. These images must have been a particularly unfortunate association when Iceland was seeking recognition as an independent state fully compatible with other European states. As Pandey (2013) demonstrates, colonization rests on a racialized division of bodies, some seen as capable of modernizing and some not. The colonized were represented as incapable of "moving forward" on the path to modernization. Loftsdóttir (2012) has shown how the reproduction of racist European imaginings in Icelandic texts in the late nineteenth and early twentieth centuries located Icelanders more firmly within the category of "civilized," even as it reflected Icelanders' anxieties about not being recognized by other Europeans or Westerners as belonging with them. The reproduction of stories of male explorers in Icelandic texts during this period, for example, allowed Icelandic intellectuals to imagine themselves as part of a progressive, civilized Europe, and furthermore to visualize the colonized parts of the world as spaces where masculinity and European-ness were enacted and reified. Even though these Icelandic writers did not themselves participate in these conquests, they could still place Icelanders within this collective "us" of a progressive Europe (see Loftsdóttir 2009). Some Icelandic schoolbooks directly identify Icelanders as part of the "white" race in the early twentieth century, but many also reflect Icelandic intellectuals' vision of themselves as intrinsically different from other Nordic people, in line with intense national sentiments at the time. Despite the shared origins, Icelandic character was seen as having been shaped over centuries by a "harsh mother," and the land and climate themselves as giving Icelanders their uniquely characteristic independence, endurance, and "roughness" (Loftsdóttir 2012). Icelanders' ability to position themselves within a particular racial category—white—and its increased reification in the late nineteenth and early twentieth century, bolstered by claims to a unique character, were necessarily important in strengthening claims to belong in the category of civilized European masculinity.

The Economic Boom in Iceland

The economic boom years in Iceland started gradually in the mid 1990s, expanded in scope and pace in the 2000s,[1] and consequently ended abruptly in 2008. Icelandic banks were privatized and capital flows liberalized in a series of neoliberal reforms (Sigurjónsson and

Mixa 2011), leading to a large influx of foreign capital and extensive public spending. The Icelandic government ignored foreign experts' warnings about the considerable expansion of the Icelandic banking system as the media and politicians alike celebrated bankers and businessmen as national heroes (Loftsdóttir 2015; Einarsdóttir 2010). Both the new privatized banks and the older, state-owned conservative banks took enormous risks with their investments (Mixa 2015). All the while, propaganda drives touted Iceland as a "neoliberal success story" and potentially a new financial capital (Johnson, Einarsdóttir, and Pétursdóttir 2013: 183). Furthermore, the economic boom period was a time of reckoning with Iceland's past as a Danish colony, and popular discourse, the media, and Icelandic politicians discussed Iceland as finally becoming an important player on the global stage (Loftsdóttir 2013; Björnsdóttir 2011). Such social discourse, focused primarily on the international success of Icelandic businessmen, also filtered into other spheres of Icelandic society, emphasizing Icelanders' unique contribution to global arts and literature (Grétarsdóttir, Ásmundsson, and Lárusson 2014) and the foreign policy arena (Björnsdóttir 2011; Loftsdóttir and Björnsdóttir 2014).

Although articulated differently in the new global environment, such discourses insistently upheld Iceland's status as a nation equal to other leading Western countries. Yet this mentality of the boom years was entangled with older historical anxieties centered on Iceland's position as a dependency of Denmark and the need to align Iceland firmly with other powerful European countries (Loftsdóttir 2012). In addition, these discourses relied on notions of Icelanders as somehow different from inhabitants of other countries due to their settlement heritage and the roughness of the Icelandic landscape. Moreover, much like discourses produced during Iceland's fight for independence in the late nineteenth and early twentieth centuries, boom-era discourses emphasized the masculine virility of men "going out" and conquering the world (Loftsdóttir 2012).

The economic boom stimulated rapid immigration to Iceland. This became particularly important once access to expanding Icelandic labor markets was facilitated by Iceland's joining the Schengen Area in 2001 (Skaptadóttir 2011). The presence of increasing numbers of immigrants from more and more distant locales stimulated Icelandic discussions on multiculturalism in Iceland that drew from and engaged with wider European discourses on the "problems" and challenges of multiculturalism (Skaptadóttir and Loftsdóttir 2009). Migrants were often referred to as a "workforce" (Icelandic:

vinnuafl) rather than as people, and their contributions to Icelandic society were still not connected to the wider ongoing discussions in Iceland that celebrated Icelandic economic prosperity. Rice (2007: 430) points out that the term *aðlögun*—immigrant assimilation or adjustment to Icelandic society—is devoid of any acknowledgment that wider Icelandic society also needs to adjust to increased plurality. Thus, concerns about how increased immigration would affect Icelandic culture and society (Skaptadóttir 2004) were raised, but not in relation to Iceland's other global integrations, such as its entry into global financial markets. Increasing immigration also intensified discussions about racism in Iceland, exposing the persistent, widespread misperception that Iceland's isolation and marginality in Europe made racism nonexistent in Iceland (Loftsdóttir 2012).

Gender Equality as a Brand

During the economic boom years, the Ministry for Foreign Affairs increased its international engagement considerably, seeking recognition as a "serious" player in the international arena. The establishment of the Icelandic peacekeeping unit (ICRU) in 2001 and its application in 2005 for a seat on the UN Security Council in 2009–2010 were part of this policy. As Björnsdóttir (2011) has elaborated, discourses of nationalism, masculinity, and development aid policy were embedded in both initiatives from the outset. The ICRU was created and structured by masculine standards and had men in all key positions. As part of the political sphere of development aid, it was promoted as Iceland's contribution to the international community. The militaristic, masculine ideology that defined the ICRU's first missions accorded with the overall masculine structure and aura of Icelandic society and the government's desire to be part of "international" society that was so palpable during the boom years.

The Ministry for Foreign Affairs upheld a policy of empowering women and emphasizing gender equality in developing countries like Afghanistan. However, these strategies seem to have mattered little inside the ICRU (Björnsdóttir 2011; Loftsdóttir and Björnsdóttir 2014) because all its positions—fire-fighters, paramedics, police—seemed to require special professional skills and training that few Icelandic women had (Björnsdóttir 2011). Thus, gender and gender equality did not become an issue in the ICRU until 2006, when the new Minister for Foreign Affairs Valgerður Sverrisdóttir, the first woman to occupy this post in Iceland, announced a change in the public image of the ICRU aimed at de-masculinizing the institution to make it more "soft" and "feminine" (Björnsdóttir 2011).

The institution's emphasis on gender equality for women in other countries continued under Sverrisdóttir's successor, Ingibjörg Sólrún Gísladóttir, who led the campaign for Iceland's candidacy for a seat on the UN Security Council in 2009–2010. The campaign placed great emphasis on "gender issues and the special needs of women and children" and women's "active participation in all levels of decision making" (Gísladóttir 2008). Lobbying for votes, the Icelandic government promised that it was "committed to being among the donors with the highest per capita contributions" (ibid.) to UN institutions such as the United Nations Entity for Gender Equality (UNIFEM) and the United Nations International Children's Emergency Fund (UNICEF). From 2001 to 2008, Iceland's contributions to UNIFEM rose from $117,000 to $854,000 (Ómarsdóttir 2010: 85).[2] The focus and emphasis were now on the status of "women and girls" (ibid.: 86) in the developing countries.

However, these actions were generally divorced from the political context of peacekeeping and Iceland's global position. Even more than before, they were framed as part of Iceland's substantial contribution to the world, an ideology and attitude that somehow defined the Icelandic self-image. The public discourse on gender equality during the "boom" years was part of the overall discourse that endorsed the ideology of the Icelandic "expansion." Gender equality became one of the brands that the Ministry for Foreign Affairs made use of during those years (Loftsdóttir and Björnsdóttir 2014). This was somewhat ironic, as at the time Icelandic women had only minor influence on major economic decisions in society and Iceland had the biggest gender wage gap in Europe (Einarsdóttir 2010; Johnson et al. 2013: 177). Nonetheless, relatively recent gender indexes (*Global Gender Gap Report* 2015) persistently ranked Iceland in the top ten globally (Johnson et al. 2013: 177). In public discourse, gender issues and especially gender equality were perceived as a "technical commodity" that Iceland could bestow upon international society, and about which Iceland could educate others. In 2007, the minister of social affairs stated in an article that at the annual UN Conference on Women, several states had requested "cooperation with us Icelanders in gender equality issues and there is a demand for our 'expansion' in that field" (Stefánsson 2007).

Governmental discourse also often linked the application for a seat on the UN Security Council to the country's status as an independent nation. Both the minister for foreign affairs and the president of Iceland claimed that the application to the Security Council could be seen as the final stage in the fight for Iceland's independence (Grímsson 2008), presumably referring to independence from Denmark. These claims were connected with the assertion that Iceland, once a poor colony, "now" had become one of the wealthiest countries in the world (Loftsdóttir 2014b). A report from the Ministry for Foreign Affairs confirms explicitly that Iceland's history as a colony was emphasized in the campaign for votes to the Security Council (Icelandic Ministry for Foreign Affairs 2009). Furthermore, in 2007 the minister for foreign affairs stated, regarding the application to the Security Council, that Icelanders could "assist former colonies in Africa, remembering that we were a colony ourselves and a developing country until the mid-20th century. It is unique in the West that as wealthy a country as Iceland does not want to take responsibility" (Gísladóttir 2008). Here Iceland is seen as taking its share of responsibility in the international community as a "developed" country, gender equality presumably being one of its contributions.

Another example of the Icelandic government's playing the gender/equality card to promote itself as a serious player in the international arena is the first female foreign minister's strategy to "soften up" and feminize the image of the ICRU, an effort that consisted of sending two health workers, a midwife, and a nurse to Afghanistan to teach local women some basics in midwifery and healthcare ("Vill mýkja ásýnd" 2006). The nature of this gesture was very much in line with the development policies of many Western governments: it carried the assumption that "Third World" women needed to be taught and "saved" from their own local and cultural knowledge or, as described by Spivak (1988), it illustrated the tendency of the West to "rescue brown women from brown men."

Icelandic Women Rescuing Iceland and the World

The economic crash created a pervasive sense of confusion, disappointment, and anxiety in Iceland, characterized as a sense of "collective shared national disaster" (Bernburg 2014: 74). The rampant discontent among the general public following the crash sparked massive protests and riots, including the "Pots and Pans" protest in front of the Parliament, and eventually resulted in the government's resignation in January 2009 (Bernburg 2014). The protesters identified corruption in the financial sector as the reason for the collapse and blamed the government for its failure to regulate it (ibid.). The series of protests continued even after the collapse of the government, though not as intensively. Two issues are particularly relevant here. On the one hand, a profound sense of Iceland's humiliation within the wider global world (Loftsdóttir 2014b; Chartier 2010) contributed to the strong self-criticism that characterized the atmosphere immediately after the crash. Although this self-criticism included a re-evaluation of pre-crash nationalism's focus on Iceland as the "best in the world," anxieties about being associated with previously colonized countries in the Global South persisted, alongside the emphasis on the need to regain Iceland's reputation (Loftsdóttir 2014a, 2014b). These anxieties did not materialize out of thin air but reflect constant hierarchies of Europeanness reflected also in discourses implying that Eastern Europeans and Southern Europeans are in some way "failed" Europeans or not fully European (Buchowski 2006). For example, some international media such as the *Globe and Mail* interpreted the International Monetary Fund (IMF) assistance provided to Iceland as evidence that Iceland's economy had dramatically "deteriorated," as it had needed to ask for "the sort of bailout more typical of the developing world than of a sophisticated Western economy" (Chartier 2010: 209). The international media furthermore claimed, as Chartier (ibid.: 208) has shown, that this request was "more typical of a developing economy than one of the wealthiest countries in the world, where measures such as soaring interest rates were more likely to be seen in places like Argentina and Thailand [but] not a country that likes to think of itself as closer to Europe."

On the other hand, the discourse in Iceland immediately after the crash, while critical of masculine traits and aggressive market values, celebrated women's important role in transforming Iceland into "a new society." This evolution in Iceland overlaps with wider discourses and practices that emerged globally in the aftermath of the global financial crisis in what Robert (2012: 90–91) has called "transnational business feminism," in which women were briefly seen as the "cure" to the capitalistic crisis. In public discourse, Icelandic businessmen were referred to pejoratively as "stock boys" who were "improvident and profit-seeking" (Magnússon 2008) and culpable for the economic meltdown. "We warned [that] it would happen," a prominent businesswoman declared (Ertel 2009). Public discussions proclaimed that it was women's turn to lead (see Helgason 2008)—at least in the financial sector. The former minister of welfare (Jóhannesdóttir 2009) argued in a speech that companies run by women were more profitable than those run by men. First, however, women had to "clean up" after the men, as usual. Or as one of our interviewees, Johanna (a middle manager in the financial sector), said: "women are always liable to clean up after adventures like this."³ In fact, it "became fashionable," as Anna (a bank employee) put it,⁴ to have women in higher management. Yet these ideas tended to slide into highly essentialist notions of Icelandic women that relied on constructions of women as "naturally" careful and honest, and intrinsically more nurturing. Thus, even as these notions seemed to recognize women as an active part of Icelandic society, they did so under specific terms. At the various protests that we attended after the economic crash, confusion and anger toward the government were often clearly evident. But there was also a sense of hope that a "new Iceland" would rise from the ashes—a better, more humane society based on different kinds of values.

Ideas rooted in the reification of women as mothers (Björnsdóttir 1997) and as a force for "improving the nation" (Halldórsdóttir 2006) have a long history in Iceland. The Woman's Alliance, a political party formed in the early 1980s, originated from the idea that women are essentially different from men and thus have something different to offer (Kristmundsdóttir 1997; Björnsdóttir and Kristmundsdóttir 1995). Even though these characteristics were originally seen as deriving from women's experiences, they were soon linked to women's "essential" characteristics, presenting women as ethically and morally superior to men (ibid.: 174). According to Björnsdóttir and Kristmundsdóttir (ibid.), "Motherhood and homemaking were seen to make women peace-loving, caring, considerate of others' needs, honest, clean, thrifty, fair, just and morally pure." Their discussion also highlights how these feminine virtues were seen as having relevance in the political arena. A speaker during one of the "Pots and Pans" protests held in downtown Reykjavík in front of Iceland's Parliament put it this way:

> The truth is that Icelandic women did not put us in this position but it is my belief that Icelandic women play a key role in rescuing us from this mess. It will be women who will clean up after this money-crazy-party (*gróðærisfyllerí*). (Oddsdóttir 2008)

To give another example, a parliamentary member claimed after the crash that in order to solve the problem of how to proceed, the leaders of different political parties, union leaders, business owners, and other leaders would have to join forces, explaining that "there should not only be men in suits; it is necessary that there are also many thrifty homemakers, women who preferably will be more in the lead than previously. We have not done such a good job, we the males." ("Steingrímur J. vill læsa" 2008).[5]

In the next section, we look into the role that gendered and racialized bodies have played in reconstituting Iceland, pointing out how the discourse—unintentionally or not—evoked global disparities of power that have historically been portrayed "white" women as active subjects and "black" women as passive subjects in need of assistance.

Auður Capital

The financial services company Auður Capital[6] was one of the few Icelandic financial companies to survive the crisis. It was founded in 2007 by Halla Tómasdóttir, former managing director of the Icelandic Chamber of Commerce, and Kristín Pétursdóttir, former investment banker at the British branch of the Icelandic bank Kaupthing Singer & Friedlander. As they explained, they "were somewhat overwhelmed by the testosterone levels in business and finance"[7] and wanted to "incorporate 'feminine' values into the world of finance by offering their clients a long-term perspective and win-win approach."[8] In 2008 Auður Capital received permission to operate from Iceland's Financial Supervisory Authority. From the beginning, the company marketed itself as a socially responsible company committed to openness, more conscious risk management, and the promotion of "feminine values" in the finance and banking sector.

Auður Capital strongly emphasized its image as a women's company, which in the post-crash months fitted well into the critical discourse on the masculine traits of the Icelandic banking and financial sector. Tómasdóttir stated, regarding Auður Capital, that "we believe that our approach and values appeal to people now" (Camila 2008). She identified independence, risk awareness, profit with principles, straight talk, and emotional capital as the company's key values. The company discourse characterized women as long-term thinkers and better team players than men, and even suggested that the economic crash would never have happened if they had been in charge of the financial and banking sector. Auður Capital's founders even pointed out that they had warned the authorities: "In early 2008 she [Halla Tómasdóttir] published a report warning Prime Minister Geir Haarde that Iceland's financial model was unsustainable" (Hewlett 2009). In an interview with *Global Economics* (Ertel 2009), Tómasdóttir went on to say that the crisis had been "man-made" by a bunch of guys who "went to the same school, they drive the same cars, they wear the same suits and they have the same attitudes. They got us into this situation—and they had a lot of fun doing it."

The feminine values emphasized in Auður Capital's policy in fact resemble the same characteristics of Icelandic women that have historically highlighted in Iceland, where women's "essential" characteristics as homemakers and mothers are seen as giving them moral superiority over men. Women's essence and the company's image were even more closely associated with each other by Tómasdóttir and Pétursdóttir in an interview in 2009 (Cameron 2009). Describing the reason the company was established, Cameron reports that "it took close to a full pregnancy term to develop their service offering, and another six months to come up with what makes them different from other financial services providers." Later the text adds, citing the founders' words: "Now that we have given 'birth' to her, we feel proud and excited ... we are happy to share her upbringing with you." Here the founders' role as mothers is strongly emphasized, thus further associating the successful businesswoman with the iconic image of the "mother" figure. Because of this, Auður Capital was often referred to, at our workplace and in informal discussions with men and women in Iceland after the crash, in highly favorable terms as exemplifying the building of a new Iceland.

As a company that boasted of maintaining "feminine" values while operating in a "testosterone-enhanced culture" (Hewlett 2009), Auður Capital received much attention in the international financial press. Its message fit well into global ideas of "transnational business feminism," in which, according to Robert (2012: 88), capitalism is naturalized and depoliticized, and women are seen as the solution to the crisis. Tómasdóttir and Pétursdóttir were not only praised as smart, socially responsible, and risk-aware but were also said to be descended from Vikings and referred to as "the Wise Viking's Daughters" (Chapsal 2011). These company founders did their best to create and maintain this Viking image, even as they distanced it from the reckless behaviors of the so-called business Vikings. For instance, Tómasdóttir stated in an interview that the company was "named after Viking woman Auður the wise" (Tómasdóttir 2010) and that the "wise moniker signifies wealth, happiness, and space" (Chapsal 2011). It is tempting to link this to Appel's (2014) ideas on the role of financial imagination, where not only men, but predominantly white men were the embodiment of the financial system. The two founders of the company Auður Capital appeared regularly in the international media and could be seen as particularly appealing representatives of "transnational business feminism" with their conservative suits, white faces, and slim figures. Connell and Wood (2005) have pointed out that because transnational business masculinity is based on particular disciplines of the body, the slim, "well-kept" body is particularly important. The association with the iconic Viking image furthermore gives this rather conservative embodiment of the new way of doing finance a more exotic and "white" appearance.

The company's reproduction of gender stereotypes intersects with ideas of both proper Europeanness and repressed and powerless women in other parts of the world who need to be assisted in some way. All the company's funds were named after the "Viking woman Auður"—underlining the feminine nature of the company—except one, established in 2008 in cooperation with the musician Björk Guðmundsdóttir to invest in "early-stage businesses concentrating on green technology, with the goal of helping spur a recovery of Iceland's economy, which was devastated by a financial crisis this fall" (Miller 2008). The private equity fund "Auður I" was intended to target profitable female-owned businesses "run by women or whose main customers are women" (ibid.), while "Auður Day-Work" (Dagsverk Auðar) focused on Icelandic community projects. These three funds all focused on local Icelandic issues, unlike "Auður's Universe" (AlheimsAuður),[9] which, as the name indicates, operates on a more cosmopolitan basis. Along with the voluntary contributions of Auður Capital's clients, the company donated 1 percent of its profits to the equity fund. Auður's Universe focuses on allocating funds to charity organizations in Iceland and abroad, mostly in Africa. Its main goal is "encouraging women to action and having initiative, especially in the developing nations" ("AlheimsAuður" n.d.). Projects that have received funds from Auður's Universe include Enza Empowering Women, which operates in South Africa, as well as projects that, like the ABC Children's Aid International Project in Africa and in developing countries elsewhere, are directed at children. This emphasis on various forms of humanitarian assistance through funds and consumption is a growing trend that has gained popularity in Iceland, fitting quite well within scholarly analysis focused on the neoliberalization of international development. The Icelandic writer Einar Már Guðmundsson (2008) portrayed this trend in an article that critically targeted "business Vikings" for, as he phrased it, "pretending to be protectors of noble causes," and their wives too for "pretending to care about the children in Africa. They said that because their husbands were so successful and lucky businessmen, they too wanted to do something good." In an interview in 2009, Tómasdóttir and Pétursdóttir stated that "our goal, ultimately, is to create a world that's more balanced in terms of gender and the distribution of opportunities, wealth and education. For us, it's not enough that our business thrives: we need to help women around the world be successful" (Mouazan 2009).

Conclusion

In this chapter, we have shown how essentialist notions of gender gained special currency during a massive economic crisis. Icelandic post-crash discourses recycled essentialized notions of gender, portraying Icelandic women as ethically and morally superior to men. Women's experience as homemakers and their more "caring" nature would thus be useful in rescuing Iceland's economy. These discourses reflect the reliance of older Icelandic gender ideas on essentialism (Björnsdóttir and Kristmundsdóttir 1995), but they also represent wider trends after the financial crisis in Europe in 2008 in which women's "natural" characteristics were seen as solutions to the problems of capitalism in general (see Robert 2012). International discourse often referred to Iceland in this regard, using Auður Capital as an example in which simply adding women and their presumed intrinsic characteristics to the upper echelons of business was seen as averting crises in capitalism. Iceland thus became a case study for understanding and reflecting on the crisis in other countries.

Even though Icelandic feminist scholars have long stressed that gender equality has not been fully realized (Pétursdóttir 2008), Iceland, along with the other Nordic countries, has a reputation of being committed to gender equality (Holli et al. 2005). We find it important to stress in our analysis that the association of gender and gender equality with the Nordic cannot be fully separated from particular racialized geographies. References to "other" women in the Global South have been used to position countries like Iceland as fully European and Western. In Iceland, such discourses have played on the historical emphasis on and anxieties around Iceland's position alongside more powerful European countries. As indicated by Loftsdóttir (2014b), race continues to be meaningful—or "endures" in Europe, to use Amin's (2010) phrase—through diverse and often distinct discourses that continue to rest on prior forms of racialization, even though they are shaped to serve the present.

Kristín Loftsdóttir is a Professor at the University of Iceland. She directs the research project "Creating Europe Through Racialized Mobilities" Her research interests include crisis, whiteness, postcolonial Europe, gender, mobility and racism. Her publications include *Crisis and Coloniality at Europe's Margins: Creating Exotic Iceland* (2019) and the co-edited of *Crisis in the Nordic Nations and Beyond* (2014) with Lars Jensen.

Helga Björnsdóttir is Adjunct in Anthropology on the Faculty of Social and Human Sciences at the University of Iceland. Her research interests are ideas and images of gender, men and masculinities, militarism, space, and homelessness. Her recent projects have focused on militarization and gender in connection to the establishment of peacekeeping in Iceland and its links to the shaping of national identity.

Notes

Our discussion here is based on data from the project Icelandic Identity in Crisis, a research project focused on the economic crash in Iceland (see http://vefir.hi.is/icelandicidentityincrisis/) that was funded by Rannís (grant number 130426-053) and the University of Iceland Research Fund.

1. The gradual deregulation of banks in the 1990s, in particular the liberalization of capital flows and the adoption of the EEA (European Economic Area) treaty in 1994, is often seen as the beginning of the boom period (Ólafsson 2008). The financial collapse caused governmental debt to rise from 23% of GDP in 2007 (Icelandic Ministry of Finance 2009) to 78% in 2009 (Icelandic Ministry of Finance 2010).
2. In 2007, the Ministry for Foreign Affairs and UNICEF in Iceland signed a mutual agreement to increase their cooperation (Sverrisdóttir 2007).
3. Interview, 2013.
4. Interview, 2013.
5. Our translation from Icelandic: "Því þarna eiga ekki bara að vera jakkafataklæddir karlar, þarna þurfa líka að vera margar hagsýnar húsmæður, konur, sem hefðu betur ráðið meiru um okkar mál en þær hafa gert, við höfum ekki staðið okkur svo vel karlarnir."
6. Auður Capital merged with the financial service firm Virðing in January 2014 and now operates under the name Virðing.
7. *BBC News*, 18 May 2009. Retrieved 6 June 2015 from http://news.bbc.co.uk/2/hi/business/8048488.stm.

8. *Cartier Women's Initiative Awards,* 2009. Retrieved 6 June 2015 from http://www.cartierwomensinitiative.com/candidate/halla-tomasdottir-kristin-petursdottir.
9. AlheimsAuður is now owned by Virðing.

References

"AlheimsAuður." n.d. *Auður Capital.* Retrieved 26 September 2013 from http://www.audur.is/. Amin, Ash. 2010. "The Remainders of Race." *Theory, Culture & Society,* 27(1): 1–23.
Appel, H. 2014. "Finance, Figuration, and the Alternative Banking Group of Occupy Wall Street." *Signs* 40(1): 53–58.
Bernburg, J. 2014. "Gambling Debt," in *Overthrowing the Government: A Case Study in Protest,* ed. E. Durrenberger and G. Pálsson, 63–79. Boulder, CO: University Press of Colorado.
Björnsdóttir, I. 1997. "Nationalism, Gender and the Body in Icelandic Nationalistic Discourse." *Nora* 5(1): 3–13.
Björnsdóttir, H. 2011. "Give Me Some Men Who Are Stout-Hearted Men, Who Will Fight, for the Right They Adore," in "Negotiating Gender and Identity in Icelandic Peacekeeping." Ph.D. dissertation. Reykjavík: University of Iceland.
Björnsdóttir, I., and S. Kristmundsdóttir. 1995. "Purity and Defilement: Essentialism and Punishment in the Icelandic Women's Movement." *European Journal of Women's Studies* 2: 171–183.
Bornstein, E., and P. Redfield, eds. 2010. *Forces of Compassion: Humanitarianism between Ethics and Politics.* Santa Fe, NM: School of Advanced Research.
Buchowski, Michal. 2006. "The Specter of Orientalism in Europe: From Exotic Other to Stigmatized Brother." *Anthropological Quarterly* 79(3): 463–482.
Bunzl, Matti. 2004. "Boas, Foucault and the 'Native Anthropologist': Notes Toward Neo-Boasian Anthropology." *American Anthropologist* 106(3): 435–442.
Cameron, L. 2009, "Financial Services: Giving Birth to a New Kind of Bank." *Canadian Business,* 26 October. Retrieved 11 June 2015 from http://www.canadianbusiness.com/business-strategy/financial-services-giving-birth-to-a-new-kind-of-bank/.
Camilla. 2008. "Auður will sparisjóð Kaupþings." *Morgunblaðið,* 16 October. Retrieved 4 June 2015 from http://www.mbl.is/greinasafn/grein/1250095/.
Chapsal, M. 2011. "The Wise Viking's Daughters." *Gender-Balanced Leadership* 6(April). Retrieved 2 December 2015 from http://www.

scoop.it/t/gender-balanced-leadership/p/4004095151/2013/07/02/the-wise-viking-s-daughters-women-on-stage.

Chartier, D. 2010. *The End of Iceland's Innocence: The Image of Iceland in the Foreign Media during the Crisis.* London and Reykjavík: Citizen Press.

Cochrane, K. 2011. "Is Iceland the Best Country for Women?" *Guardian*, 11 October. Retrieved 4 April 2015 from http://www.theguardian.com/world/2011/oct/03/iceland-best-country-women-feminist.

Connell, R., and J. Wood. 2005. "Globalization and Business Masculinities." *Men and Masculinities* 7(4): 347–364.

Durrenberger, P., and G. Pálsson. 1989. "Introduction," in *The Anthropology of Iceland*, ed. P. Durrenberger and G. Pálsson, ix–xxvii. Iowa City, IA: University of Iowa Press.

Einarsdóttir, Þ. 2010. "Kreppur og kerfishrun í ljósi kyngerva og þegnréttar." *Íslenska þjóðfélagið* 1(1): 27–48. Retrieved 22 November 2015 from http://www.thjodfelagid.is/index.php/Th/issue/view/6.

Ertel, M. 2009. "Women Reach for Power in Iceland." *Spiegel Online*, 24 April. Retrieved 5 June 2015 from http://www.businessweek.com/globalbiz/content/apr2009/gb20090424_328219.htm.

Escobar, A. 1995. *Encountering Development: The Making and the Unmaking of the Third World.* Princeton, NJ: Princeton University Press.

———. 2007. "Worlds and Knowledges Otherwise: The Latin American Modernity/Coloniality Research Program." *Cultural Studies* 21(2–3): 179–210.

Ferguson, J. 2006. *Global Shadows.* Durham, NC: Duke University Press.

Gísladóttir, I. 2008. "Address at the Formal Opening Session of the High-Level Roundtable on International Cooperation for Sustainable Development in Caribbean Small Island Development States." *Icelandic Ministry for Foreign Affairs*, 25 March. Retrieved 11 June 2015 from http://www.utanrikisraduneyti.is/frettaefni/raedurISG/nr/4181.

The Global Gender Gap Report: 2015. 2015. *World Economic Forum.* Retrieved 29 August 2016 from http://www3.weforum.org/docs/GGGR2015/cover.pdf.

Goudge, P. 2003. *The Power of Whiteness: Racism in Third World Development and Aid.* London: Lawrence and Wishart.

Grétarsdóttir, T., Á. Ásmundsson, and H. Lárusson. 2014. "Creativity and Crisis," in *Gambling Debt: Iceland's Rise and Fall in the Global Economy*, ed. E. Paul Durrenberger and G. Pálsson, 93–109. Boulder, CO: University Press of Colorado.

Grímsson, Ó. 2008. "Interviewed by Sveinn Helgason." *RÚV* [Ríkisútvarpið – The Icelandic National Broadcasting Service], 12 March.

Gullestad, M. 2002. "Invisible Fences: Egalitarianism, Nationalism and Racism." *Journal of the Royal Anthropological Institute* 8(1): 45–63.

Gupta, A., and J. Ferguson. 1997. "Discipline and Practice: 'The Field' as Site, Method, and Location in Anthropology," in *Anthropological Locations: Boundaries and Grounds of a Field Science*, ed. A. Gupta and J. Ferguson, 1–46. Berkeley: University of California Press.

Guðmundsson, E. 2008. "Herhvöt úr norðri." *Morgunblaðið*, 16 October. Retrieved 11 June 2015 from http://www.mbl.is/greinasafn/grein/1250149/.

Hálfdánarson, G. 2000. "Iceland: A Peaceful Secession." *Scandinavian Journal of History* 25(1–2): 87–100.Halldórsdóttir, E. 2006. "Constructing Identity: A Critical Assessment of the Gender Perspective in Icelandic Historiography," in *Professions and Social Identity: New European Historical Research on Work, Gender and Society*, ed. B. Waaldijk, 135–151. Pisa: Edizioni Plus-Pisa University Press.

Hartigan, J. J. 1997. "Establishing the Fact of Whiteness." *American Anthropologist* 99(3): 495–505.

Helgason, Þ. 2008. "Nýja Ísland." *Morgunblaðið*, October 18. Retrieved 15 May 2015 from http://www.mbl.is/greinasafn/grein/1250540/?item_nu m=34&searchid=0c1a12c3ee279020961b2c3da7bfbb4f9a923d81.

Hewlett, S. 2009. "Too Much Testosterone on Wall Street?" *Harvard Business Review*, January 7. Retrieved 6 June 2015 from http://thedowningstreetproject.ning.com/profiles/blogs/would-more-women-in-financial.

Holli, A., E. Magnusson, and M. Rönnblom. 2005. "Critical Studies of Nordic Discourses on Gender and Gender Equality." *Nora* 13(3): 148–152.

Holter, Ø. 2003. *Can Men Do It? Men and Gender Equality: The Nordic Experience*. Copenhagen: Temanord.

Holter, Ø., H. Svare, and C. Engeland. 2009. *Gender Equality and Quality of Life: A Norwegian Perspective*. Oslo: The Nordic Gender Institute (NIKK). Icelandic Ministry for Foreign Affairs. 2009. *Skýrsla um framboð Íslands og kosningabaráttu til sætis í öryggisráði Sameinuðu þjóðanna, 2009–2010* [Report on Iceland's application and campaign for a seat on the UN Security Council]. Reykjavik: Ministry for Foreign Affairs.

Icelandic Ministry of Finance. 2009. "Fylgiskjal um eignir og skuldir ríkissjóðs-", *Icelandic Ministry of Finance*. Retrieved 22 November 2015 from http://www.fjarmalaraduneyti.is/media/Utgefin_rit/Fylgiskjol_um_eignir_og_skuldir_rikissjods_20090626.pdf.

Icelandic Ministry of Finance. 2010. "Um skuldastöðu ríkissjóðs. Fréttatilkynning nr. 8/2010" [On the debt situation of the state treasury, 15 March 2010 press release nr. 8/2010], *Icelandic Ministry of Finance*, 15 March. Retrieved 22 November 2015 from http://www.fjarmalaraduneyti.is/frettir/frettatilkynningar/frettatilkynningar/nr/12988.

Jacobs-Huey, Lanita. 2002. "The Natives are Gazing and Talking Back: Reviewing the Problematics of Positionality, Voice and Accountability

among 'Native' Anthropologists." *American Anthropologist* 104(3): 791–804.
Jóhannesdóttir, Á. R. 2009. "Endurreisn samfélagsins krefst jafnréttis kynja." *Icelandic Ministry of Welfare*, March 8. Retrieved 12 April 2016 from https://www.velferdarraduneyti.is/radherra/raedur_og_greinar_arj/nr/4282.
Johnson, J., Þ. Einarsdóttir, and G. Pétursdóttir. 2013. "A Feminist Theory of Corruption: Lessons from Iceland." *Politics and Gender* 9(2): 174–206.
Keskinen, S., S. Tuori, S. Irni, and D. Mulinari, eds. 2009. *Complying with Colonialism: Gender, Race and Ethnicity in the Nordic Region*. Surrey: Ashgate.
Kristmundsdóttir, S. 1997. *Doing and Becoming: Women's Movement and Women's Personhood in Iceland 1870–1990*. Reykjavík: Háskóli Íslands.
Loftsdóttir, K. 2009. "'Pure Manliness': The Colonial Project and Africa's Image in 19th Century Iceland." *Identities: Global Studies in Culture and Power* 16(3): 271–293.
———. 2012. "Colonialism at the Margins: Politics of Difference in Europe as Seen through Two Icelandic Crises." *Identities: Global Studies in Culture and Power* 19(5): 597–615.
———. 2013. "Republishing 'Ten Little Negros': Exploring Nationalism and Whiteness in Iceland." *Ethnicities* 13(3): 295–315.
———. 2014a. "Building on Iceland's 'Good Reputation': Icesave, Crisis and Affective National Identities." *Ethnos*, 81(2): 338–363. DOI: 10.1080/00141844.2014.931327.
———. 2014b. "Iceland, Rejected by McDonald's: Desire and Anxieties in a Global Crisis." *Social Anthropology* 22(3): 340–352.
———. 2015. "The Danes Don't Get It: The Economic Crash and Iceland's Postcolonial Engagements." *National Identities*. DOI: 10.1080/14608944.2016.1095491.
Loftsdóttir, K., and H. Björnsdóttir. 2014. "Nordic Exceptionalism and Gendered Peacekeeping: The Case of Iceland." *European Journal of Women's Studies*, 22(2): 208–222. DOI: 10.1177/1350506814543839.
Loftsdóttir, K., and L. Jensen. 2012. "Introduction," in *Whiteness and Postcolonialism in the Nordic Region: Exceptionalism, Migrant Others and National Identities*, ed. K. Lofttsdóttir and L. Jensen, 1–11. Surrey: Ashgate.
Magnússon, G. 2008. *Nýja Ísland*. Reykjavík: Forlagið.
Matthíasdóttir, S. 2004. *Hinn sanni Íslendingur: Þjóðerni, kyngervi og vald á Íslandi 1900–1930*. Reykjavík: Háskólaútgáfan.
McIntosh, L. 2015. "Impossible Presence: Race, Nation and the Cultural Politics of 'Being Norwegian.'" *Ethnic and Racial Studies* 38(2): 309–325.
Miller, C. 2008. "Bjork, Icelandic Singer and…Venture Capitalist?" *New York Times*, 23 December. Retrieved 11 June 2015 from http://bits.

blogs.nytimes.com/2008/12/23/bjork-icelandic-singer-and-venture-apitalist/?_r=0.
Mixa, M. 2015. "A Nation of Money and Sheep," in *The Routledge Companion to Cross- Cultural Managements*, ed. N. Holden, S. Michailova, and S. Tietze, 294–303. London and New York: Routledge.
Moran, M. 2010. "Gender, Militarism, and Peace-Building: Projects of the Postconflict Movements." *Annual Review of Anthropology* 39: 261–274.
Mouazan, S. 2009. "Halla Tómasdóttir & Kristin Pétursdóttir: Founders AuDur Capital; Financial Services Based on Feminine Values." Retrieved 11 June 2015 from http://bit.ly/1RiH6xu.
Narayan, Kirin. 1993. "How Native Is a 'Native' Anthropology?" *American Anthropologist* 95: 671–684.
Naum, M., and J.M. Nordin, eds. 2013. *Scandinavian Colonialism and the Rise of Modernity: Small Time Agents in a Global Arena*. New York: Springer.
Oddsdóttir, K. 2008. Stjórninni gefið viku til að boða til kostninga. RÚV, November. Retrieved 11 June 2015 from http://www.ru.is/lisalib/getfile.aspx?itemid=11485.
Ólafsson, S. 2008. "Íslenska efnahagsundrið: Frá hagsæld til frjálshyggju til fjármálahruns." *Stjórnmál og stjórnsýsla* 4(2): 233–256.
Ómarsdóttir, S. 2010. "Áhrif feminisma á utanríkisstefnu Íslands 1999–2009." *Stjórnmál og stjórnsýsla. Veftímarit* 1(6): 75–94. Retrieved 22 November 2015 from http://rafhladan.is/bitstream/handle/10802/403/%C1hrif%20feminisma%20%E1%20utanr%EDkisstefnu%20%CDslands%201999-2009.pdf?sequence=1.
Otto, D. 2006. "A Sign of 'Weakness'? Disrupting Gender Certainties in the Implementation of Security Council Resolution 1325." *Michigan Journal of Gender and Law* 13: 113 –175.
Pandey, G. 2013. *A History of Prejudice*. Cambridge: Cambridge University Press.
Pétursdóttir, G. 2008. "Within the Socially Desirable Aura of Gender Equality: Division of Domestic Labour and Child Care," in *Rannsóknir í Félagsvísindum IX.*, ed. G. Jóhannesson and H. Björnsdóttir, 213–223. Reykjavík: Félagsvísindastofnun Háskóla Íslands.
Popular Memory Group. 1982. "Popular Memory: Theory, Politics, Methods," in *Making Histories: Studies in History Writing and Politics*, ed. R. Johnson, G. McLennan, B. Schwarz, and D. Sutton, 205–52. Minneapolis, MN: University of Minnesota Press.
Rastrick, Ó. 2013. *Háborgin: menning, fagurfræði og pólitík í upphafi tuttugustu aldar*. Reykjavík: Háskólaútgáfan.
Rice, J. 2007. "The Charity Complex: An Ethnography of a Material Aid Agency in Reykjavík, Iceland." Ph.D. dissertation. St. John's: Memorial University of Newfoundland.
Robert, A. 2012. "Financial Crisis, Financial Firms…and Financial Feminism? The Rise of 'Transnational Business Feminism' and the

Necessity of Marxist-Feminism IPE." *Socialist Studies/Études socialistes* 8(2): 85–108.

Sigurðsson, G. 1996. "Icelandic National Identity: From Romanticism to Tourism," in *Making Europe in Nordic Contexts*, ed. P. Anttonen, 41–75. Turku: Nordic Institute of Folklore, University of Turku.

Sigurjónsson, Þ., and M. Mixa. 2011. "Learning from the 'Worst Behaved': Iceland's Financial Crisis and the Nordic Comparison." *Thunderbird International Business Review* 53: 209–223. DOI: 10.1002/tie.20402

Skaptadóttir, U. 2004. "Mobilities and Cultural Difference: Immigrants' Experiences in Iceland," in *Topographies of Globalization: Politics, Culture, Language*, ed. V. Ingimundarson, K. Loftsdóttir, and I. Erlingsdóttir, 133–148. Reykjavík: University of Iceland.

———. 2011. "The Context of Polish Immigration and Integration in Iceland," in *Integration and Assimilation? Polish Immigrants in Iceland*, ed. M. Budyta-Budzyńskas, 18–28. Warsaw: Wydawnictwo Naukowe Scholar.

Skaptadóttir, U., and K. Loftsdóttir. 2009. "Cultivating Culture? Images of Iceland, Globalization and Multicultural Society," in *Images of the North*, ed. S. Jakobsen, 205–216. Amsterdam: Rodopi.

Spivak, G. 1988. "Can the Subaltern Speak?" in *Marxism and the Interpretation of Culture*, ed. C. Nelson and L. Grossberg, 271–313. Urbana, IL: University of Illinois Press.

Stefánsson, M. 2007. "Sátt um mikilvæg skref í jafnréttisbaráttunni." *Icelandic Ministry of Welfare*, 8 March. Retrieved 11 June 2015 from http://www.velferdarraduneyti.is/radherra/RaedurMS/nr/3118.

"Steingrímur J. vill læsa hóp forystufólks inni í Höfða þar til það nær saman um lausnir". 2008. *Eyjan*, 2 October. Retrieved 12 September 2013 from http://eyjan.pressan.is/frettir/2008/10/02/steingrimur-j-vill-laesa-hop-forystufolks-inni-i-hofda-thar-til-hann-naer-saman-um-lausnir/.

Stoler, A. L. 2008. "Imperial Debris: Reflections on Ruin and Ruination." *Cultural Anthropology* 23(2): 191–219.

———. 2013. "Preface," in *Imperial Debris: On Ruins and Ruination*, ed. A. L. Stoler, ix–xi. Durham, NC: Duke University Press.

Sverrisdóttir, V. 2007. "Ræða Valgerðar Sverrisdóttur utanríkisráðherra í tilefni undirskristar á rammasamningi milli utanríkisráðuneytisins og Landsnefndar UNIFEM á Íslandi," *Icelandic Ministry of Foreign Affairs*, 8 May. Retrieved 11 June 2015 from http://www.utanrikisraduneyti.is/frettaefni/RaedurVS/nr/3540.

Tómasdóttir, H. 2010. "A Feminine Response to Iceland's Financial Crash." *TED*, 8 December. Retrieved 11 June 2015 from https://www.ted.com/talks/halla_tomasdottir/transcript?language=en.

"Vill mýkja ásýnd íslensku friðargæslunnar." 2006. *Morgunblaðið*, 23 August, p. 6.

2

"Latvians do not understand the Greek people"

Europeanness and Complicit Becoming in the Midst of Financial Crisis

Dace Dzenovska

Becoming European

In January 2014, Latvia joined the Eurozone. Europoliticians and Eurofunctionaries congratulated Latvia on this achievement and remarked that Latvia has now joined the "core of Europe" (Grundule 2014). Such use of the notion of the "core of Europe" suggests that today's Europe is at heart a monetary union governed by the rules of finance capitalism. Moreover, it is not a homogenous but rather a differentiated entity, governed through hierarchically arranged distinctions, such as that between the core and peripheries.

However, joining the Eurozone is no guarantee that one has become fully European. In 2015, Latvia's Europeanness came into question in the context of Europe's "migration/refugee crisis," that is, the set of European states' politically and ethically contested responses to the millions of people from Syria, Somalia, Afghanistan, and sub-Saharan Africa who, fleeing unlivable lives due to war and other forms of dispossession, crossed the Mediterranean in hopes of reaching Europe, many of them dying en route. This series of events, widely referred to as crisis, was also governed through distinctions. First, the people on the move were sorted into migrants and refugees with the aim of enabling the latter to enter or remain while keeping most of the former out. Second, European states and peoples were sorted according to their response to the crisis. Thus, for example, Central and Eastern European states, including Latvia, lost some of their Europeanness insofar as their peoples' and politicians' reluctance, even refusal, to accept and welcome refugees left those states open to criticism of their apparent lack of compassion and undermining of European values (Krastev 2015; Simecka and Tallis 2015; see also Dzenovska 2018a, 2017, 2016).

This suggests that besides meeting the criteria of formal membership in political and monetary unions and fitting the identity-related markers of Europeanness, peoples and states can become more or less European depending on their political and ethical conduct in particular circumstances (Dzenovska 2013a; Böröcz 2006). Moreover, gaining and losing Europeanness is a relational process. Thus, Latvia—along with the rest of Central and Eastern Europe—was deemed less-than-European in the context of the migration/refugee crisis relative to the moral superiority asserted by Sweden and Germany (Dzenovska 2017). In contrast, Latvia succeeded in becoming European in the context of the 2008 financial crisis by demonstrating exceptional fiscal discipline and implementing severe austerity measures—unlike Greece, which was widely thought of as failing the test of Europeanness, because its citizens protested against the austerity measures instead of behaving as responsible economic subjects (Mufti 2014; see also De Genova 2016; Herzfeld 1987, 2013). Europeanness, then, is an unstable and relational articulation of often racialized identity markers, institutional membership, and political and economic conduct. Moreover, it tends to be distributed as a marker of civilization by those propelled to the position of proper Europeanness in particular historical moments (see also Loftsdóttir, Smith, and Hipfl this volume).[1]

In this chapter, I analyze how Europeanness was negotiated in the context of financial crisis in Europe. In particular, I am interested in how moralized economic conduct played a role in the distribution of Europeanness, as well as in how marginalized Europeans, such as Latvians and Greeks, negotiated Europeanness in relation to each other. For example, I trace the emergence of a subject position from which it was possible to claim that "Latvians do not understand the Greek people" in the context of Greece's sovereign debt crisis. This statement was made by Jānis Reiris, Latvia's Minister of Finance, but the sentiment was shared beyond political discourse. It emerged in response to the definitive "no" to austerity measures that Greek voters delivered in a referendum held on 5 July 2015.[2] Importantly, in tracing the contours of this subject position, I do not offer a representative analysis of the views of Latvia's citizens and residents about debt, Europeanness, and the the Greek sovereign debt crisis. Rather, I offer analysis of how the hegemonic subject position of "Latvians do not understand the Greek people" was formed in the context of public debates about the financial crisis in Latvia and Greece. There were dissenting voices among Latvians and among Latvia's Russian-speakers that contested this normative subject position, but such dissenting voices were not heard in the mainstream public discourse at the time and did not translate into sustained protest actions of the kind that occurred elsewhere in Europe, most notably Greece.

The bailout negotiations and debates about them within the European public and political space suggested that the Greek handling of the sovereign debt crisis was not thought of as merely an economic issue, but also as a moral and cultural one. Many commentators emphasized that no reform would be successful in Greece unless institutional and cultural practices changed (e.g., Paalzow 2015). Similarly, the primary concern of many Eurozone taxpayers who feared the burden of Eurozone solidarity was not whether the bailout was economically sustainable in the long run or whether people in Greece were able to withstand the debt burden, but rather whether Greece and Greeks behaved as proper economic, moral, and thus European subjects. In that light, the Latvian minister's statement itself should be viewed not only as a commentary on the incomprehensible economic conduct of the "Greek people," but also as an instance of *becoming European* that reinforces forms of power that shape the material and discursive contours of Europeanness. Insofar as such becoming European reproduces hegemonic ways of distributing Europeanness via civilizational—and often racialized—hierarchies, it is a form of *complicit*—rather than radically transformative—becoming. To put it another way, the Latvian way of becoming European does not carry an inherently transformative potential in relation to history "as a set of preconditions that one leaves behind in order to 'become', that is, to create something new" (Deleuze in Biehl and Locke 2010: 317), but can be and often is complicit with history.

Latvian assertions of Europeanness in the context of the Greek sovereign debt crisis drew on recognizable civilizational hierarchies, but at the same time they were also aided by an unexpectedly lucky historical contingency: the stories that Latvians tell themselves about themselves coincided with the markers of Europeanness that emerged as important amidst the crisis. For example, the virtue of endurance in the face of harsh conditions (such as World War II, Soviet deportations, and poor economic conditions), which is central to the Latvian self-narrative, facilitated proper economic—and thus moral and European—conduct, namely living by the rules and within one's means regardless of how constraining or devastating these rules and means may be. The financial crisis was, one might say, the Latvian moment to shine as proper Europeans.

In what follows, I draw on observations made during my ethnographic research on tolerance promotion in the context of post-socialist democratization, conducted between 2005 and 2010 (Dzenovska 2018a, 2013a), and that on outmigration, conducted between 2010 and 2012 (Dzenovska 2018b, 2013b), to consider how hegemonic forms of power were both reproduced and reinvented in Latvia vis-à-vis public reasoning about the Greek sovereign debt crisis.[3] On the one hand, I show how the Latvians becoming European in relation to Greece's sovereign debt crisis reinforced the hegemony of well-worn civilizational hierarchies of people and places through which Europe is constituted as a normative and aspirational space. On the other hand, I suggest that in conditions of neoliberalization and financialization of capitalism, these civilizational hierarchies became visible in relation to economic conduct.

The problem of debt, whether private or sovereign, is not and has never been merely an economic issue. It has always had a moral and a civilizing dimension (see also Graeber 2011; Peebles 2010; Gregory 2012). Debates about the sovereign debt crisis in Greece have revealed how morality and economics intersect in the current historical moment, as well as how this particular intersection of morality and economics works to distribute credentials of Europeanness, in the process obscuring the operations of contemporary forms of capitalism.

For example, Maurizio Lazzarato (2012) argues that the current form of finance capitalism, which depends heavily on debt as the source of capital accumulation, has produced the figure of the "indebted man." The "indebted man," first, considers debt to be part of a healthy economic life and, second, is willing "to assume the costs, as well as the risks of a flexible and financialized economy, costs and risks, which are not only—far from it—those of innovation, but also and especially those of precariousness, poverty, unemployment, a failing health system, housing shortages, etc." (ibid.: 51). The "indebted man" is a Weberian ideal type and a figure that characterizes the tensions that animate contemporary forms of capitalism (Weber 1897, 1930). At the same time, it entails normative elements, insofar as being in debt and living responsibly in indebtedness have become measures of proper economic and thus moral and European conduct.

In order to draw the historically specific contours of Latvian complicity with the civilizational hierarchies through which Europeanness is upheld, and to point out the potential consequences of such complicit becoming, I first discuss the intersection of morality and nationhood in the context of post-Soviet nation-building in Latvia. I continue with a discussion of morality and indebtedness in relation to Latvia's own financial crisis and its consequences, such as extensive outmigration. In the process, I trace the emergence of the enduring subject as the normative subject of the current historical moment in Latvia, a subject that perseveres through difficulties for the sake of the nation and in the name of a better future, a subject that "does not understand the Greek people," and, finally, a subject that facilitates Latvia's ascendency to Europeanness in the midst of Europe's financial crisis.

A National Way of Life

Latvia's post-Soviet transformations were characterized by two distinct yet related trajectories, namely nationalism and neoliberalism (Dzenovska 2007). To make sense of the claim that "Latvians do not understand the Greek people," it is crucial to understand how nationalism and neoliberalism not only coexisted in the political and policy domains, but also converged in the realm of ethical conduct. In the context of post-socialist democratization and liberalization projects, nationalism was widely thought of as a problem that manifests in the register of conventional politics (e.g., voting), or as a problem of exclusion of minorities from public institutions, spaces, or the body of citizenry. However, focusing on nationalism as a political and policy problem overlooks the importance of nationalism as an ethical framework that produces subjects who equate the good life to a life led within confines of the nation as a moral community. Thus, in Latvia, being national involves more than holding Latvian citizenship. It is also a way of being in the world that, first, assumes that a historically formed cultural community is fundamentally constitutive of the self and, second, posits a moral contract between such a historically formed and embedded self and the state that guarantees the existence of the cultural community.[4]

Throughout the Soviet period, many Latvians cultivated a national way of being as an alternative to Soviet socialism. This way of being emphasized rootedness in place, care for language and culture, and, at crucial moments, privileging the collective interests of the cultural community over individual ones. Despite Latvians being the "titular nation" of a Soviet republic (Martin 2001), the absence of full political and economic independence was thought to be detrimental to the existence of the cultural community. It therefore fell to individuals to ensure the continued existence of the Latvian nation by cultivating themselves as national beings, that is, as individuals who see themselves as shaped by a particular culture and aspiring to realize themselves and the collective in a political entity—the national state. Several generations of Soviet Latvians were socialized with this embattled sense of Latvianness. During that time, the virtue of enduring harsh political and economic conditions became central to the Latvian sense of self and to the collective effort to sustain the Latvian nation.

Many in Latvia perceived cultivating a national way of life during the Soviet period as an oppositional project necessarily at odds with Soviet socialism. This is not entirely accurate, however. The Soviet state did in fact explicitly cultivate cultural and linguistic difference, but the way this related to the Soviet state and the socialist project remained ambiguous (Martin 2001; Hirsch 1995; Slezkine 1994). In Latvia, for example, the Soviet state struggled to enforce the boundary between nationalism as a national form with socialist content and nationalism as a dangerous aspiration for self-determination that threatened the Soviet socialist project. The national way of being, therefore, was solidified as an ethical orientation in a simultaneously complementary and oppositional relationship with the Soviet state. For many Latvians, the "other" of this way of being was the Russian-speaking Soviet person, sometimes also referred to as the "migrant," who was thought to be concerned with the socialist future and defined good life economically rather than via a relationship with place, culture, and history (Dzenovska 2013b).

The collapse of the Soviet Union allowed the national way of life as an ethical orientation to converge with the political nationalism of the post-Soviet Latvian state, which in turn enabled the state to appeal to Latvian self-narratives, including the virtue of endurance, in an effort to forge popular consent for various policies, including the austerity measures following the financial crisis. The convergence of the national way of life and political nationalism after the Soviet Union's demise also meant that something had to be done about the Russian-speaking Soviet person—the "migrant," who was seen as a threat to the new political order and the national way of life. Thus, in the late 1980s and throughout the 1990s, Russian-speaking residents became targets of the Latvian state's "reawakening efforts," an ethical and political project that aimed to recruit national minority subjects from among Soviet people in order to boost support for the Latvian state as a national state (Dzenovska 2018a). Importantly, becoming a national minority subject did not mean becoming Latvian, but rather becoming a subject who understands the importance of a national way of life and strives to be a good national minority subject, that is, someone who cultivates himself or herself as a member of a particular cultural community while recognizing this community's political subordination to Latvians within a national state.

In independent Latvia, forming individuals into national subjects, be they minority or majority, is a project that spans the family, the school, and public and political space. National subjects are tied to each other and to the state through the moral framework of belonging to the Latvian nation as a cultural community that has realized itself politically. This political realization, in turn, is seen as crucial to the cultural community's continued existence. This, then, is the moral bond that conjured up the enduring subject in the context of the 2008 financial crisis and the Greek sovereign debt crisis, inadvertently also facilitating the Latvians' ascendancy to Europeanness.

Financial Crisis and Moral Bonds

Not unlike other states subjected to neoliberalization and fiscal discipline, the Latvian government implemented severe austerity measures to overcome the 2008 financial crisis, thus off-loading the burden of the crisis onto the public sector and the broader society (Paalzow 2015; Hudson and Sommers 2012). The government's exceptional fiscal discipline propelled Latvia into the international limelight as an exemplary apprentice of neoliberal economics. Latvia's success was celebrated in various international forums. Prime Minister Valdis Dombrovskis delivered lectures to international audiences and cowrote a book about Latvia's success story (Åslund and Dombrovskis 2011).[5] Success was measured by economic growth indicators and the government's ability to repay the IMF bailout loan early, that is, at the end of 2012. This early loan repayment enabled the government to cut public spending even further. Two weeks after repaying the loan, the guaranteed minimum income dropped to the point that even the IMF began defending the poor by criticizing the government's reduction of the guaranteed minimum income (Eglītis 2013; see also Eihmanis n.d.).

A less publicly discussed but more noteworthy measure of "success" was that there was no sustained protest in response to the austerity measures. One organized demonstration in January of 2009 erupted in violence when some youths began to vandalize cars and shop windows after a peaceful gathering involving speeches and singing in the Old City of Riga. The incident was quickly contained both physically and symbolically, and politicians, intellectuals, and media pundits came together to dismiss violence by suggesting that it was not a Latvian way of expressing dissatisfaction, but rather something done by Europe's immigrants or people with a "Mediterranean mentality," such as Greeks. Moreover, even though the demonstration had been organized by an opposition party with the alleged aim of protesting cuts in social spending, it led to the replacement of the old government—thought to be corrupt—with a new government lead by Valdis Dombrovskis, who shortly thereafter implemented even harsher, if transparent, austerity measures.

Enjoying public support, this new government called on Latvia's residents to express solidarity with the state in the midst of crisis. In making such an appeal, the government invoked the stories that Latvians tell themselves about themselves, that is, about enduring harsh conditions to ensure the continuity of the nation and achieve political self-determination in the form of their own national state. Thus, the government appealed to Latvia's residents to express solidarity with *their* state, the state that they had so painstakingly restored following the collapse of the Soviet Union, the state that guaranteed their collective existence as a people, that was *them*, as many civil servants emphasized, and that now was in existential danger. The crisis animated renewed efforts to assert moral bonds between the state, the nation, and individuals. From within this moral framework, solidarity was manifested as a "tightening of belts" for the sake of a collective future. Latvia's residents were called upon to sustain their lives with severely diminished resources—to persevere with living in the present—in order to enable a collective flourishing in a distant future. Many of Latvia's residents took up this call. A few pensioners offered to donate their meager pensions to the state to boost its budget. In internet commentaries and newspaper articles one could encounter references to how Latvians, as a nation, "survived multiple wars, survived the Soviet gulag, and thus will survive the crisis as well."[6] Most people, however, simply continued surviving as they had done before the crisis.

At the same time, Latvia's residents did not wish to merely survive, but rather to lead "normal lives," a concept widely used in post-socialist contexts to demarcate an aspirational mode of life (e.g., Fehervary 2002; Dzenovska 2014). For example, the interlocutors of my ethnographic project on outmigration differentiated between "living" and "surviving" in ways similar to those of the Sarajevans analyzed by Stef Jansen (2014) in an article on "not moving well enough." They described "living" as a mode of being exceeding attempts to persevere, in which one was not constantly confronted with profound challenges to existence in the form of shortage of money, jobs, or time, or a sense of not going anywhere. During my fieldwork, the ability to survive and surviving itself—what I refer to in this chapter as endurance—variously appeared as part of a collective habitus formed in relation to a history of multiple foreign dominations. A necessary tactic for living in the present, it increasingly became a normative mode of conduct of living the crisis (see Hage 2009). Endurance, then, was part of the collective self-narrative of Latvians and a virtue that came to characterize a good national subject.

Not everyone was willing or able to endure in this way, however, and many people emigrated. When migration reached such a level that most everyone in Latvia knew someone who had emigrated, had family members who had emigrated, had themselves emigrated or considered emigrating, emigration erupted on the political agenda as a problem that needed to be addressed (Dzenovska 2012).[7] The initial public and political reactions to the news that emigration was becoming a mass phenomenon interpreted departure as betrayal. Even prior to the crisis, in 2004, the then Prime Minister of Latvia Aigars Kalvītis had said: "Let them go, they are consumers by nature anyway," suggesting that the emigrants were failed members of the nation as a moral community because they related to it merely as consumers. Some years later, when it was suggested that people might be leaving because they felt the state had not created the conditions for building normal lives at home, Speaker of the Parliament Solvita Āboltiņa responded by saying: "I want to ask only one question of all those who are leaving. What have you—you in particular—done to make Latvia a different place?" These moral arguments juxtaposed consumption with production, suggesting that emigrants wished to consume and receive rather than produce and give. Such arguments entirely overlooked the fact that most emigrants left in order to be productive laborers, and many left to earn money with which to repay the debts accumulated during the pre-crisis period, when they were on their way to becoming proper economic subjects (see next section).

But as more and more people left, driven by onerous debt, job shortages, insufficient income, and general hopelessness about the future (Dzenovska 2012), the government realized that the Great Departure, as post-European Union accession emigration was colloquially referred to, was to have lasting effects. Working against the trope of betrayal that had saturated earlier reactions to departure, concerned government officials set out to govern Latvia's mobile subjects through diaspora programs and re-emigration plans. They argued that the state needed the mobile subjects—formally all Latvia's citizens, but especially cultural Latvians among them—in order to revive the economy, reproduce the cultural community, and legitimate the national state. This task initially proved difficult, as many of those who had emigrated also felt that the state had betrayed them, insofar as it did not create conditions within which they could craft "normal lives."

These feelings of mutual betrayal suggest that imagined moral bonds existed between individuals and the state, and that they became most visible at the moment when they were thought to be broken. These bonds imagined by those who stayed and those who left alike, can also be thought of as relations of indebtedness. These relations of indebtedness link individuals in the present to a collective past and a collective future. Such relations might assume that individuals are indebted to the moral community and to its steward, the state; or they might assume that the state is indebted to individuals and the moral community, or that individuals are in debt to each other as members of the moral community. Appeals to the public to put up with economic discomfort in the context of financial crisis therefore assumed the state and individuals were united in solidarity as members of an enduring moral community whose well-being was at risk. In the name of this community one was summoned to become an "enduring subject."

Importantly, this enduring subject was not only expected to survive the crisis, but also to use the crisis as an opportunity to unleash previously untapped creativity and contribute to the revival of the economy and thus to the flourishing of the community. To illustrate this type of conduct, political and intellectual elites introduced success stories (*veiksmes stāsti*) into the public discourse. For example, several publications and TV shows, including the popular weekly *Ir*, began to feature interviews with successful entrepreneurs who had either persevered through difficulties or managed to find a niche business that helped them strive. Their success stories marginalized narratives of poverty, emptiness, and abjection, depicted these as products of negativist thinking rather than aspects of social reality. It was hoped, it seemed, that the success stories would counter negativist thinking, heal the collective psyche, and motivate people to help themselves and thus the nation and the state.

The success stories emphasized individual ingenuity, through which people could lift themselves out of collective misery. The message was that the crisis should provide an opportunity to capitalize on human creativity and entrepreneurship. To put it another way, while enduring, the good national subject was not supposed to just wait, but to do something, to keep moving, be active, become an entrepreneur. In policy circles, such emphasis on doing something and not expecting things from the state was considered a necessary remedy to the enduring Soviet legacy, understood here as state-dependency. Combined with this valorization of individual entrepreneurial activity, endurance amounted to withstanding hardship while working on oneself to harness the possibilities that the crisis might provide. Enduring subjects were loyal: they honored their commitment to the collective and worked to remake themselves as entrepreneurial subjects who contributed to collective well-being. But the enduring-cum-entrepreneurial subject valorized by the state was at cross-purposes with the indebted subject, an individual who, in order to honor a contractual relationship and repay debt, had to find work elsewhere to earn enough money to make the loan payments. While at cross-purposes, these two different subjects nevertheless converged in the ethical orientation of playing by the rules and working hard.

I now turn to a more detailed consideration of this indebted subject to consider how learning to live with and without debt—and financial indebtedness more generally— in post-Soviet Latvia came to be judged within the moral framework forged at the intersection of nationalism and neoliberalism.

Learning to Live with and without Credit

One of the most characteristic features of the 1990s post-Soviet landscape in Latvia was the *sadzīves tehnikas veikals* (household electronics shop) (Beliaev and Dzenovska 2009). People purchased irons, washing machines, mixers, juicers, kitchen combines, and whatever else they found appealing after years of beating egg whites by hand. Kitchens and bathrooms were overloaded with household technologies, many of which were rarely used. It was in the sphere of household electronics that people first learned to buy on credit. Competing for customers who were filling their small living spaces with Bosch, Electrolux, and Zanussi items of various sizes, stores advertised in-store credit with no down payment: you walked into the store with no money and walked out with the steam-spewing iron you always wanted. And want it you did, because back in the Soviet times you simply could not get it. As Krisztina Fehervary (2002) has pointed out in the context of post-socialist Hungary, Western household appliances and other items of material culture were part of the measure of "normal life" in both socialist and post-socialist contexts. "Normal life," in turn, constituted a horizon of aspirations and marked specifically post-socialist, if varied, understandings of the good life (Jansen 2014; Rausing 2004; Dzenovska 2014; Fehervary 2002).

The understandings of the good life forged during the socialist period facilitated the expansion of credit culture in post-socialist societies. By obtaining credit in relatively small amounts, people got used to the idea that the good life, a middle-class life, could be achieved through credit. Indeed, an explicit concern of the post-socialist transition was the creation of a middle class of young, upwardly mobile citizens, who would fulfill their aspirations to middle-class life by taking out mortgages and living on credit. As Mateusz Halawa (2015: 715, 719) has written with regard to mortgages in Warsaw, those who took out mortgages were thought of as coming of age, as maturing into responsible citizens. Eager to extend credit to un-indebted populations, the banking industry also promoted these aspirations, for example by advertising credit as the road to a middle-class existence. As Halawa (2015: 720) notes, one bank advertisement read: "For all those who grew up (enough) to own a home" [sic].[8]

Similar processes took place in Latvia. Though much of the older generation acquired private property via privatization of their Soviet-era apartments (resulting in an unprecedented level of home ownership that does not accurately reflect overall prosperity or quality of life), this was not the case for their children.[9] At the same time, post-Soviet individuals were instructed that renting was unwise because it meant throwing money away and not maturing into adulthood. Buying your own property was thought of as a wise investment and a way to make your money count. As Mateusz Halawa (2015: 720) writes,

> such narratives of maturing into homeownership resonate with the hegemonic discourse of the post-socialist transformation, which promoted a

new kind of model citizen: active, enterprising, and able to fend for him or herself. Since 1989, journalists, public intellectuals, and sociologists have been invested in looking for, or actively fabricating, "the middle class" ... Rooted in private property, consumer choice, and aspirations toward the lifestyles of the West, this new class was expected to develop individualistic, responsible, proactive attitudes. It was also expected to distinguish itself from the maligned *homo sovieticus*, who demanded things—including housing—from the government ... .

But credit did not just pave the way to post-Soviet adulthood; it was also thought to lay the groundwork for economic growth and development. For example, agricultural specialists acknowledged that extensive credit was needed to modernize agriculture (Cimdiņa and Raubiško 2012: 81). Farmers had not been able to accumulate capital in any way other than credit or European Union grants (which nevertheless required co-financing)—credit was the only way for agricultural business to expand to the point of being able to generate profit. Credit was a crucial component of the post-Soviet middle class and post-Soviet market economy. It was also indispensable to the expansion of finance capitalism (Choonara 2009). Thus, capitalism needed indebted subjects as much as post-socialist subjects needed capitalism—and credit—to satisfy their aspirations for a "normal life."

While some Latvians behaved as good entrepreneurial subjects by buying family homes and taking out loans to develop their businesses, there also emerged rogue subjects willing to imitate the profit-making possibilities of finance capitalism to try to make a "quick buck," or *uzvārīties* (to boil up, in Latvian). These people took loans and invested them for short-term returns. For example, some purchased apartments and sold them a little while later (renovated or not). Real estate prices were going up, so the returns were rewarding. One could wait longer, but it was better to sell quickly in order to generate profit, which could be used to make more money.

The real estate boom and the rising prices and wages of the early 2000s made the temporary seem permanent. These became known as the *treknie gadi* (fat years). People borrowed more and more money to finance vacations abroad, country homes, apartment renovations, and even medical operations, so much so that taking on debt seemed like an endless source of wealth—an end in itself. Both private and public entities seemed to be living on speed. Politician Ainārs Šlesers urged Latvians to "put the pedal to the metal" (*pedāli grīdā*), that is, to take advantage of all the opportunities offered by the free-market economy. People began to gain faith in living on credit. This did not necessarily represent greater certainty about the future, however. Instead, they developed faith in the permanence of the present—in the permanent cycle of credit-based existence (Lazzarato 2012; Halawa 2015; Beliaev and Dzenovska 2009).

And then came the crisis. When the housing bubble burst, many people lost their jobs and could not repay their debts. Banks repossessed their homes, and many left for Ireland or the United Kingdom to find jobs so as to make their payments. When I began fieldwork on outmigration in 2012, leaving had become the subject of public debates and private conversations. My interlocutors—those who stayed behind—often talked about debt-related departures in hushed tones: "You know, they took all those loans and now they have to leave. Thank God, I managed to repay mine." Or, "I never took any loans; I knew no good would come of it." Individuals who had taken loans and had defaulted as a result of the crisis, were no longer seen as maturing into adulthood and a middle-class existence, but viewed as having failed to withstand the temptations of capitalism. Even as people understood that credit was a product that banks were marketing quite aggressively (some recounted how bank employees were given bonuses for selling more credit), in the end they nevertheless saw a loan as something one asks for, and thus always a matter of choice (Halawa 2015; Gregory 2012).

My interlocutors articulated insightful critiques of the post-socialist *pedāli grīdā* living as a systemic problem rather than an individual one. They also understood that financial institutions ultimately benefited from the crisis, or at least suffered less from it than the population did. Yet they still held the view that once individuals had entered into a credit-debt relationship—that is, once they had asked for and received loans—the responsibility for repaying the debt was not negotiable. For example, Inta and Aija, two small-scale entrepreneurs I met in Kurzeme, told me that they had not taken on debt because "debt must be returned, returned regardless of circumstances. Big, small, all wanted to be rich. Very tempting. Now they have to leave." For Inta and Aija, taking on debt amounted to pretending to be rich. Though they, too, confirmed that loans must be given back regardless of circumstances, they did not elaborate on whether this was so because it was morally or juridically right, or because banks would not have it any other way. Strikingly, in the midst of systemic crisis, my interlocutors subscribed to the view that one has to manage oneself—that if you get into trouble, it is your fault and thus your responsibility to get out of that trouble. In addition to converging with the neoliberal emphasis on individual responsibility, I suggest this was a historically overdetermined stance boosted by both the imperative to overcome the Soviet past, remembered as excessively reliant on the state, and a collective memory of suffering and resilience as the only reliable tactics of survival in such difficult moments as multiple wars, post-Soviet deportations, and the daily grind of Soviet socialism.

As Latvia's residents, recently crushed by their own economic crisis and the subsequent austerity measures, tried to make sense of the Greek sovereign debt crisis, many transposed the moral frameworks that governed their personal relations onto the sovereign debt crisis. In doing so, they affirmed the power relations of capitalism without allowing for political critique of capitalism and its underlying moral frameworks. In his acclaimed book *Debt: the First 5,000 Years*, David Graeber (2011) interrogates the now nearly universal moral premise underlying global forms of finance capitalism: "one has to repay one's debts." Drawing on Graeber, Deborah James (2015: 11) puts it as follows: "Something originally thought of as 'reciprocity,' in which gifts or favours, once given, are returned only after long delays or are transferred onward over generations, has been transformed by the modern financial system, backed up by the power of the state, into a relationship of unequal power and of enduring hierarchy in the modern world: between first-world and third-world nations, rich and poor."

By privileging the moral obligations of a credit-debt relationship over a critique of financial capitalism and its dependency on indebtedness, Latvians became complicit with the normative framework of finance capitalism. Moreover, by conflating the moral obligation to repay debt with Europeanness, Latvians became complicit with its companion civilizational project. As I show next, the crisis proved an especially productive site for such a position.

Proper Economic, Moral, and European Subjects

In July 2015 in Rēzekne, a small town in the southeast of Latvia, I found myself in a crowd watching a concert held as part of the International Folklore Festival Baltica. The people in the crowd, some dressed in folk costumes, were in high spirits. I was standing next to a group of people engaged in light banter who all seemed to be near retirement age when I suddenly overheard someone declare: "Oh, this is so that the Greek pensioners could live better." I had missed the first part of that exchange, but the response generated laughter and further exchange about how the Latvian pensioners were getting by on so much less, and how it was ridiculous that Greeks were protesting austerity measures that, in the view of those conversing, were aimed at mitigating a situation that the Greeks themselves had created.

I overheard many such conversations in the summer of 2015, when the Greek sovereign debt crisis was used as a rhetorical device to point simultaneously to Latvian pensioners' resilience on the one hand and the unfairness of Greek demands on the other, given the perception that Greek living standards were much higher than those of Latvia's pensioners. Similar discourse was reproduced in the media. For example, following the pattern of using Latvia as an exemplary case of fiscal discipline, one Latvian and one Lithuanian journalist wrote a piece for *The Guardian* headlined: "In Latvia and Lithuania, pensioners and other poor people wonder why they are being asked to pay to bail out their far richer Greek counterparts" (Černiauskas and Raudseps 2015). The article quotes Milda, a Latvian pensioner who is surprised that Greeks cannot get by on €120 per week in a climate where people need not heat homes or buy winter boots, and where vegetables and fruit must be cheaper. The authors of the article note that Milda's pension is €293 per month, well under half of current Greek levels. They go on to explain the results of the even harsher austerity measures imposed by the Latvian government: the country suffered 20 percent unemployment, output fell by a quarter, and the "population left in droves." Now, the authors continue, Latvia is well on its way on recovery. Yet they cite GDP growth and export growth without so much as touching upon the social costs incurred. According to the journalists, most Latvians want to know: "If we did it, why can't the Greeks?" It is here that they quote Latvia's Finance Minister Jānis Reiris as saying, "Latvian people do not understand the Greek people." Milda ultimately concludes: "Anyway, if they borrowed all that money, they should pay it back, that's the way I see it." Nowhere does the article even raise the question of whether Greeks alone are to blame for the current situation, or whether Latvians could perhaps have done things differently themselves. The message is clear: We tightened our belts, suffered even more than the Greeks are suffering right now, and are now asked to show solidarity to bail them out. This is unfair.

Articles republished on Latvian Internet sites from the foreign press—for example, Slavoj Žižek's take on the Greek referendum—generated a slew of critical, often offensive commentary ("Slavojs Žižeks par Grieķijas referendumu" 2015). Here, too, the sovereign debt crisis was discussed through analogies with personal relationships. Someone rhetorically asked whether a neighbor would lend a cent to a severely indebted and unemployed Žižek, if he were unprepared to find a job and prove he was able to pay it back. "Does finding a job amount to Eurozone terrorism or loss of Žižek's independence?" the commentator asked.

This popular sense of unfairness fed into political demands that Greeks take on responsibility and play by the rules. In July 2015, in an episode of the weekly TV show *Sastrēgumstunda* (Rush Hour), financial consultant Gundars Kuļikovskis pointed out that "the EU is a club of countries based on rules. And now Greece says: we will not play by the rules."[10] Sitting next to Kuļikovskis, Ilmārs Rimšēvics, the president of the Bank of Latvia, stressed that "the responsibility lies only with the government of Greece." He continued: "Latvia has positive experience with austerity measures. We did it in two years. You have to involve all sectors of society. We regained trust, and the economy recovered. All those who borrow money know the rules. And if you do not follow the rules, there are consequences. One has to be very responsible on the large Euro ship." Andris Sprūds, Associate Professor of International Relations at the Riga Stradiņš University, tried to broach the possibility that responsibility might be shared, but even this mild attempt met with absolute denial and reiteration that Greeks alone were to blame.

Furthermore, in an article published on the Internet site *Delfi.lv*, Inese Vaidere, a Latvian member of the European parliament, suggested that Greeks have something to learn from the Latvians. She pointed out that Latvians cannot understand why Greeks refuse to be frugal, because "we are used to saving and living within our means. Germans, too, are used to spending as much money as is within their means. Similarly, if borrowed, the money has to be returned within a foreseeable period of time. But Greeks want it otherwise: they think they can borrow all the time and not repay."[11] Moreover, Vaidere continued, "tightening of belts corresponds to European values. Why is it so difficult for Greeks to do it? Perhaps it is lack of information, perhaps it is tradition, perhaps it is the Southern sun, which makes people more relaxed than in Latvia. But within Europe and within the European Union, all have to adhere to the same rules.... European rules stipulate that debt has to be repaid. Not repaying debt amounts to theft."

This is not a uniquely Latvian stance (in fact, Latvians soon turned away from upholding the community of rules in the context of the refugee crisis). References to a community of rules resounded in a variety of European and global forums, so it is noteworthy that a commentator for the *New York Times* invoked precisely Latvian and Lithuanian politicians to make these points. Rankin (2015) quotes the Lithuanian president as saying that for the Greeks it is always *manana* (tomorrow), and the President of the Bank of Latvia as ironically referring to the "brave Greeks" who had voted themselves out of the eurozone. Latvian government officials, politicians, and pensioners seemed to provide quotes that aptly illustrated the conduct of proper economic, moral and European subjects. What could be a better validation of Europeanness than its endorsement by aspiring Europeans?

The Shining Moment of Europeanness

In any historical moment of asserting or distributing Europeanness, competing and contested notions of Europeanness are at play. In the context of the financial crisis, Europeanness took on a very particular form, namely following rules, adhering to financial discipline, and tightening belts. It so happened that the Latvian historically formed self-narrative (one of suffering, resilience, and putting up with things) aligned quite well with the hegemonic vision of Europeanness in the context of the crisis. The financial crisis was the Latvians' moment to be European; indeed, to be better Europeans than the Europeans themselves. The collective memory of suffering, in conjunction with the neoliberal call for the post-Soviet nation to endure for the sake of the collective, had prepared Latvians to heed the call of a Europe in crisis and to become exemplary economic subjects.

From street conversations to media articles to policy discourses and political statements, Latvia's residents seemed united in asserting their momentarily acquired Europeanness against the Greeks' failure to conduct themselves as proper economic subjects and thus as proper Europeans. This articulation of proper conduct and Europeanness obscured the forms of power that governed European public and political space. Insofar as experts, political commentators, and ordinary people in Latvia reproduce these powers in their critiques of "the Greek people's" handling of the crisis, they were complicit with them.

There is another element of the Latvian self-narrative that might be interesting to consider in relation to this instance of complicit becoming. It is common to hear references to something called "serf mentality" in debates about Latvia's stance toward Russia in the international political arena, and in the public and political attitudes toward Russian speakers at home. The notion of the serf mentality is meant to refer to a submissive disposition produced in contexts of domination—for example, under the Baltic German administrative, economic, and cultural rule of the territory of today's Latvia from the thirteenth until the early twentieth century, or under the Soviet regime in the twentieth century (e.g., Matīsa 2005). Believed to be passed on from generation to generation via socialization, the serf mentality is thought of as a postcolonial mentality that prevents Latvians from becoming mature political subjects who are independent, rather than submissive.

Against the backdrop of the debates about economic crises such as those faced by Greece and Latvia, it might be argued that the two elements of the collective self-narrative—namely endurance and the serf mentality defined as a postcolonial disposition to submit to the dictates of powerful elites—work at cross purposes. In emphasizing the virtue of endurance, politicians, policymakers, commentators, and ordinary people overlook that in a context of economic crisis, this amounts to adhering to dominant economic ideologies and, in the context of the Greek sovereign debt crisis, to reproducing what Ulrich Beck (2013) has called the German Europe. Not unlike the way Latvians in the late nineteenth and early twentieth centuries strived to show the Germans that they were cultured people by imitating German song festivals (now a major part of Latvian public performances of identity) (Ījabs 2010), today's Latvians who claim "not to understand the Greek people," are once again imitating a dominant power in a quest to approximate Europeanness. The Greeks' refusal to tighten belts, to implement austerity measures, or to endure, and their contrary stance of protesting the austerity measures, must therefore remain incomprehensible to Latvians. This incomprehension is the ultimate performance of Europeanness, a becoming more European than the Europeans themselves.

Dace Dzenovska is Associate Professor of Anthropology of Migration, University of Oxford. She writes about re-bordering and migration in the context of European Union enlargement, as well as tolerance promotion and the post-socialist democratization agenda in Latvia. Her book *School of Europeanness: Tolerance and Other Lessons in Political Liberalism in Latvia* is forthcoming from Cornell University Press. She is also preparing a book manuscript entitled *The Great Departure: Staying and Leaving after Postsocialism*.

Notes

Parts of the section "Learning to Live with and without Credit" were previously published in Beliaev and Dzenovska (2009). Material included in this chapter was authored by Dzenovska, and is reprinted with permission. A couple of paragraphs from the section "Proper Economic, Moral, and European Subjects" are from the forthcoming book manuscript *School of Europeanness: Tolerance and Other Lessons in Political Liberalism in Latvia* and are reprinted with permission from Cornell University Press.

1. For example, Beck (2013) has recently suggested that today's Europe is a German Europe.
2. Despite the vote, the bailout package, which demanded implementation of severe austerity measures and privatization of public assets, was approved by the Greek parliament in the early morning hours of 16 July 2015. Much of the package was likely to go toward financing the unsustainable public debt (acknowledged as such even by the IMF), built up through a combination of government mismanagement of financial affairs and the Eurozone's refusal to let Greece default in 2011, instead providing more unsustainable loans with which to pay back private creditors. For background, see Blyth (2015), Knight (2015).
3. It should be noted that I did not conduct ethnographic research on debt; these reflections are based on the observations I have accumulated in the course of other ethnographic projects in Latvia and on analysis of public discourse.
4. The Latvian state is often referred to not as a nation-state, but as a national state (*nacionāla valsts*), that is, as a state that gains legitimacy from ensuring the existence and flourishing of the cultural community of Latvians.
5. It should be noted that Valdis Dombrovskis took over the post of the European Commissioner for Financial Stability, Financial Services, and Capital Markets Union after the Brexit vote and the resignation of Jonathan Hill.
6. See Power (2015) for resonant observations of the Irish response to the crisis.
7. About 10% of Latvia's residents are estimated to have emigrated in the last ten years (Hazans 2011).
8. The collapse of Soviet and Eastern European socialisms enabled an unprecedented expansion of finance capitalism, not only in Eastern Europe and the former Soviet Union, but also in other places, such as South Africa (James 2015), where the 1990s introduced watershed changes.
9. Statistics show an 80.9% home ownership rate in Latvia (which peaked at 87% in 2009), which is well above that of the Euro curency zone (66.6%), USA (63.7%), and UK (64.6), but about the same level as Russia (83.50) (Latvia Home Ownership Rate 2007–2015 n.d.). See Zavisca

(2012) for an extensive analysis of housing in Soviet and post-Soviet Russia.
10. The title of the broadcast was "Who Will Be the Last Sirtaki Dancer?" The show is available here in Latvian: http://ltv.lsm.lv/lv/raksts/08.07.2015-sastregumstunda.-krize-griekija.-kurs-dejos-sirtaki-pedejais.id52470/.
11. http://financenet.tvnet.lv/viedokli/567005grieki_varetu_pamacities_no_latviesiem_dazas_noderigas_lietas.

References

Åslund, A., and Dombrovkis, V. 2011. *How Latvia Came Through the Financial Crisis*. Washington, DC: Peterson Institute for International Economics.

Beck, U. 2013. *German Europe*. Cambridge: Polity Press.

Beliaev, A., and D. Dzenovska. 2009. "Some Reflections on the 'Global' Crisis in Latvia." *Newsletter of the Institute for Slavic, Eastern European and Eurasian Studies, University of California, Berkeley* 26(2): 3–6.

Biehl, J. and P. Locke. "Deleuze and the Anthropology of Becoming." *Current Anthropology* 51(3): 317-351.

Blyth, M. 2015. "A Pain in the Athens: Why Greece Isn't to Blame for the Crisis." *Foreign Affairs*, 7 July. Retrieved 22 November 2015 from https://www.foreignaffairs.com/articles/greece/2015-07-07/pain-athens.

Böröcz, J. 2006. "Goodness is Elsewhere: The Rule of European Difference." *Comparative Studies in Society and History* 48(1): 110–138.

Buchowski, M. 2006. "The Specter of Orientalism in Europe: From Exotic Other to Stigmatized Brother." *Anthropological Quarterly* 79(3): 463–482.

Černiauskas, Š., and P. Raudseps. 2015. "Poorer than Greece: The EU Countries that Reject a New Athens Bailout." *The Guardian*, 9 July. Retrieved 22 November from http://www.theguardian.com/world/2015/jul/09/poorer-than-greece-the-eu-countries-that-reject-a-new-athens-bailout.

Choonara, J. 2009. "Interview: David Harvey—Exploring the Logic of Capital." *Socialist Review*, April. Retrieved 22 November 2015 from http://socialistreview.org.uk/335/interview-david-harvey-exploring-logic-capital.

Cimdiņa, A., and I. Raubiško. 2012. *Cilvēks un darbs Latvijas laukos: sociālantropoloģisks skatījums*. Riga: Zinātne.

De Genova, N. 2016. "The 'European' Question: Migration, Race and Postcoloniality in Europe." *Social Text* 34(3): 75–102.

Dzenovska, D. 2007. "Neoliberal Imaginations, Subject Formation and Other National Things in Latvia, the Land that Sings," in *Representations on the Margins of Europe: Politics and Identities in the*

Baltic and South Caucasian States, ed. T. Darieva and W. Kaschuba, 114–138. Frankfurt: Campus Verlag.

———. 2012. *Aizbraukšana un tukšums Latvijas laukos: Starp zudušām un iespējamām nākotnēm*. Riga: Biznesa apgāds Turība.

———. 2013a. "Historical Agency and the Coloniality of Power in Postsocialist Europe." *Anthropological Theory* 13(4): 394–416.

———. 2013b. "The Great Departure: Rethinking National(ist) Common Sense." *Journal of Ethnic and Migration Studies* 39(2): 201–218.

——— 2014. "Bordering Encounters, Sociality, and Distribution of the Ability to Live a Normal Life." *Social Anthropology* 22(3): 271–287.

———. 2016. "Eastern Europe, the Moral Subject of the Migration/Refugee Crisis, and Political Futures." *Near Futures Online* 1(March).

———. 2017. "Coherent Selves, Viable States: Eastern Europe and the Migration/Refugee Crisis." *Slavic Review* 76(2): 297–306.

———. 2018a. *School of Europeanness: Tolerance and Other Lessons of Political Liberalism in Latvia*. Ithaca, NY: Cornell University Press.

———. 2018b. "Maintaining Life and Seeking Futures Past: Staying and Leaving as Tactics of Life in Latvia." Forthcoming in *Focaal: Journal of Global and Historical Anthropology*.

Dunn, E. 2004. *Privatizing Poland: Baby Food, Big Business, and the Remaking of Labor*. Ithaca, NY: Cornell University Press.

Eihmanis, E. n.d. "An Ever Wider Gap: The Ethnic Divide in Latvian Party Competition," in *European Party Politics in Times of Crises*, ed. S. Hutter, and H. Kriesi. Manuscript in preparation.

Eglītis, A. 2013. "Latvian Austerity Fervor Outstrips IMF After Loan Payback." *Bloomberg Business*, 3 January. Retrieved 22 November 2015 from http://www.bloomberg.com/news/articles/2013-01-02/latvian-austerity-fervor-outstrips-imf-after-early-loan-payback.

Fehervary, K. 2002. "American Kitchens, Luxury Bathrooms, and the Search for a 'Normal Life' in Post-Socialist Hungary." *Ethnos* 67(3): 369–400.

Graeber, D. 2011. *Debt: The First 5,000 Years*. New York: Melville House.

Gregory, C. 2012. "On Money Debt and Morality: Some Reflections on the Contribution of Economic Anthropology." *Social Anthropology* 20(4): 380–396.

Grundule, L. 2014. "ES augstākās amatpersonas noņem cepuri Latvijas priekšā" [EU's highest functionaries tip their hats to Latvia], *Diena*, 10 January. Retrieved 10 January 2015. http://www.diena.lv/latvija/zinas/es-augstakas-amatpersonas-nonem-cepuri-latvijas-prieksa-14039553.

Hage, G. 2009. "Waiting Out the Crisis: On Stuckedness and Governmentality," in *Waiting*, ed. G. Hage, 1–9. Melbourne: Melbourne University Press.

Halawa, M. 2015. "In New Warsaw." *Cultural Studies* 29(5–6): 707–732.

Hazans, M. 2011. "Latvijas emigrācijas mainīgā seja 2000–2010," in *Latvija. Pārskats Par tautas attīstību. 2010./2011. Nacionālā Identitāte,*

Mobilitāte, Rīcībspēja, ed. SPPI, 70–91. Riga: Institute of Social and Political Research, University of Latvia.

Herzfeld, M. 1987. *Anthropology through the Looking Glass: Critical Ethnography in the Margins of Europe*. Cambridge: Cambridge University Press.

———. 2013. "The European Crisis and Cultural Intimacy." *Studies in Ethnicity and Nationalism* 13(3): 491–497.

Hirsch, F. 1995. *Empire of Nations: Ethnographic Knowledge and the Making of the Soviet Union*. Ithaca, NY: Cornell University Press.

Hudson, M., and J. Sommers. 2012. "Latvia Is No Model for an Austerity Drive." *Financial Times*, 21 June. Retrieved 22 November 2015 from http://www.ft.com/cms/s/0/73314cbe-baee-11e1-81e0-00144feabdc0.html#axzz3goIQ67wG.

Ījabs, I. 2010. "Strange Baltic Liberalism: Paul Schiemann's Political Thought Revisited." *Journal of Baltic Studies* 40(4): 495–515.

James, D. 2015. *Money from Nothing: Indebtedness and Aspiration in South Africa*. Stanford, CA: Stanford University Press.

Jansen, S. 2014. "On Not Moving Well Enough: Temporal Reasoning in Sarajevo Yearnings for 'Normal Lives.'" *Current Anthropology* 55(S9): S74–S84.

Knight, D. 2015. *History, Time, and Economic Crisis*. New York: Palgrave Macmillan.

Krastev, I. 2015. "Eastern Europe's Compassion Deficit." *New York Times*, 8 September. Retrieved 22 November 2015 from https://www.nytimes.com/2015/09/09/opinion/eastern-europes-compassion-deficit-refugees-migrants.html.

"Latvia Home Ownership Rate 2007–2015." n.d. *Trading Economics*. Retrieved 22 November 2015 from http://www.tradingeconomics.com/latvia/home-ownership-rate.

Lazzarato, M. 2012. *The Making of the Indebted Man: Essay on the Neoliberal Condition*. Cambridge, MA: MIT Press.

Martin, T. 2001. *The Affirmative Action Empire: Nations and Nationalism in the Soviet Union, 1923–1939*. Ithaca, NY: Cornell University Press.

Matīsa, K. 2005. "Latvieši – kalpa dvēseles vai revolucionāri?" *Neatkarīgā Rīta Avīze*, 17 January. Retrieved 22 November 2015 from http://www.tvnet.lv/zinas/viedokli/292944-latviesi_kalpa_dveseles_vai_revolucionari.

Mufti, A. 2014. "Stathis Gourgouris Interview, Aamir Mufti." *Greek Left Review*, July. Retrieved 22 November 2014 from http://greekleftreview.wordpress.com/2014/07/14/stathis-gourgouris-interviews-aamir-mufti/

Paalzow, A. 2015. "Latvian Lessons: Here's How Riga Overcame Its Own Economic Crisis—and What That Says about Greece." *Foreign Affairs*, 20 July. Retrieved 22 November 2015 from https://www.foreignaffairs.com/articles/latvia/2015-07-20/latvian-lessons.

Peebles, G. 2010. "The Anthropology of Credit and Debt." *Annual Review of Anthropology* 39: 225–240.

Power, S. 2015. "To Understand the Eurozone Crisis, Consider Culture." *Capital Ideas*, 17 June. Retrieved 22 November 2015 from http://www.chicagobooth.edu/capideas/magazine/summer-2015/to-understand-the-eurozone-crisis-consider-culture.

Rankin, J. 2015. "Eurozone Tells Greece Not to Expect Debt Relief in Near Future." *The Guardian*, 7 July. Retrieved 22 November 2015 from http://www.theguardian.com/business/2015/jul/07/eurozone-calls-on-athens-to-get-serious-over-greece-debt-crisis.

Rausing, S. 2004. *History, Memory and Identity in Post-Soviet Estonia: The End of a Collective Farm*. Oxford: Oxford University Press.

Simecka, M., and B. Tallis. 2015. "Fighting the Wrong Battle: A Crisis of Liberal Democracy, Not Migration." *Eurozine*, 4 September. Retrieved 22 November 2015 from https://www.opendemocracy.net/can-europe-make-it/michal-simecka-benjamin-tallis/fighting-wrong-battle-central-europe%E2%80%99s-crisis-is-o.

"Slavojs Žižeks par Griekijas referendumu: 'grieķi izdarījuši pareizo izvēli.'" 2015. *Delfi Bizness*, 8 July. Retrieved 22 November 2015 from http://www.delfi.lv/bizness/pasaule/slavojs-zizeks-par-griekijas-referendumu-grieki-izdarijusi-pareizo-izveli.d?id=46193343#ixzz3fln89TDE.

Slezkine, Y. 1994. "USSR as a Communal Apartment, or How a Socialist State Promoted Ethnic Particularism." *Slavic Review* 53(2): 414–452.

Weber, M. 1897. "'Objectivity' in Social Sciences." *Marxist Internet Archive*. Retrieved 22 November 2015 from https://www.marxists.org/reference/subject/philosophy/works/ge/weber.htm#s2.

———. 1930. *The Protestant Ethic and the Spirit of Capitalism*, trans. T. Parson. London: G. Allen and Unwin.

Zavisca, J. 2012. *Housing the New Russia*. Ithaca, NY: Cornell University Press.

3

Fairness and Entitlement in Neoliberal England, 2005–2015

Steve Garner

Who gets what, why, and under what conditions? These questions form the core of discussions about national identity, attached as they are to the relationship between citizens and the State in terms of rewards and responsibilities. In a period characterized as an "economic crisis" and by the UK's governing party as one of necessary "austerity," these questions are posed more pointedly: the threat of cuts in public services looms large in the narrative of sensible governance. The central assertion of this chapter is that discourses about entitlement, partly attached to the "fairness" agenda developed by former PM David Cameron (2010–16) provide a frame for understanding some of the dynamics of inequality currently shaping British people's view of themselves. This process produces and reproduces the distinction between the "deserving" and the "undeserving" poor (classed and racialized others), and is thus inscribed into a historical pathway of determining belonging to the nation(s).

The "fight for fairness" (as the Conservative Party called the policy) thus seems to have produced a "moral economy," where groups are produced via moral judgments: the dominant group constructs the subjugated one by attaching negative characteristics to it (in opposition to the characteristics it attaches to itself). However, I argue that the lines of division between deserving and undeserving lie not only between and within classes, but are also racialized. My own research on the racialization of white identities (Garner 2015) has identified the micro-functioning of that moral economy.

I am a white researcher engaged in qualitative fieldwork on the racialization of white identities, especially in England, since 2004. I have written in detail about my racialized, gendered and classed experiences of the field elsewhere (Garner 2015), but two points are relevant for this chapter. First, the title indicates my unwillingness to generalize findings from a set of provincial English sites to the UK as a whole. The local-ness of identifications is an important part of the story my respondents tell, and entitlement works largely on a national scale and with a particular idea of Englishness rather than Britishness (Garner 2015). Second, the production of the interview material from which the section 'Fairness is the opposite of equality' is drawn is predicated on white respondents talking to a white interviewer about immigration and community in England. I am certain that had the same projects been carried out by black and/or Asian researchers, a different discourse would have emerged due to self-censorship.

The moral economy, which existed before Cameron's fight for fairness had been articulated, incorporates a strand that extends into a critique of political correctness and produces a white Englishness that establishes itself in opposition to multicultural Britishness. This critique is based more on affect than on engagement with the details of discursive subjects such as immigration. Moreover, the equality agenda (i.e., the policies and ideas aimed at establishing racial equality) is understood as the opposite of fairness because it redistributes funding and status away from white English people toward ethnic minorities.

Given that this is the context in which the Conservatives' "fight for fairness" is received, I suggest that "fairness" accomplishes multiple ideological labor. Moreover, fairness plays a significant role in the meta-level strategy of "austerity" by identifying people to blame and providing a rationale for cuts in public spending. Indeed, austerity is not a logical response to a situation but one choice among ways to frame a set of economic and social policies: it actually functions as a Foucauldian "technology," that is, as part of a neoliberal project aimed at withdrawing the state's obligation to fund the welfare system, while enabling the effective conditions for the market to flourish.

We will look at the fairness agenda before examining how the discourse incorporates a racializing strand. The final section broadens the analysis of fairness with reference to the Coalition and Conservative administrations' (2010–15) use of the concept of austerity.

The UK state and the Crisis

We begin with the State—the focus of claims of entitlement. In Omi and Winant's (1994: 83) formulation of the state, there is more to it than simply the government: "The State is composed of institutions, the policies they carry out, the conditions and rules which support and justify them, and the social relationships in which they are imbedded." This is admittedly a wide-ranging definition, and full coverage of all these aspects is beyond this chapter's remit. However, I would emphasize the link between the policies and "the social relationships in which they are imbedded." This chapter identifies and analyzes the overlapping classed and racialized ways of understanding membership of the larger nation.

The story of the crisis in Britain dates back to the 2007–08 period and the emergency measures to support the banking system instigated by the new PM and former Chancellor Gordon Brown. In the 2015 general election and Labour leadership election alike, the political interpretation of the causes of this crisis was still a live issue. On one hand, Labour have generally argued since 2007 that the effects of a global recession deriving from North America were mitigated by Brown's swift and decisive action. The Conservatives (and latterly the New Labour candidates in the 2015 leadership election), however, have consistently argued that New Labour, once in power (1997–2010), overspent its way into deficit. The latter argument seems to have been the more compelling for English, if not for other UK voters, in the general election.

After the Conservative / Liberal Democrat Coalition took power in 2010, twin rival narratives emerged: Labour's economic profligacy versus reckless practices in the financial services sector. The former is code in UK politics for borrowing money and public spending. It should also be noted that this Conservative critique has been made of every Labour government going back to the 1920s, and that the 2007–08 crisis merely enabled the critique to be focused on a particularly tangible set of circumstances.

From the beginning of the 2010 general election campaign, the necessity of addressing the public spending deficit has formed the basis of the Conservatives' "austerity" discourse. They have since been the governing party (in coalition 2010–15), with a majority from May 2015 to June 2017. This is the context for then Prime Minister David Cameron's delineation of "fairness," the key concept guiding government strategies on public spending. We shall now examine the definition of fairness deployed in his interventions.

What Is Fairness?

The use of the term fairness vis-à-vis policy derives from Cameron's speeches in the run-up to the 2010 election campaign, and it was further emphasized in the 2010–12 period. However, D'Ancona (2012) links it to a speech by the then Shadow Chancellor George Osborne in 2008 at a Demos (think tank) event: "A fair society, argued Osborne, would have three characteristics. First, people would be 'properly rewarded for their effort and ability.' There would be equality of opportunity. And 'the current generation should not saddle the next generation with the costs of its own mistakes, be they environmental, social or fiscal.'" The presentation of the Conservative Party as the "party of working people" in the 2015 election relied strongly on the recycling of the concept of fairness and the associated epithet "hardworking," which we shall examine in the next section.

The version of fairness as a policy term in UK Conservative thinking derives from the coalition period (2010–15). The thirty-page program of the Coalition Government (2010) contains twenty-four mentions of "fair," "unfair," or "fairness." David Cameron used the phrase repeatedly in speeches since 2010, defining it firstly in this way: "Fairness means giving people what they deserve—and what people deserve depends on how they behave" (Mulholland and Wintour 2010).

This concise summary raises the question of what behaviors are considered deserving. The Conservative Party began featuring a "Fight for Fairness Agenda" in January 2012 (Montgomerie, 2012), followed up by two detailed articles published on the same day in the *Daily Telegraph* (D'Ancona 2012; Hennessey 2012). D'Ancona concludes that Cameron's aim was to save capitalism from itself (with the "fairness project"), as he wanted people to perceive their society as fair (in relation to both bankers' extravagances and public spending). Cameron situated the fairness project in a context of concrete measures such as reform—of executive pay and of the welfare system—and a campaign for change in the European Court of Human Rights' (ECHR) powers to override UK court and government rulings, notably around the 1998 Human Rights Act (Hennessey 2012). The ECHR occupies a central place in the popular 21st-century anti-EU discourse, being viewed as direct, unwelcome, and relentless competition for British sovereignty. The Human Rights Act is drawn from the ECHR's remit, and the court is seen as imposing "extreme" versions of human rights that afford more rights to defendants, offenders, and groups seen as undeserving, such as migrants and Roma. However, though the Conservatives certainly targeted the Human Rights Act in the immediate post-2015 election victory, the overriding emphasis in 2010–15 was on reform of the welfare system. Note the development of the behavioral theme first evoked in 2010: "… [the welfare system] was invented to help people escape poverty, but has trapped too many people in it. It was meant to be a stopgap in hard times, but has become a lifestyle choice for some. It was designed to bring us together, but is causing resentment" (David Cameron in Oakeshott 2013).

"Let's face it," says Wendy (Plymouth), "there's plenty of white English people, or not just saying white, but English people in this country, or British people in this country who really, if you set the criteria of not being useful members of society, you'd kick out of the country anyway." Her frustration with benefit-recipients is shared by Barry (Bristol). "No one wants to work," he complains. "There's people walking round the streets who haven't worked for years and years and years." This resentment stems from the mismatch of outcomes, summarized by the Prime Minister in the same speech when he suggested it was "crazy" that claimants could have a bigger income on benefits than from paid work, and argued that it is "fair that we all play by the same rules" (*Sky News* 2013).

Cameron's development of the theme of fairness leads people to a simple conclusion: welfare needs to be reformed so that fairness can be reinstated. The Coalition Government indeed enacted a series of welfare reforms, including the universal credit system, increased benefit sanctions, the tax on extra bedrooms in social housing (referred to as "the bedroom tax" in the media), and reforms to disability benefits, all of which, combined with the media focus on benefit recipients analyzed by Jensen (2014) and characterized as "poverty porn," has generated an appetite for reform (see next section). "Poverty porn" is a media focus on the lives of people living in poverty that portrays them as irresponsible absorbers of resources, thus providing putative evidence of the argument that public spending on benefits should be cut. In this televised scrutiny of the poor, Jensen (ibid.) argues, "life on the breadline was transformed from a profound social injustice to an opportunity to scrutinise the habits of the poor and assess how deserving they are."[1]

Thus, by Autumn 2014, when policy was put forward for the 2015 electoral campaign, the conclusion to the fight for fairness had been transformed into a proposal to finally remove the outstanding source of resentment articulated by Cameron in 2013. The household benefits cap (of £23–26,000 per annum) is aimed at ensuring that a household where no one has paid work cannot have more income than a household where someone is working (as of March 2015 the minimum wage was £6.70, and the average national wage was £26,500).[2] Cameron refers to this principle as "a basic fairness" (BBC News 2014). Reference to the theme of fairness continued after the 2015 election victory, when the PM commented on the Cabinet reshuffle that: "It will be our task to renew a sense of fairness in our society—where those who work hard and do the right thing are able to get on" (BBC News 2015).

The "fight for fairness" policy is strongly linked to the principle of "less eligibility." The idea that anyone doing waged work should be better off than anyone not doing it, —that is, independent of, rather than dependent on the State, goes back to the nineteenth century.[3] The crucial distinction in this philosophy lay between the "deserving" and "undeserving": the former characterized either by actual work or willingness to work, or by serious impediment to work, and the latter by active avoidance of work when capable of doing it. Both New Labour and Conservatives have generated summary binaries in recent political soundbite history. Jensen (2014) observes that the Gordon Brown administration's former Chief Secretary to the Treasury Liam Byrne, used the pairing, "shirkers" and "workers" at the 2011 Labour Party conference, while a more recent article cites him as "admitting" that people see the Labour Party as more supportive of "shirkers than workers" (Hall 2013). The Conservatives' couplet, "strivers" and "skivers"[4] (Jensen 2014), has also circulated widely. These rhyming pairs of terms seem to exemplify the "deserving" versus "undeserving" distinction originally asserted in the principle of "less eligibility."

This terminology should alert us to the multiple functions of such soundbites. Cameron's emphasis on behavior being rewarded is a statement of not only economic, but also moral intent. Chancellor George Osborne's criticism of people with their blinds down "sleeping off" the benefit lifestyle (Mason 2013)[5] removes these debates from the rather more complex and contested picture of who gets benefits (and questions such as what counts as "benefits" and what counts as "subsidies"), to a relative and hierarchical binary index generated by, and subject to a moral, rather than a material economy.

Having outlined the development of the fairness agenda, we will next examine "fairness" more critically.

Is Fairness for "Hardworking People"?

Polling shows the electorate's widespread support for the Coalition and Conservative governments' welfare-cutting reforms. The British Social Attitudes survey's exploration of public attitudes toward benefits and welfare sketches a long-term decline in public appetite for welfare spending on benefits for working-age people (especially unemployment), from 61 percent in 1989 to 30 percent in 2014, including a 3 percent rise after 2009 (Taylor-Gooby and Taylor 2014: 1). The other element of the picture is increasing divergence along party lines, with only 17 percent of Conservative supporters in favor of more spending on welfare (pensions excluded), vis-à-vis 44 percent of Labour supporters. Additionally, 71 percent of Conservative supporters, compared to 38 percent of Labour supporters, feel that benefits are too high and discourage people from seeking work. Overall, 52 percent of those interviewed felt this to be the case, while another 59 percent thought the unemployed could find work if they "really wanted to." The benefits cap referred to above has the support of 73 percent of those polled. These seem unambiguous figures: a clear majority supports the key assumptions underlying the "fight for fairness": that it is behavior that leads to poverty or success, and good behavior should thus be rewarded.

Yet there are actually some areas of ambiguity. It is unclear whether the PM's central argument (behavior determines reward) is as neatly embedded as those figures suggest. Although there is majority support, when broken down by class (Rogers 2014) the figures show a statistically significant distinction between upper and lower segments, even if both are more than 50 percent in favor of reducing housing benefits for people under twenty-five, and for families with three or more children.

Moreover, in the Joseph Rowntree Foundation's qualitative fieldwork on attitudes toward poverty, a point of tension derives from discussion of behavior and deservingness (Hall, Leary, and Greevy 2014: 5). People challenge the reading of poverty as resulting *solely* from behavior. Indeed, this research shows that in the understandings of the interviewees, even though individuals do have a role to play, poverty is seen as "structural." In other words, it is the outcome of a social system rather than purely the reflection of an individual's poor decisions.

> Some participants, typically those who lived in areas of high deprivation, felt that what others might view as poor choices and priorities could

be seen as manifestations of the long-term structural and current economic barriers experienced by people living in poverty. If poverty was to be partly defined by a lack of opportunity and aspiration then, they argued, what some may see as poor personal choices were the outcomes of poverty, not the cause... (ibid.: 24)

This reading of poverty stands in opposition to the one underpinning "fairness," which is about attitudes and choices. So this returns us to the question of what the "fight for fairness" discourse does. Is it an opportunist reflection of shifting public attitudes, a major element producing that shift, or something more complicated? First, fairness appears to be a means of rationalizing policy by categorizing people into two groups, them and us, the former undeserving and the latter deserving. The route by which we arrive in these groups is asserted as being due to individual choices, expressed in patterns of behavior.

Fairness shares the ideological territory of "less eligibility." It also elicits feelings of being beleaguered among those *not* on benefits, articulated through notions of "welfare cheats" fiddling the system (Allen and Blinder 2013). In the British Social Attitudes survey, one in three believes this to be the case (Taylor-Gooby and Taylor 2014). The spectacle and judgment of people's entitlement is a 21st-century British television hook (Jensen 2014), with the trend for "poverty porn," now overlying the type of class-transformation reality television described by Skeggs and Wood (2011). However, in both genres of classed television, the focus is placed on bad behavior: being unjustly rewarded in "poverty porn," and being "transformed" into good behavior in the class-transformation shows.

Spending and the Material Economy

The argument in this chapter revolves around the discrepancy between material and non-material dimensions of welfare. Hills (2015) asserts that according to the government's own figures, only 4 percent of total state spending goes on unemployment benefits. Moreover, unemployment benefits, tax credits, and all other out-of-work benefits *combined* account for less than 20 percent of spending. Pensions make up the largest spend (20 percent), with all forms of welfare totaling around 15 percent of all government spending as of 2015. Indeed, the public vastly overestimates the proportions of spending on unemployment benefits, the number of fraudulent claims, and the idea of an ongoing "culture" of benefit dependence.

Jobseeker's Allowance (JSA) is the main unemployment benefit: 2.9 percent of JSA claims are fraudulently overpaid, as are just 0.7 percent of all benefit claims. Lastly, 94 percent of JSA claims last for less than one year. These figures contrast starkly with ideas of a culture of permanent "lifestyle" dependents receiving half the welfare spend, the majority of it by fraudulent means.

Data on the performance of the UK economy and the government's role in it could be the subject of an entire book. Here I merely attempt to identify some key issues relevant to the concept of fairness. During the Coalition Government's first weeks in June 2010, the new chancellor, George Osborne, claimed that the government's transformation of deficit into surplus was feasible by 2015, if the correct spending cuts were enacted. However, while the deficit was reduced from £153 billion to £98 billion (2010–14), the reduction targets were missed every year. This was not because cuts were not as ferocious as promised (spending on some government departments was more than halved in the 2010–15 period), but because tax revenues fell below the predicted level, due to lack of growth in the economy. Simply put, the UK economy did not grow enough to generate taxation sufficient to enable Osborne's spending plan to come to fruition.

This basic mismatch between growth and cuts is explained by three important trends observed in the post-crisis economic restructuring. The first is that wage levels are stagnating, and the second is that many of the newly created jobs are low-paid and/or part-time. As of 2015, the threshold for personal income tax was £10,600, that is, no income tax is payable on salaries below that level (*Economist* 2014). So while "zero hours" contracts[6] are increasing (they rose 19 percent in 2014–15 and now account for 2.4 percent of the workforce) and 16.2 percent of part-time workers cannot get full-time jobs (ONS 2015a), it seems clear that the major growth area has been low-income work. Moreover, a third trend is now observable. In June 2015, 17.2 percent of workers were employed in the public sector vis-à-vis the 82.8 percent in the private sector (ONS, 2015b): a record low since in 1999, when the ONS started collecting such figures. So, while the number of jobs is expanding, they are shifting from the public to the private sector, and the majority of new jobs are at the lower end of the income bracket.

There are a number of ways that the consequences of the public spending cuts could imaginatively be measured, and one of these is the use of food banks. In April 2015, the Trussell Trust, the only nationwide food bank organization, released figures that showed that in 2014–15, it had provided enough meals to feed 1.1 million people for three days (Butler 2015). The same organization's historic figures showed a rise from "2,814 in the 2005–06 financial year to 61,468 in 2010–11, 346,992 in 2012–13," and "913,138 in 2013–14" (Grice 2015). Trussell is of course not the only source of foodbanks in the country, so the actual figure for the nationwide use of foodbanks is higher.

Not only have cuts to spending on benefits been implemented, they have been supported by an increasingly punitive sanctions regime. According to criminologist David Webster (2015), in his evidence to the Parliamentary Committee on Benefits, the sanctions regime of the post-2010 administrations has been particularly severe, with more than 1 million sanctions (a record) applied in 2013, affecting one in four benefit recipients. Webster also points out that although the sanctions are more far-reaching than court sanctions, they are implemented by government officials in secret, in a context where the claimant has no rights except an appeal, months after the original sanction has come into force. When placed next to the introduction of the "bedroom tax" and changes in the assessment of disability, aimed at returning people to the workforce, what emerges is a particular and punitive focus on the lower end of the income range entailed in the welfare and spending regime, which we might shorthand as the "material economy," which I am going to juxtapose later with the "moral economy."

The fight for fairness therefore promotes a binary (those on benefits / those not on benefits) in the place of the complex relationships and realities attached to benefit access. A large proportion of UK residents are recipients of some benefits, even if it is only Child Benefit. Moreover, if subsidies for various industries are included as "benefits," this proportion will increase. A number of state transfer payments are specifically called "benefits," such as those compensating unemployment or disability, pension payments, topping up or paying for rent, and additional payments to go toward expenditure incurred through caring for children under eighteen. However, other types of state transfer, particularly those paid to various industries—either as ongoing payments aimed at protecting them in developmental stages (e.g., non-fossil energy production), or tax breaks to entice companies to come to or remain in the UK—are referred to as "subsidies." Other payments, such as those received by landowners and farmers (a total of around £3 billion as of 2013) through the Common Agricultural Policy, to which UK taxpayers contribute, can bring in hundreds of thousands of pounds to business and self-employed farmers on an annual basis. Moreover, when land is owned by a non-domiciled owner, no tax is payable on it.[7] The distinction between "benefit" and "subsidy" is therefore social and judgmental rather than operational. The UK state paid out £93 billion in corporate welfare in 2014–15 (Chakraborty 2015) including tax breaks, procurement subsidies, direct subsidies, travel subsidies and others.

The fight for fairness thus seems to have produced a "moral economy," where one group judges another relationally. However, despite what we have seen so far, the lines do not only lie between "respectable" and "unrespectable" working classes. My own research has focused on how white UK people in provincial towns "make" racialized identities (Garner 2015), and I suggest that one of the ways they do so is exactly by "working" in this "moral economy" that existed before Cameron's fight for fairness had been articulated.

Fairness Is the Opposite of Equality

This section is based on two working hypotheses. First, in the exploration of "fairness" as a policy term, the public's engagement with it is rooted in the moral rather than the material economy: facts are secondary, and it's all about representations.

Second, the terms "migrant," "immigrant," and "asylum seeker" are not used in their technical senses but are parts of a racialized vocabulary that amalgamates a wide spectrum of diverse people, from those that actually fall into these categories at one end, through to British citizens who by now are two or even three generations out of migration at the other. Certainly, throughout media and in most political coverage of immigration these terms are utilized inaccurately, and immigration is posed as problematic per se. Indeed, the findings of the projects in which I have been involved (Garner 2015) lead me to assert that when UK people talk about "immigration" they are actually talking about a political space into which they are pouring a set of frustrations and resentments about inequality. Moreover, they attribute causal explanations to immigration, rather than responding to actual material bases.[8] In other words, immigration is credited exclusively with a set of negative impacts ranging from putting a strain on the National Health Service and taking British workers' jobs, to absorbing excessive proportions of welfare, to changing the country's culture for the worse. This pattern of understanding starts with a contested outcome and then reduces multi-causal phenomena to a single explanation, ignoring other possible factors. People's anxieties about falling living standards, increasing employment precariousness, and the changing demography of the UK are channeled in particular ways toward the conclusion that immigration is responsible.

"The Brits, those born and bred here, shall we say," states Mary (Bristol), "feel that we're being squeezed out of our own country." In this evocative statement, Mary encapsulates a cultural, economic and spatial resentment, picked up by Adam (Bristol), who cannot imagine a time when he would be able afford a house: "… when I think of immigrants … I think of just someone that's come into the country, that's obviously not allowed to come into the country but they're living like what we are … And I think it's unfair on British citizens, established British citizens … It's not fair, it's not fair at all. Just don't like it." The perception that public money is channeled toward migrants and Black and Minority Ethnic (BME) groups, and that white English people are in an unfair struggle for resources, is very powerful. This image is nicely expressed in Beryl's (Plymouth) account of collecting her pension from the Post Office in the city centre:

> I don't like all the immigrants coming to this country. And you're in the Post Office waiting for your pension which you've worked for. And you're standing there, and immigrants come in, go to another counter and they're seen right away, and you're standing in a big queue, and you're feeling tired and that, and then you see other people getting better treatment than what you are.

The battle for resources between those entitled through birth and bloodline, and those who are not is played out in a variety of figurative ways (Garner, 2015).

Taxpayers' money is spent, or indeed, the payment of tax is avoided, in a number of ways that could be sources of resentment about cutbacks. Yet it is immigration and a particular narrow range of benefits that are the main focus of comments and anxieties. A substantial minority are also interested in protesting the practices of corporate (and individual) tax evasion, which have provoked some legislative response from the UK Tax Office. So the interesting question here is not why people are feeling angry about the economy and public spending cutbacks, but why specific elements of spending, specifically those whose beneficiaries are poor and/or migrants, are viewed as more ripe for extended attention than other areas that cost taxpayers just as much, if not more, but whose beneficiaries are typically much wealthier.

What has this discussion got to do with fairness and entitlement? The long-term trend of opinion polling on attitudes toward immigration (and to increased welfare spending) is one of increasing hostility over the same period. Overall, a substantial majority wants to stop migration from rising, and expresses reservations about some kinds of migrants (particularly the undocumented, the low-skilled; Africans, and asylum seekers) (Ford, Morrell, and Heath 2012). Importantly, in the British Social Attitudes survey (Taylor-Gooby and Taylor 2014), majorities also want to prevent both EU and non-EU workers accessing the benefit system.

Below we will review a small number of examples from fieldwork (Garner 2015) that encapsulate some of the micro-level expressions of these sentiments. However, it is useful first to hear an assessment of the equality agenda (official legislative action against racial discrimination) by the then incoming Home Secretary (now Prime Minister) Theresa May in November 2010, who stated that "in recent years, equality has become a dirty word because it meant something different. It came to be associated with the worst forms of pointless political correctness and social engineering" (May 2010). According to the majority of our interviewees, May has pinpointed a common sentiment among white UK people, namely that "equality" is not for them. However, people expressing impatience with the existing forms of resource allocation by no means focus solely on BME groups and migrants. Typically, on our interviews, two groups are identified: non-contributing white people, and minorities/migrants.

In Bristol, Patricia says:

> I'm not racist. I'm not racist... but I'm prejudiced. I am prejudiced, but I'm not only prejudiced against people that are black, I'm prejudiced against people who are on the dole who don't do nothing, and still get it all. And there's like me and my husband, who work hard ... who keep our house nice ... I mean we're only council tenants ... but we don't get nothing.

Stanley in Birmingham tells a common story. He is dismayed at the number and scope of holidays that his benefit-recipient neighbor is taking (Bhattacharyya et al. 2012: 73):

> The person who used to live next door to me ... he couldn't read or write ... and he was claiming for all this money. At Easter he went to Brean [a seaside resort] with it for a fortnight. Then at Whitsun he went to Brean again for a week. Then he decided 'I've always wanted to see the Pyramids'... So he got some more and he went to Egypt. And then

he claimed again. He went for three weeks cruising round the Spanish Islands ... Now you're sitting thinking—I've worked all my life!

Many tell of undeserving people receiving resources and living envied lifestyles. It should however be pointed out that the assumption is always that the speaker has an excellent knowledge of someone else's personal finances. The next complaint, drawn from the same fieldwork as Patricia's interview (above) shows one version of this story:

> The Somalians, they're having everything ... the lady across the road [Somali] ... Now I know they're mucking about with the social. You know they're claiming they don't get this and don't get that ... and they're all working. And the two things I ask for, they got ... And I think hang on a minute, is it right that you look after your house, go to work, pay your council tax, pay your rent, pay your taxes and you're not rewarded? Yet those that do nothing ... they get it because they show you the racist card... (Hoggett, Wilkinson, and Beedell 2008: 19).

This is the point at which the fairness discourse is most clearly racialized. In this model, local authorities and the Department of Work and Pensions (DWP, the ministry responsible for paying out and monitoring most benefits) would be threatened with equality legislation by ethnic minorities and their advocacy groups if they are not accorded resources. The systems for delivering resource allocations appear in this discourse to be perpetually biased in favor of racialized and abject others because they are under the threat of with 'unreasonable' legislative procedures. So a consensus in our interviews about access to resources was, in the words of John (Bristol), that "the pendulum has swung too far the other way."

This perception produces resentment (as David Cameron himself states above). "Everywhere you look there's refugees" says Maureen, a low-paid worker in Birmingham whose son lived with his girlfriend and four-year-old daughter in Maureen's small council house. She maintains that they eventually split up because of this overcrowding: "and they're getting the houses ... that's been allocated to asylum seekers. Why are they getting it when our own kids can't get nothing? It's just so, so ... annoying." Indeed, access to housing is a particularly thorny and emotive issue (Garner 2009) whose complexity is often reduced to a deserving/undeserving binary. The amount of housing stock available in the social housing sector is far below the level of demand, and multiple factors increase the likelihood that the housing available to most migrants will be of poor quality (Robinson 2010); further, asylum seekers have a different, weaker status than other benefit recipients. Subletting of social housing and letting of former council houses may also give people the impression that migrants are accessing social housing "ahead of" them and their families. However, it has to be noted that you cannot tell someone's immigration status just by looking at them: many of the assumptions rest on the idea that particular bodies are a priori foreign.

The idea of tables being unfairly turned manifests itself in how people articulate racism: as equally available to minorities as to white people. A woman in Milton Keynes (Garner, 2015) asks:

> Why should we have to be politically correct all the time when they're not, when they get away with it. Why should we? Why should we have to be the ones that step back and have to change it all the time, because that's what's happening! We have got nowhere to go. We don't have a white race relations board. But they have a black relations board or an ethnic race relations board they can go to and complain about us, but we haven't.

Neoliberal governance ideologically minimizes the role of social differences (e.g., class, gender, race) and contexts in favor of the individual rational actor. Success or failure emerges as a direct function of responsibility and hard work. In the UK, one outcome of applying this frame to the legislative grid on equality since 2010 is a withering of state interest in "race" as a basis for discrimination (Kapoor 2013). The "race equality duty" incumbent on public authorities and employers under the 2000 Race Relations (Amendment) Act has been removed, no policy has replaced the area that until 2010 was referred to as "community cohesion," and the Commission for Racial Equality—a body set up to oversee race equality legislation—has been merged into the Equality and Human Rights Commission, which deals with several grounds for discrimination rather than focusing on one. Taken together with Theresa May's comments about "equality" vis-à-vis fairness (above), the picture is one in which the state's involvement in enforcing anti-discrimination legislation has been deprioritized since the Conservative–Liberal Democrat Coalition took power. The irony is that just at the moment when neoliberal governance formally de facto banishes race to a space where it is either obsolete or irrelevant to individuals, the people we spoke to see resource allocation very clearly as a racialized game (with local variations); and importantly, a game in which whiteness no longer guarantees privileged access.

The othering in the entitlement game, or the fight for fairness, is not one-dimensional (class), but at least two- (class and gender), or three-dimensional (class, gender, and race). By underscoring the fairness or unfairness of the current allocation structure, the interviewees who argue that it is disadvantageous to white UK people are arguing that the previous thirty years of the "equality" agenda (racial and sexual equality legislation and agencies to monitor said legislation) have resulted in a *reversal* of power relations. In our interviews, the script in which politically correct local authorities and central government have conspired to de-resource white UK people in favor of ethnic minorities and other migrants is strikingly ubiquitous. Many of the white UK people interviewed in Milton Keynes in 2008 believed that the local authority would rather be seen as not "racist" than be "fair." This had contributed to and "caused a lot of resentment in the area" (Garner et al. 2009: 41).

The powerful affective frameworks through which people make sense of topics such as poverty, welfare, and immigration (Ioanide 2015) means that the ideological labor entailed in rebutting myths with figures has poor returns. Fairness thus emerges as a more complex idea than had first been suggested. The way David Cameron originally pitched it is that fairness means not being rewarded for unproductivity. According to many of those interviewed in our projects, "equality" is the opposite of "fairness." And because equality is spoken of directly in relation to British ethnic minorities as well as migrants, then "fairness" has a racialized subtext. For these interviewees, restoring the status quo in which white UK people were advantaged vis-à-vis others should be one of the objectives of fairness: once that advantage begins to evaporate, the situation becomes "unfair."

"Fairness" and "Austerity"

We have so far examined how fairness is portrayed as part of a political agenda aimed at reducing the crisis-level deficit by reforming welfare, and explored some of the ambiguities and clarities in the public's reception of these ideas. Finally, we saw how one of the ways in which people make sense of the welfare reform fairness logic is by resisting what they see as the imposition of unfairness ("equality") that rewards people for poor behavior and / or identity politics.

In this section I will marshal some framing and contextual arguments enabling us to understand "the fight for fairness" as a "technology" (in the Foucauldian sense) of austerity, i.e. a discourse aimed at simultaneously abrogating the state's obligation to fund the welfare system, and maximising the operation of the free market.

Far from signalling the state's retreat in toto from the front lines of governance, these "austerity" conditions indeed necessitate ongoing state actions. These have not ceased but shifted: toward increased subsidies, in the forms of tax breaks, enabling legislation for the pursuit of individual and corporate profit to be made in originally state-owned economic spaces.

The role of the fairness agenda is to win consent from the electorate for the austerity project, and focus attention on specific areas of spending by prioritizing elements for discussion. For the ruling parties, politics is about prioritizing spending. The post-2010 UK administrations have, for example, instituted a new higher education fee regime that actually costs taxpayers more than the system it replaced (while justifying it in terms of saving money; see Malik 2014); fined people on benefits with extra bedrooms—ostensibly to bring those rooms back into the public domain for the needy—when no homes were available for people to downsize into; and simultaneously provided financial packages (subsidies or benefits?) for people buying very expensive housing on the private market (Dorling 2014).

Indeed, fairness has less to do with financial egalitarianism and equitable management of state resources than with the emotional politics of affect (Wetherell 2012) activated behind a particular political project. Fairness is about moral obligation and perceived respectability. In effect, fairness pits people against the poor because the latter receive particular types of benefits, and suggests they do not share the values of respectable, hardworking "us." In terms of spending and loss to the public purse per se, however, corporate and individual tax evasion, and various subsidies to farmers, construction, landlords, and so forth would be more logical targets for reform. Fairness is thus a very useful hook because it is part of an "emotional circuit" (Ahmed 2001) or "emotional economy" (Ioanide 2015) in which an array of "figures" and behaviors form the constitutive points.

Austerity is not the only possible response to an act of God, but an ideological blanket under which a set of policies promoting the reorganization of the economy and redistribution of wealth upwards can be pursued on the basis that there is no other way to rebuild the economy. Yet creating such a project is neither a foregone conclusion, nor easy to achieve. It relies on convincing people of different things at different moments, such as the necessity of taking austerity measures; who is to blame for the economic crisis; how long austerity measures will take to be effective; where the cuts should fall and why, and so on. In effect, the permanent state is shrinking (Warner 2014), and this not a temporary response to a crisis but a policy objective. The outsourcing and privatization of government functions has increased rapidly since 2010. The (contested) shifting of blame away from bankers and onto New Labour and welfare dependents (Clarke and Newman 2012), along with the collective sacrifice made to shrink the state until better times, actually turns out to be a project in and of itself instead of a pragmatic response, as David Cameron's speech at the Mansion House in November 2013 demonstrates (Watt 2013). After arguing that better services could be provided with less, he stated: "We are sticking to the task. But that doesn't just mean making difficult decisions on public spending. It also means something more profound. It means building a leaner, more efficient state. We need to do more with less. Not just now, but permanently."

This statement contradicts earlier statements made about the desirability of cuts in public spending, and should alert us to the momentum accumulated by the fight for fairness. By the end of 2013 the focus had readjusted from the banking sector's practices to New Labour's profligacy and the need for hardworking people to get value for money. The fact that many benefit recipients are actually working complicates the message of "fairness," which dichotomizes the population into productive workers and unproductive benefits recipients. The Social Mobility and Child Poverty Commission (Chakelian 2015) estimated that the cuts in tax credits (produced by lowering the threshold for taxation of people on low incomes) announced in the July 2015 budget will impact negatively on 45 percent of families in work.

Conclusions

"Fairness" thus emerges as a technique meant to bind voters around a punitive neoliberal political agenda while simultaneously reproducing and reconfiguring lines of inequality, thereby generating a concomitant emotional othering. For some groups, accessing resources paid for by the taxpayer is transformed into a moral failing, made all the more profound by the idea that everyone else is collectively sacrificing, even though they are consistently contributing. Benefits aimed at the unemployed and the working poor are those earmarked for most attention, and form the subject matter of "poverty porn." Yet these are by no means the largest burden on the tax payer: tax evasion and subsidies to industry also account for billions of pounds' annual spending, while outsourcing public functions to private sector companies is passed off as a saving, but merely displaces the cost elsewhere.

Work in the "moral" economy consists of creating the identity of a respectable, contributing and deserving person vis-à-vis the non-respectable, unproductive and undeserving other. The fairness agenda is constructed on the principle and practice of the moral economy trumping the material economy. The moral judgements made about the idle poor are based on ostensibly reasonable claims and policies: capping benefits-derived income, encouraging people back to work, and providing disincentives for having unused rooms in your home. Yet the new welfare regime has a consequential punitive aspect. The figure of the "idle poor" does not stem solely from a discursive set of judgments consolidated by television shows. It is also the fruit of the new sanctioning regime, which has removed benefits from millions of people since 2010 (Webster 2015). Moreover, initial research indicates that people who are removed from Jobseeker's Allowance—for example, due to failure to demonstrate that they are actively seeking employment—do not actually end up in work, though their employment is the stated objective of sanctioning them in the first place (Loopstra et al. 2015). Ideological and discursive patterns result in material consequences: the degradation and humiliation caused by benefit sanctions can have drastic results, including ill health (both physical and mental) and possibly death.[9] The crisis management tool of austerity converges with the fight for fairness and a narrow understanding of dependency. It reconfigures old ideas about entitlement in new ways, such as the racialization of claims for deserving-ness observed in our fieldwork, where citizens of color, economic migrants, and asylum seekers were often amalgamated into a group whose claims on the common wealth were viewed as less compelling than those with a "birth right."

The electoral successes of the Scottish Nationalist Party and of Jeremy Corbyn in the Labour leadership election (in May and September 2015 respectively) demonstrate that there is an audience for the version of fairness that prioritizes corporate and individual tax avoidance, and ditches austerity measures in favor of targeted spending. In the last forty years, however, the moral economy's overall trajectory has been toward producing and reproducing figures of shame, embodying failings attributed to lifestyle choices. Poverty porn makes us visualise poor bodies and behaviors, and compels the viewer to judge them. A similar frame places migrants and minority ethnic groups in the same position of vulnerability: as foreign versions of the idle poor, they are even less entitled because they are someone else's responsibility.

The othering discourses conveyed in the constituent strands of the fairness project are meant to place distance between "us" and "them," to confer permanence on these divisions, and to rest the case for further ongoing welfare reform and thus for ongoing austerity, a strategy whose objective can never quite be achieved. So the fight must continue.

Responding to the Archbishop of Westminster's criticisms of his welfare policy, David Cameron declared that "seeing these reforms through is at the heart of our long-term economic plan—and it is at the heart too of our social and moral mission in politics today" (*Guardian* 2014). The social and moral mission of "fairness" was a central plank of austerity policy in the Cameron-led Coalition and Conservative administrations. This chapter has argued that "fairness" is not a neutral, rational set of ideas but in fact identifies particular groups whose behavior and deservingness are subject to scrutiny, whereas other groups that absorb public funds are not singled out for scrutiny—a situation reflecting the power relations involved.

The UK is in a transitional phase of "winning consent" for the fight for fairness as part of the neoliberal project. On one hand, attitudes are settling into a new consensus around key parts of the fairness agenda (especially but not exclusively in England), while on the other, the oversimplified binary of "strivers" and "skivers," or of "hardworking people" and their others, has helped produce a moment in which to challenge the messages being conveyed. The focus on class that underpins the fight for fairness is refracted through notions of respectability, and its discourse maps directly onto one binding racialized immigration to nationalism (Garner 2015). Our interviewees seem to have hit the nail on the head: "fairness" does seem to be the opposite of equality, but maybe not in the way they meant.

Steve Garner is Professor of Critical Race Studies and Head of the Department of Criminology and Sociology at Birmingham City University, UK. He has published widely on whiteness as well as racism and its intersection with class and nation in a variety of geographical contexts (including England, Ireland, the USA, and Guyana). He is the author of *A Moral Economy of Whiteness* (2015). *Whiteness: An Introduction* (2007), *Racism in the Irish Experience* (2004), and numerous book chapters and articles in journals such as *Ethnic and Racial Studies*, *Ethnicities*, and *Sociology*. He is currently working on skin lightening practices and discourses.

Notes

1. Poverty porn examples given by Jensen include "Benefits Street" (Channel 4, 2014); "On Benefits and Proud" (Channel 5); "Benefits Britain, 1949" (Channel 4, 2013), "Britain on the Fiddle" (BBC, 2013), and "We Pay Your Benefits" (BBC, 2013). Maybe equivalent programmes about immigration could be considered "immigration porn"? I would suggest "UK Border Force" (Sky, 2008–), "The Big Immigration Debate" (Channel 5, 2014), "Immigrant Street" (Channel 4, 2015), and "Tom and Margaret: Too Many Immigrants" (BBC 1, 2014).
2. Between 2012 and 2015, the average wage fell 0.2%. The average wage is earned by Prison Officers. Plenty of professionals and part-time workers do not earn £26,000. Based on ONS figures. Retrieved 11 September 2017 from http://www.icalculator.info/news/UK_average_earnings_2014.html.
3. Typically associated with Jeremy Bentham, it actually derives from the Noetics (Cambridge Christian political economists), who were influential in the Poor Law Commission of the early 1830s.
4. "Strive" means to work hard toward a particular goal. "Shirk" and "skive" both mean to avoid working.
5. Osborne's comment is a normative one that recalls Nicolas Sarkozy's repeated claim during the 2012 presidential election, that he was on the side of "people who get up at seven in the morning to go to work," a French equivalent of the Conservatives' "hardworking people" riff.
6. Zero hours contracts are employment contracts where no hours of work are guaranteed over a specific period, yet the employee must be available to work. They are defended by some as offering both employer and employee a maximum of flexibility, and criticized by others as jeopardizing the employee's expectation to earn a feasible amount of money from employment.
7. Iain Duncan-Smith's son and in-laws, for example, benefit from such transfer payments as the owners of Swanbourne Home Farms in Buckinghamshire, an estate that has received more than 1.5 million in EU subsidies over a ten-year period (Muir 2013).
8. See my three connected *Open Democracy* blogs published as part of the run-up to the 2015 general election: "What Is This Political Space We Call Immigration?" 23 March, https://www.opendemocracy.net/ourkingdom/steve-garner/what-is-this-political-space-we-call-'immigration; "Integration: Different Logics and Local Factors," 27 March, https://www.opendemocracy.net/ourkingdom/steve-garner/integration-different-logics-and-local-factors; "Immigration Views: How the Marginal Has Become Mainstream," 2 April, https://www.opendemocracy.net/ourkingdom/steve-garner/immigration-views-how-marginal-has-become-mainstream.
9. In April 2015, the Information Commissioner's Office (2015) upheld a claim that the Department of Work and Pensions should regularly

publish the number of people who die after being taken off benefits. There is a controversy about what proportion of them would not have died had the DWP not removed their benefits.

References

Ahmed, S. 2001. "The Organisation of Hate." *Law and Critique* 12(3): 345–365.
Allen, W., and Blinder, S. 2013. *Migration in the News: Portrayals of Immigrants, Migrants, Asylum Seekers and Refugees in National British Newspapers, 2010–2012*. Oxford: Migration Observatory, COMPAS.
BBC News. 2014. "David Cameron: Freezing Benefits 'a Basic Fairness.'" 30 September. Retrieved 11 September 2017 from http://www.bbc.co.uk/news/uk-politics-29421957.
———. 2015. "Cabinet Reshuffle: Amber Rudd and Sajid Javid Promoted." 11 May. Retrieved 11 September 2017 from http://www.bbc.co.uk/news/election-2015-32683868.
Bhattacharyya, G., et al. 2012. "Understanding and Defining Poverty and Deprivation: the Challenges of Political Disengagement and White Identities across Six Birmingham Wards." *Birmingham City Council / Aston Centre for Research on Languages and Diversity*. Retrieved 11 September 2017 from http://www1.aston.ac.uk/EasySiteWeb/GatewayLink.aspx?alId=116455.
Butler, P. 2015. "Those Food Bank Data: Complicated Yes; Exaggerated, No." *Guardian*, 4 May. Retrieved 22 November 2015 from http://www.theguardian.com/society/patrick-butler-cuts-blog/2015/may/04/those-food-bank-data-complicated-yes-exaggerated-no.
Chakelian, A. 2015. "Budget 2015: What Welfare Changes Did George Osborne Announce, and What Do They Mean?" *New Statesman*, 9 July. Retrieved 22 November 2015 from http://www.newstatesman.com/staggers/2015/07/budget-2015-what-welfare-changes-did-george-osborne-announce-and-what-do-they-mean.
Chakraborty, A. 2015. "The GBP93bn Handshake: Businesses Pocket Huge Subsidies and Tax Breaks." *Guardian*, 7 July. Retrieved 22 November 2015 from http://www.theguardian.com/politics/2015/jul/07/corporate-welfare-a-93bn-handshake.
Clarke, J., and J. Newman. 2012. "The Alchemy of Austerity." *Critical Social Policy* 32(3): 299–319.
D'Ancona, M. 2012. "David Cameron Won't Let the Socialists Have Fairness All to Themselves." *Daily Telegraph*, 7 January. Retrieved 22 November 2015 from http://www.telegraph.co.uk/news/politics/david-cameron/9000153/David-Cameron-wont-let-the-socialists-have-fairness-all-to-themselves.html.

Dorling, D. 2014. *All That Is Solid: The Great Housing Disaster.* London: Allen Lane.
The Economist. 2014. "The Tax-Free Recovery: Why Britain's Economic Recovery Has Not Yet Filled Its Coffers." 20 September. Retrieved 11 September 2017 from https://www.economist.com/news/britain/21618820-why-britains-economic-recovery-has-not-yet-filled-its-coffers-tax-free-recovery.
Ford, R., G. Morrell, and A. Heath. 2012 "'Fewer but Better?' Public Views about Immigration." *British Social Attitudes.* 29 Retrieved 22 November 2015 from http://www.bsa.natcen.ac.uk/latest-report/british-social-attitudes-29/immigration/introduction.aspx.
Garner, S. 2009. "Home Truths: The White Working Class and the Racialization of Housing in Contemporary Britain," in *Perspectives: Who Cares About the White Working Class?* ed. K. Sveinsson, 45–50. London: Runnymede Trust.
———. 2015. *A Moral Economy of Whiteness: Four Frames of Racializing Discourse.* London: Routledge.
Garner S., J. Cowles, B. Lung, and M. Stott. 2009. *Poor White People's Attitudes toward Immigration.* London: National Community Forum / Department of Communities and Local Government.
Grice, A. 2015. "Food Banks: One Million Britons Will Soon Be Using Them, according to Trussell Trust." *Independent*, 15 April. Retrieved 22 November 2015 from http://www.independent.co.uk/news/uk/home-news/one-million-britons-using-food-banks-according-to-trussell-trust-10186142.html.
The Guardian. 2014. "David Cameron Defends 'Moral Mission' on Welfare." 19 February. Retrieved 11 September 2017 from http://www.theguardian.com/society/2014/feb/19/david-cameron-moral-mission-welfare-archbishop-westminster.
Hall, M. 2013. "Party Is Over for Benefit Skivers." *Daily Express*, 9 January. Retrieved 22 November 2015 from http://www.express.co.uk/news/uk/369554/Party-is-over-for-benefit-skivers.
Hall, S., K. Leary, and H. Greevy, 2014. *Public Attitudes to Poverty.* York: Joseph Rowntree Foundation.
Hennessey, P. 2012. "David Cameron: My Vision for a Fair Britain." *Daily Telegraph*, 7 January. Retrieved 22 November 2015 from http://www.telegraph.co.uk/news/politics/david-cameron/9000249/David-Cameron-my-vision-for-a-fair-Britain.html.
Hills, J. 2015. "Welfare Myths and Their Consequences." *Discover Society*. Retrieved 22 November 2015 from http://discoversociety.org/2015/01/03/welfare-myths-and-their-consequences/.
Hoggett, P., H. Wilkinson, and P. Beedell. 2013. "Fairness and the Politics of Resentment." *Journal of Social Policy* 42(3): 567–585.
Information Commissioner's Office. 2015. "Freedom of Information Act 2000 (FOIA)."

Information Commissioner's Office. Retrieved 22 November 2015 from https://ico.org.uk/media/action-weve-taken/decision-notices/2015/1424160/fs_50557638.pdf

Iaonide, P. 2015. *The Emotional Politics of Racism: How Feelings Trump Facts in an Era of Colorblindness*. Stanford, CA: Stanford University Press

Jensen, T. 2014. "Welfare Commonsense, Poverty Porn and Doxosophy." *Sociological Research Online* 19(3): 3. Retrieved 22 November 2015 from http://www.socresonline.org.uk/19/3/3.html.

Kapoor, N. 2013. "The Advancement of Racial Neoliberalism in Britain." *Ethnic and Racial Studies* 36(6): 1028–1046.

Loopstra, R., A. Reeves, M. McKee, and D. Stuckler. 2015. "Do Punitive Approaches to Unemployment Benefit Recipients Increase Welfare Exit and Employment? A Cross-Area Analysis of UK Sanctioning Reforms." Sociology Working Papers, Paper Number 2015-01. Oxford: University of Oxford. Retrieved 11 December from http://www.sociology.ox.ac.uk/materials/papers/sanction120115-2.pdf

Malik, S. 2014. "Student Fees Policy Likely to Cost More than the System It Replaced." *Guardian*, 21 March. Retrieved 22 November 2015 from http://www.theguardian.com/education/2014/mar/21/student-fees-policy-costing-more.

Mason, R. 2013. "Will the Benefit Squeeze Hit the 'Strivers' or the 'Skivers with Their Blinds Down'?" *Daily Telegraph*, 8 January. Retrieved 22 November 2015 from http://www.telegraph.co.uk/news/politics/9787734/Will-the-benefit-squeeze-hit-the-strivers-or-the-skivers-with-their-blinds-down.html.

May, T. 2010. "Equality Strategy Speech." *GOV.UK*, 17 November. Retrieved 22 November 2015 from https://www.gov.uk/government/speeches/theresa-mays-equality-strategy-speech.

Muir, H. 2013. "Diary: Will IDS Speak Out against 'Income Support' for Farmers?" *Guardian*, 30 May. Retrieved 22 November 2015 from http://www.theguardian.com/politics/2013/may/30/hugh-muir-diary-iain-duncan-smith.

Montgomerie, T. 2012. "David Cameron Begins Fight for Fairness Agenda." Conservative Home, 8 January: Retrieved 11 September from https://www.conservativehome.com/thecolumnists/2012/01/david-cameron-begins-fight-for-fairness-agenda.html.

Mulholland, H., and P. Wintour. 2010. "Fairness Means Giving People What They Deserve, Cameron to Tell Tory Conference." *Guardian*, 6 October. Retrieved 22 November 2015 from http://www.theguardian.com/politics/2010/oct/06/david-cameron-fairness-people-deserve.

Oakeshott, I. 2013. "Cameron Warns Welfare System Has Lost Its Way." *Sunday Times*, 7 April. Retrieved 22 November 2015 from onhttp://www.thesundaytimes.co.uk/sto/news/uk_news/Society/article1242060.ece.

Omi, M., and H. Winant. 1994. *The Racial State: Racial Formation in the USA from the 1960s to the 1990s*, 2nd ed. New York: Routledge.

ONS (Office of National Statistics). 2015a. "Employee Contracts that Do Not Guarantee a Minimum Number of Hours: 2015 Update." *Office of National Statistics*, 2 September. Retrieved 22 November 2015 from http://www.ons.gov.uk/ons/dcp171776_415332.pdf.

———. 2015b. "Statistical Bulletin: UK Labour Market." *Office of National Statistics*, November. Retrieved 11 December 2015 from http://www.ons.gov.uk/ons/dcp171778_421089.pdf.

Robinson, D. 2010. "New Immigrants and Migrants in Social Housing in Britain." *Policy & Politics* 38(1): 57–77.

Rogers, M. 2014. "All Parties Stand for 'Fairness', but What Voters Perceive to Be 'Fair' Is Up for Grabs." Retrieved 11 December 2015 from LSE blogs: http://eprints.lse.ac.uk/48432/1/blogs.lse.ac.uk-All_parties_stand_for_fairness_but_what_voters_perceive_to_be_fair_is_up_for_grabs.pdf.

Skeggs, B., and H. Wood. 2011. *Reality Television and Class*. Basingstoke: Palgrave.

Sky News. 2013. "Cameron: Welfare Reforms 'Put Fairness Back.'" 7 April. Retrieved 11 September 2017 from http://news.sky.com/story/1074902/cameron-welfare-reforms-put-fairness-back

Taylor-Gooby, P., and E. Taylor. 2014. "Benefits and Welfare: Long-Term Trends or Short-Term Reactions?" *British Social Attitudes* 32. Retrieved 22 November 2015 from http://www.bsa.natcen.ac.uk/latest-report/british-social-attitudes-32/welfare.aspx.

Warner, J. 2014. "George Osborne's Plan to Shrink the State is Big News." *Daily Telegraph*, 4 December. Retrieved 22 November 2015 from http://www.telegraph.co.uk/finance/autumn-statement/11271781/George-Osbornes-plan-to-shrink-the-state-is-big-news.html.

Watt, N. 2013. "David Cameron Makes Leaner State a Permanent Goal." *Guardian*, 12 November. Retrieved 22 November 2015 from http://www.theguardian.com/politics/2013/nov/11/david-cameron-policy-shift-leaner-efficient-state.

Webster, D. 2015. *Written Evidence Submitted by Dr David Webster, Honorary Senior Research Fellow, Urban Studies, University of Glasgow (SAN0110)*: Retrieved 11 September 2017 from https://publications.parliament.uk/pa/cm201314/cmselect/cmworpen/479/479vw36.htm. Wetherell, M. 2012. *Affect and Emotion: A New Social Science Understanding*. London: Sage.

Wood, H., and B. Skeggs. 2011. *Reality Television and Class*. Basingstoke: Palgrave Centre.

4

Debating Refugee Deservingness in Post-Celtic Tiger Ireland

Shay Cannedy

Introduction

In the spring of 2014, I volunteered to help a previous asylum seeker run for local office in a Dublin suburb. I regularly went canvassing with him, knocking on doors and handing out pamphlets in his predominantly immigrant neighborhood. Originally from DR Congo, Albert[1] was the first candidate of African origin to represent Sinn Féin, a nationalist political party capitalizing on widespread public frustration over government and EU-imposed austerity measures. Although many welcomed him to Irish politics, he was not without critics who took advantage of social media to call into question his right to participate as an African newcomer. In one particularly insulting Facebook post, a detractor digitally altered Albert's campaign poster to read: "Sinn Féin: Brits Out! Blacks In! More Welfare! Rent Allowance! Open Borders! Vótáil [Vote] Albert: Your Plantation Candidate for the African Township of Mulhuddart."

Responses to this racist post were swift and angry. One person exclaimed, "He has more respect for Ireland than whatever sap runs this page. Grow up ya fool" while another responded, "Albert is Irish because he is an Irish citizen. Even if he weren't, by virtue of being a human being, he has a right to be in this country and participate in politics. He represents the interests of ordinary working people in Dublin 15. Criticize the bankers, politicians and developers who have bleed [sic] this country dry."

The heated Facebook exchange surrounding Albert's candidacy exemplifies current debates in the Republic of Ireland (hereafter called "Ireland"): How should the country respond to newcomers in an era of economic uncertainty? Does immigration benefit or harm Ireland? What are Ireland's obligations to those seeking political asylum? Are some more deserving of a life in Ireland than others?

This chapter takes up the last question by examining how different stakeholders in Ireland assess "refugee deservingness" in terms of who deserves the state's protection and the sort of reception conditions that should be in place for asylum applicants—a category of immigrants applying for legal recognition as refugees based on fear of persecution in their home countries. Questions of this nature are relatively new for Ireland, as it has historically sent its own people abroad in the face of colonialism, famine, and poverty rather than receive other people's diasporas. However, during the Irish economic boom of the mid 1990s and early 2000s, Ireland became a net-importer of people, and like other EU members at the time, it received a higher than normal number of asylum applications, albeit still relatively few given its geographic location. In response, the Irish electorate voted in 2004 to abolish birthright citizenship, signaling the continued relevance of "whiteness" to Irish national identity (Garner 2004; Lentin 2008). Significantly, widespread anti-immigrant sentiments (especially targeting asylum seekers) in Ireland emerged in the context of an economic boom rather than recession, distinguishing it from other European contexts. Since the economic crash of 2008, survey data have shown that hostility toward immigrants in general has increased (Turner and Cross 2015), and my research points to the persistence of anti–asylum seeker discourses, even though this population has greatly decreased in recent years (RIA 2014).

This chapter focuses on "deservingness" rhetoric to analyze the current debate about Ireland's treatment of asylum seekers, many of whom have waited years for a final decision on their cases and have, in the meantime, started families and become involved in local communities. On one hand, pro-migrant activists and asylum seekers themselves argue that Ireland, by virtue of its own subaltern past, should extend better reception conditions and residency to this population. However, others claim that they are "undeserving" of a place in the nation by virtue of being truly "bogus" asylum seekers in a country that is struggling to support "its own" in times of economic recession.

As the editors note in the Introduction to this volume, crisis can result in radical power shifts or bolster the status quo and exclusionary notions of belonging. In the case of Ireland, I illustrate how the economic crisis entailed the latter scenario. However, I argue that other factors besides the economic downturn played into public and state reactions to asylum seekers—namely, Ireland's place in Europe as a postcolonial country and the transnational circulation of disparate discourses related to the moral worth of asylum seekers. Thus, the debate that I discuss below is rooted in a complex array of factors and ultimately signals competing notions of inclusion, exclusion, and cosmopolitanism in the political and public spheres. Moreover, it points to ambiguity over the meaning of Irishness, which may or may not be tied to "whiteness."

My theoretical orientation is based on scholarship that highlights how questions of moral deservingness interact with prevailing ideologies of inclusion and exclusion to impact the lives of the disenfranchised. Sarah Willen (2012: 813–814) theorizes notions of deservingness as the "flip side of rights." Unlike a conception of "rights" where commitments are codified in law and which "presumes universality and equality before the law, deservingness claims are articulated in a vernacular *moral* register that is situationally specific and often context-specific" (see also Garner's discussion in this volume). In addition, Willen (ibid.) explains that whereas rights discourse presumes to take no heed of individual particularities, deservingness discourses are relational: assessments are made according to one's own sense of deservingness as well as one's perceived or actual social distance from those whose deservingness is in question. Deservingness assessments are also conditional in that individuals may be deemed as more or less deserving based on presumed or actual characteristics (ibid.). Lastly, Willen highlights how these assessments are closely tied to extrinsic factors such as geopolitics, labor markets, and national ideology but also stem from personal ethics and commitments. As such, she notes how they are dynamic and can change over time as new circumstances and knowledge arise (ibid.).

I also situate my analysis within postcolonial theories that critically examine the past to understand present configurations of power. Located within this work is recognition of the agency of the colonized, who variously resist and manipulate colonial power to meet their own ends. Thus, colonized and formerly colonized people take up the subject positions of both the oppressed and the oppressor. As Bhabha (1994: 122) notes, this points to an ambivalence toward the colonizer, where subaltern populations mimic imperial behavior in an effort to attain recognition as "authentic"—a status that colonial power denies them. In the case of Ireland, I show how the Irish successfully appropriated the powerful "white" identity of "civilized" Europe to gain independence, and how this identity is now employed to deny the deservingness of racialized asylum seekers. Yet I will also discuss how some challenge this stance through a different subject position, as colonized subjects. Ireland is not unique in this regard, as evidenced in the case of Iceland, which shares a history of colonization, a sense of being peripheral to Europe, ideas of ethnic purity, new multiculturalism, and recent economic fluctuations (Loftsdóttir 2011; see also Loftsdóttir and Björnsdóttir in this volume). Like Ireland, Iceland has responded to its relatively few newcomers as a "threat" to its unmarked "whiteness," thus pointing to the powerful, if tenuous, nature of "whiteness" as a resource in formerly colonized European countries.

Material for this chapter is based on twelve months of ethnographic research conducted in 2014, which included unstructured and semi-structured interviews with asylum seekers, immigrant rights activists, and government officials; observation of political rallies, local conferences, and public meetings; and document analyses of government speeches and media offerings including newspaper opinion pieces, online newspaper comments sections, and television news programs. Researching the construction and material effects of "whiteness" poses methodological and analytical challenges. First, there is the challenge of how to understand racial discourse that repudiates racism yet supports racist ideology masked by objections to "culture" or other differences. Second, I found that my own social position as a white researcher from the United States impacted how interlocutors related to me. For instance, some African asylum seekers perceived my whiteness as an association with a colonial past and current neocolonial relations, which limited my access to certain research participants. On the other hand, some white Irish government officials assumed that I shared their notions of African incommensurability vis-à-vis (white) Western culture. Ultimately, it is important for white researchers to recognize their own positions as racial actors. This entails consideration of how external readings of whiteness may grant symbolic and material advantages—as well as limitations—and how one's subject position at the top of a racial hierarchy may produce blind spots when it comes to fully apprehending these advantages.

To contextualize discourses of refugee deservingness in Ireland, I first provide a brief examination of the historic formation of "race" in Ireland, and then move on to discuss the recent economic fluctuations and general attitudes towards immigrants in this context.

Next, I delve into the specifics of how asylum seekers are received in Ireland in terms of policy and living conditions, and discuss how these configurations culminated in a series of protests by asylum seekers and their advocates aimed at securing greater rights for the displaced. I conclude with an analysis of the discourses surrounding these protests and how they illuminate notions of "refugee deservingness" in the Irish context.

"Race" and the Irish Colonial Past

In the heart of Dublin Docklands, a memorial features emaciated figures in bronze walking hunched over and barefoot toward an imagined ship bound for the United States; some clutch a few belongings while one carries a child, draped over his shoulder. This haunting scene of the potato famine of the 1800s serves as a reminder of Ireland's painful past of colonialism, starvation, and poverty — poverty and underdevelopment that endured until relatively recently, and which some fear will re-emerge in the wake of austerity. Pointing to their own history of oppression and relative powerlessness in the global order today, some claim that the Irish are "immune" to being racist themselves (cf. Loftsdóttir and Björnsdóttir in this volume). This assertion, however, ignores institutionalized and everyday racism against asylum seekers, as well as older discrimination against internal "others." The denial of racism has provoked academic rebuttals, such as that of Lentin and McVeigh (2002), who argue that today's racism is simply a new articulation of discrimination that has long existed in Ireland. They locate its antecedents in the contradictory ways that the Irish have been racialized throughout history, as victims of anti-Irish racism in the colonial encounter and as empowered by their whiteness and Europeanness.

The negative racialization of Irish society is a process that can be traced to several historical moments, including subjugation under Protestant British colonists who initially deemed the Irish "barbaric" and "wild" pagans to justify land seizure in the late sixteenth century (Garner 2004). Later, nineteenth-century scientific racism proclaimed that Celts occupied a "non-white" position in the racial hierarchy due to supposedly objective physical characteristics (Luibhéid 2013). Due to their purportedly pre-modern religion, Catholic Irish who arrived in the United States during this time were also considered a lesser "white race"; there, as in Britain, whiteness was tied to a white, Anglo-Saxon, Protestant (WASP) identity (Garner 2004).

The Irish in the USA eventually managed to secure a place in the American racial hierarchy as "white" by distancing themselves from black "others." In turn, this had repercussions for the Irish nationalism emerging in the late 1800s and early 1900s (ibid.). For example, drawing on diasporic racial ideologies, the Irish independence movement sought to create a new, respectable national identity based on the revalorization of the Celtic "race" defined through its whiteness, Catholic morality, self-sufficiency through ties to the land, and shared language and history (McVeigh 1992). Thus, Irishness was understood in ethnic terms, constructed against internal "others" such as Travellers and Jews, who did not meet these norms.

As I illustrate later in the chapter, this perceived homogeneous Irish identity based on "whiteness" influences discourses surrounding refugee deservingness, where racialized asylum seekers are deemed a threat to the nation. On the other side of the debate, however, others argue for solidarity with asylum seekers as co-subalterns. These two views derive from two historical traditions in Ireland: anti-imperialism/nationalism, which supported racism; and anti-racism, which found common ground with other subjugated peoples of the world. As Rolston (1999) notes, contradictory attitudes and behaviors are characteristic of colonized people. Drawing on Albert Memmi, he writes that the Irish had various and "schizophrenic" responses to their British colonizers because of two polar options available to them: to either attempt to assimilate into the superior model of the colonizer, for example by becoming "white"; or, that failing, to revolt. Because of this historic legacy, Lentin and McVeigh (2002: 11) describe Ireland as "'between two worlds'—both perpetrator and survivor of racism, both thoroughly racist and determinedly anti-racist."

From Boom to Bust to Recovery? The Irish Economy, circa 1996 to 2014

Ireland's "economic miracle" began in the mid-1990s with increased exports made possible by EU assistance and foreign multinational investment drawn to the island by low tax rates. There was a general sense that Ireland had finally arrived, having finally escaped economic dependency and successfully entered the globalized world, where in 1998, Ireland's GDP overtook the EU national average (Delhey 2001). Ireland was heralded as an EU "success" story given its purportedly wise usage of European funds to stimulate growth (ibid.).

Exports slowed after 2000, but the economy continued to grow due to credit-fueled construction financed by Irish banks via international lending institutions. During this period, residential real estate values increased threefold from 1994 to 2006 (Mercille 2014). Government, bankers, property developers, and the media benefited from the property market bubble, and as Mercille (ibid.) notes, the government colluded with the other parties to keep property prices high. But when the US financial crisis went global in 2008, the property market crashed, leading to banking and fiscal crises that culminated in a financial crisis in 2010 (Donovan and Murphy 2013). The government initially responded by socializing private bank debt and imposing austerity measures that included severe cuts in health, education, science, and social welfare. After conditions further deteriorated in 2010, the government took an €85 billion EU/IMF bailout that required more "structural reforms," limiting Irish control over the financial restructuring. Consequently, spending on social programs was slashed further, as has been the course in other European countries (Mercille 2014).

By 2015, Ireland was supposedly emerging from the recession. Pointing to a drop in unemployment (from a high of 15.2% in January 2012 to 9.8% in May 2015), the IMF declared that "Ireland's economic rebound is in full swing" owing to the government's response to the crisis (IMF 2015; CSO n.d.). Newspaper headlines and government officials frequently echoed the same optimism, but others pointed to the illusory nature of these indicators. In a letter written to the people of Greece in July 2015, over a hundred Irish academics argued that austerity had been devastating for Ireland and should not be replicated in Greece or anywhere else (Storey et. al. 2015). They noted that although GDP had grown due to Ireland's open economy, this wealth had not "trickled down." Moreover, the drop in unemployment masked the fact that emigration exceeded that drop and wages continued to fall.

The addition of cuts in social services and higher taxes (including the introduction of a controversial water charge) to economic insecurity on the ground has resulted in mass protests and anger at the existing political guard and the EU. New political parties have emerged, including the left-leaning Anti-Austerity Alliance and the right-leaning Identity Ireland—a party that aims to protect Ireland's "full sovereignty" against EU mismanagement and "mass immigration." In the following section, I take up the topic of immigration and particularly public attitudes toward asylum seekers in the contexts of Ireland's economic boom and bust.

Attitudes Toward Asylum Seekers
In Pre- and Post-Crash Ireland

It is notable that in the Irish context, fear of (particular) immigrants reached a fever pitch during the economic boom or so-called Celtic Tiger (1996–2008), rather than during the recession, thus challenging patterns that link xenophobia to perceived economic decline (cf. Espenshade and Hempstead 1996). Beginning in the mid 1990s, Ireland witnessed marked and swift demographic changes with the arrival of immigrants who came as workers, asylum seekers, students, and dependents. The 2002 census revealed, for example, that 5.8 percent of the population was "non-national"; this figure increased to over 10 percent in 2005 (Lentin 2008). The vast majority of immigrants came as workers recruited by the government to fill labor shortages, initially through liberal work permit policies and later via the opening of the labor market to the 2004 EU accession states (ibid.).

According to the 2003 Eurobarometer survey (n = 1,004), overall attitudes toward immigrants during the economic boom were welcoming; most thought that immigrants had made Irish society better through their cultural and economic contributions (Haynes, Devereux, and Breen 2008). Yet this welcome was limited—the number of arrivals, the cultures brought, and the duration of stay were all cited as factors that should be controlled (ibid.). A possible explanation for the increased mistrust of certain "others" during this time is that the Celtic Tiger did not benefit everyone equally. Rather, Garner and Moran (2009) observe, wealth was unevenly distributed, and the gap between rich and poor widened. Other possible factors include perceptions of incommensurable difference, fear of economic recession, and resentment over EU-imposed multicultural directives (ibid.; Tormey 2007).

Asylum seekers, whose numbers rose from 39 in 1992 to a peak of 11,634 in 2002 (ORAC 2014), were considered an especially threatening group. Many have observed how the media (mainly tabloids) and state officials created a moral panic over their arrival (Haynes et al. 2008; Kenny 2010). Assertions not supported by evidence framed them as "bogus" and truly "illegal" immigrants who falsely claimed persecution in order to gain entry to the country, have children on Irish soil, and thereby obtain residency through Ireland's birthright citizenship law. The state argued that the supposed drove of pregnant asylum seekers threatened the "integrity" of Irish immigration law and, if allowed to persist, would attract more illegal immigration, ultimately incapacitating medical services and social provision (Luibhéid 2013). Noting that EU membership is based on citizenship in a member state, officials also claimed that Irish birthright citizenship was a loophole for accessing Europe, and that it was thus "common sense" for Ireland, as a good neighbor, to fall into line with European citizenship norms by removing it (Lele 2008).[2]

As a result, by the early 2000s all asylum seekers had become morally suspect and were considered a population in need of control, despite their low numbers compared to labor migrants, who outnumbered them 4 to 1 in 2002 (Mancini and Finlay 2008). Moreover, although many ethnicities were represented in the asylum process, the legal category "asylum seeker" became racialized, so that Africans were routinely conflated with asylum seekers and the bodies of pregnant African women became sites of surveillance and ridicule, and symbols of "illegality" (Luibhéid 2013; Lele 2008). In 2004, these views culminated in a highly popular referendum (with 79.4% approval) to amend the Constitution to remove birthright citizenship from those whose parents are not Irish nationals, thereby "limiting temporal and ethnic change in the composition of 'the Irish nation'" (Mancini and Finlay 2008: 581).

Since the recession, negative attitudes towards immigrants have increased due to concerns over jobs and the economy (Turner and Cross 2015). O'Flynn, Monaghan, and Power (2014) find that certain groups have been discursively constituted as causing the recession, thus preserving the interests of the bankers, business, and government. According to their analysis, the finger is typically pointed at one of three groups: (1) "we" the Irish, who collectively "went mad with borrowing" due to lust for home ownership; and specific groups who are perceived as a "drain" on the system, including (2) unionized public-sector workers and (3) recipients of social welfare, including the unemployed, single mothers, and labor migrants. Labor migrants are scapegoated through discourses that frame them as "welfare cheats" who supposedly travel to Ireland to illegally claim social benefits before returning to their home countries. Indeed, as O'Flynn et al. note, group conflict theory posits that prejudice toward outgroups is related to perceived resource competition, whether over housing, employment, or power and status (cf. Blumer 1958; Bobo 1988).

My research indicates that asylum seekers are also denigrated as a burden on state coffers because they are purportedly given scarce resources at a time when Irish citizens are suffering unemployment and homelessness. Thus, negative discourses have shifted from the drain on state resources caused by asylum seekers' childbearing to the expense of feeding and housing "undeserving" people in a recession. This latter discourse surfaced in public debate in late summer 2014, when asylum seekers staged protests against a number of issues, including the extremely long refugee determination process and their living conditions in state-provided housing.

After a brief discussion of Ireland's system for receiving asylum seekers, I turn to how various actors framed their protests, some drawing on national economic hardship to form negative moral valuations of asylum seekers articulated through an idiom of exclusionary deservingness.

The Refugee Reception System in Ireland

Until 2000, asylum seekers had the same access to the Irish welfare system as Irish citizens, including access to public housing and welfare payments. However, amid rising numbers of asylum seekers and moral panic over their alleged "welfare abuse," the government instituted the direct provision system, which provides room, board, and a small weekly allowance (€19.10 per week per adult and €9.60 per week per child) while claimants wait for their refugee status to be determined. They are also entitled to free medical care, two exceptional needs payments of €100 per year (unless they are suspected of having other means of support), and free schooling for children under age eighteen (Thornton 2014). They are not legally obliged to stay in direct provision centers, but living in private accommodation is not an option for many, given high living costs and Ireland's blanket ban on employment for all asylum seekers. Furthermore, if they choose to live on their own they are not entitled to any state support, not even the weekly allowance and medical card.

In July of 2017, a total of 4,340 asylum seekers throughout the country were living in thirty-two centers consisting mainly of repurposed hotels and guesthouses that are privately owned and managed (RIA 2017).[3] Asylum seekers cannot choose their centers (although they can request transfers, which may or may not be granted), and human rights organizations have long criticized the system for its restrictive and questionable living conditions (cf. FLAC 2003; IRC 2012). In the majority of centers, for example, residents cannot cook their own food; living conditions can be overcrowded, with up to five people sharing a room; movements are monitored with CCTV and sign-out sheets; and those living in remote locations have difficulty accessing services such as medical appointments (IRC n.d.).[4]

These conditions are worsened by the long time asylum seekers live in direct provision waiting for decisions on their cases. In 2014, the average stay was four years, and 17.7 percent of all residents had been there for more than seven years (RIA 2014). Reasons for the extremely long determination process were multiple but stemmed in part from a dysfunctional system that required various applications for different legal statuses, instead of a single procedure.[5] At the end of 2016, the International Protection Act of 2015 finally came into effect, which partially rectified the situation by instating a single procedure. However, the process is still slow, with an average stay of two years due to large backlogs and the state's failure to provide the resources needed to hear appeals in a timely manner (RIA 2017; Mac Cormaic 2014).

Long waits coupled with forced idleness, isolation, and poverty have led to widespread frustration and documented mental health issues (Uchechukwu n.d.). Despite asylum seekers' vulnerability and well-founded fear of government retaliation, protests erupted at eight direct provision centers starting in the summer of 2014. Finally forced to respond to calls for change, the government instituted a working group comprised of government officials and immigrant rights NGOs to suggest improvements to the protection process, including direct provision. The working group delivered its McMahon Report, which recommended instating a single-procedure system, residency for those who have been in the system for more than five years, and increased allowance among other things. With the exception of the single-procedure system, it remains to be seen which (if any) recommendations the government will adopt, given concerns over "cost effectiveness" and protection of borders in hard economic times.

Calls for the Rightful Presence of Asylum Seekers

One fall morning I headed out to see Sephora, a friend who was living in a large, rambling direct provision center that had once been a convent. Her center was the latest to join the string of protests happening at other centers around the country. As I walked up to the building, men and women stood outside the barricaded driveway holding hand-written placards reading, "Ten Years is Too Much," "Release Us From Hostels," and "We Need Freedom." Occasionally passing cars honked in support, at which the residents cheered. This was day three of the protest.

The tipping point had occurred a few days prior when residents noticed the staff busily sprucing up the entrance and learned that this was in preparation for a top ministerial visit. Desperate to get the government's attention, they decided to draft and hand-deliver a letter outlining their concerns to him, and to offer tours of their rooms so he could witness conditions first hand. He received the letter, but in the end he stayed only a few minutes, claiming he had to attend another function. Viewing his visit as an empty gesture, the residents staged a protest a few days later by taking over the center and preventing staff from entering. When I arrived, the general mood was optimistic and energetic. For the first time, outside visitors could freely enter residents' rooms, there was no staff to monitor residents' comings and goings, and they were happily cooking donated chicken and fish for themselves.

Although there was some initial disagreement over demands, their letter (and basis for protest) ultimately centered on the difficulty of living for so long in legal limbo in an environment not conducive to mental or physical health—specifically, in buildings segregated from Irish society in what they called an "open prison." They argued that as humans, they should be treated with dignity, which would include quick knowledge of the outcome of their cases (decided within "the norms of human rights"), the means to cover basic living expenses, and ample, private living space. They also highlighted widespread depression due to long delays, as well as discord and fear between residents, which they attributed to cultural and lingual incommensurability. Thus, they protested not only their living conditions, but also the entire direct provision system itself. Finally, they argued rhetorically: "May we ask, if a child [is] born on this island, are they not entitled to some form of protection? Where else would you send them? Back to a country which is alien to them?"

As Arendt (1966/1951: 296) says, stateless people have lost "the right to have rights" and function as the citizen's "other." This makes it incredibly difficult for those without citizenship to make claims on the state. Even so, as we see here, protestors challenged dominant statist discourses by employing a cosmopolitan conception of socio-economic rights rooted in international human rights rather than national belonging. Yet their arguments were not exclusively post-national, as evidenced in their critique of the 2004 Citizenship Referendum, which removed *jus soli* citizenship. They argued that it was an immoral act to deport children who have deep links to Ireland by virtue of birthplace and residence, and therefore they—along with their caretakers—deserved a life in Ireland. In this way they challenged the notion that birth is a tenuous link to the nation and located their legitimacy within older, existent values and ideas in Irish society—namely, powerful conceptions of Irish national belonging as rooted partly in territory as well as Catholic and constitutional emphasis on the inviolability of family (Conway 2006; Garner 2004).

Other discourses appealed to popular memory and sentiment by drawing analogies between Irish emigration and the plight of asylum seekers that have circulated in the public sphere since the late 1990s (Gray 2004). Sitting in her small single room at the Waterford center, my friend Sephora said in exasperation, "They're emigrants. The story of Irish is one [where] they've been all over the world and no one closed doors. No one. All American presidents are Irish." Despite well-documented Irish experiences of racism and social exclusion in the diaspora (Garner 2004; Ignatiev 1995), Sephora's larger critique is that given a long history of emigration, it is hypocritical for the Irish not to be more welcoming to outsiders.

Pro-immigrant activists also drew parallels between direct provision and Irish institutions of the nineteenth and twentieth centuries, such as workhouses and the Magdalene laundries. Both institutions existed to deal with the "undesirables" of society, the former ostensibly created to provide relief for the poor and the latter to reform "fallen" women such as prostitutes and unwed mothers through prayer and (unpaid) hard labor, mainly in laundry services. By drawing comparisons between direct provision and these institutions, which in the popular imagination symbolize a cruel past, activists and some government officials argued that Ireland has a moral obligation to protect asylum seekers. They claimed that rather than being something of the past, inhumane institutionalization with no state accountability continues today as evidenced in the way vulnerable asylum seekers are segregated, treated poorly, and forgotten by society. Thus, they obliged a (once again) complicit citizenry and state to take a stand to stop the long, still ongoing legacy of containing "problematic" populations, which in this case consists of locking up the "'human waste' of a fragile global economy" (Titley 2012).

Significantly, the asylum seekers' rights movement consisted of various demands based on various understandings of deservingness, and their wishes ranged from improved conditions to the closure of the entire system while keeping deportability on the table in the case of failed asylum seekers. Yet others in the movement called on the government to not only shut down the system, but also rethink the ethics of deportation and the discriminating line that is typically drawn between "deserving" refugees and "undeserving" economic immigrants. These differences caused friction between individuals and organizations and point to the heterogeneity of anti-racism more generally. However, the movement was united in its call for better treatment for asylum seekers and a more inclusive, cosmopolitan Ireland, even in times of recession. As one academic activist noted, "It is an easy argument that 'we must look after our own,' especially in an acute recession. However, the history of the 'Irish gulag' [Magadelen Laundries] illustrates the thinness of any such national fiction" (Titley 2012).

Delegitimizing Asylum Seekers' Deservingness

In midsummer 2015, a meeting was held at a Dublin hotel to launch Identity Ireland as a new political party favoring exit from the EU and strict immigration control in order to regain what they see as the loss of Irish sovereignty. However, the launch descended into a shouting match when anti-racism activists interrupted the proceedings with speeches accusing the group of purposefully holding the event on the anniversary of the 2011 Anders Behring Breivik murders in Norway, which the party denied. Hotel personnel escorted the activists out of the building, and Identity Ireland has since referred to them as "fascists" who try to quash democratic debate through accusations of racism.

Irish politics are unusual in that a sharp left-right ideological divide is absent among their parties. Scholars trace this in part to the historical development of the two main institutional players, Fianna Fáil and Fine Gael, which emerged out of civil war politics rather than class struggles, as is the case in other European countries (Garner 2007; O'Malley 2008). In Garner's (2007) estimation, a far-right party would be superfluous in this context given the hegemony of these center-right blocs, which tend to promote nationalism tinged with racial ideology.

Overtly anti-immigrant parties have so far failed to gain political traction but nonetheless influence immigration discourse through a strong Internet presence (Garner 2007; Lentin and McVeigh 2006). According to Identity Ireland, though, the time is ripe for their party to enter government. They claim to represent a majority of the population who want stricter immigration control but remain silent for fear of being labeled a racist or enacting a double standard vis-à-vis Irish emigration—a sentiment I found echoed in newspaper op-ed pieces and online news comments. Spokesman Ted Neville (2015) explained:

> There has been an unquestioning mantra amongst the political and media establishments ... that all immigration is good. We must take on immigration. There's a certain guilt complex about it that because we went abroad and founded America with all the other countries in the world, we should take everybody from Africa and Asia. Our purpose was to get people a choice in electoral terms.

Individuals on this side of the debate generally constructed war victims as deserving of safe haven in Ireland, but in keeping with discourses leading up to the 2004 referendum, they doubted the veracity of most claims. This allowed asylum seekers to be framed as truly opportunistic economic immigrants who posed a threat to Irish sovereignty and economic well-being. Proponents drew on several pieces of evidence to support their assertion: first, a question often asked was, "How did these so-called asylum seekers get here?" They pointed to the Dublin Regulation, which establishes a hierarchy for determining which EU member state is responsible for processing asylum claims. This is primarily determined by family links, followed by the country where an asylum seeker first enters the EU. Noting Ireland's remote location, anti-immigrant activists claimed that Ireland could not have been their first entry point and thus was not responsible for harboring them. Rather, in all likelihood, they were immoral "asylum shoppers" applying in Ireland after their applications had been denied elsewhere in Europe, which is against EU law.

Another argument used to discredit the authenticity and hence deservingness of asylum seekers is that they don't "act" like real refugees. Referencing their calls for the right to work and an end to the direct provision system, O'Doherty (2014) wrote in an op-ed piece, "For people who are supposedly escaping from grievous persecution in their homelands, that's a pretty ambitious list of demands. Since when did anyone fleeing for their life feel entitled to issue 'demands' of their safe haven? Genuine asylum seekers don't arrive with 'demands.'" A retired barrister, Sean Deegan (2015), provided another image of the "genuine refugee" when he said in a televised interview that in his six years on the Refugee Appeals Tribunal, he granted refugee status to just two people out of an estimated five hundred cases. He explained: "It is clear that the majority of people were actually trafficked into this country and then that these people obviously had to have money to get this far. And one's to surmise that the real refugees are left back at home. Those who can't afford to pay the trafficker." Taken together, these discourses tread the well-worn trope of "true" refugees as poor, helpless individuals who, given their miserable position, should be grateful receivers (rather than demanders) of humanitarian charity (Harrell-Bond 1999). Yet according to Malkki (1995), this reification of "the refugee" obscures the sheer heterogeneity of refugees' histories and personal backgrounds and has real consequences for those applying for international protection.

The last piece of "evidence" presented to prove the bogus nature of asylum seekers was the length of time they spent in direct provision. Rather than seeing the long process as evidence of a broken system or a culture of disbelief (Conlan, Waters, and Berg 2014), immigration skeptics argued that true refugees were given a quick decision that on average took 15.3 weeks for non-priority cases in 2014 (ORAC 2014). All others, they noted, were simply economic immigrants who lodged appeals and judicial reviews to cynically gain backdoor entry to Ireland through other humanitarian statuses. Thus, they recognized neither the legitimacy of these other statuses nor the right of asylum seekers to pursue them. Áine Ní Chonaill (2015), a spokeswoman for the NGO Immigration Control Platform (ICP) summed up this argument by saying: "The citizens of Ireland are very abused by the system in that—people talk about the length of time that people are in the system but that is an abuse of us as well as the genuine among them.... Most of it is their fault, not ours. People don't seem to realize that decisions have been made and this has been the case for quite a few years."

By conflating those seeking international protection with undeserving economic immigrants, these critics dismiss the entire asylum process as illegitimate and deem reforms unnecessary. In fact, Chonaill (2015) of ICP stated that the asylum system, like a borderless EU, was a "massive imposition" on Ireland, marking an end to Irish sovereignty. At the very least, she argued, Ireland should swiftly deport those denied refugee status. Moreover, it was ludicrous that some members of the government were pushing for amnesty on the basis of an inefficient process and government culpability.

Securing borders against outsiders was framed as a "commonsense" solution in times of economic recession in a country with "limited resources"—a powerful, long-standing discourse also found in Britain, most recently expressed through the Brexit vote. Drawing on notions of "us" versus "them," immigrants were perceived as posing an economic threat through job competition. Newcomers who arrived in Ireland without a visa, such as asylum seekers, also presented a security and moral threat in that they were not abiding by the rule of law, which Chonaill (2015) framed as a "justice issue" and "abuse" of Irish people. Despite Ireland currently having negative net migration, there was significant apprehension that the tide could quickly turn, with Ireland turning into a version of Calais with its build-up of unwanted immigration (cf. O'Doherty 2014). Both ICP and Identity Ireland rejected claims that these views were antithetical to the history of Irish emigration, noting that it was the duty of any government to protect the nation—implied as indigenous (white) Irish—against outside threats.

Proponents of strict border control generally argued that a proper response to border issues entailed refusal to kowtow to various hegemonic forces, particularly the EU, the international human rights regime, and domestic anti-racist groups, which together were believed to compromise Irish sovereignty and not to have "our" people's interests at heart. As O'Doherty (2014) opined, controlled migration can be a good thing because it infuses needed skills, but Ireland is not obliged to

> provide refuge for everyone who comes demanding a home and a job, particularly when they haven't bothered to go through the proper procedures. Inevitably, the lobbyists, quangos [quasi-autonomous NGOs] and special interest groups will squawk that we have to abide by international laws and treaties. But you don't see France or Australia worrying about their international "obligations" when those obligations run contrary to the best interests of their own people.

O'Doherty's comment points to the tension between legal and moral obligations—the latter of which are to '"we," the Irish.' Moreover, it reveals deep resentment of Ireland's place in the global order as a relatively powerless nation. As I discuss below, these anxieties are related not only to the economic crisis, but also to fears over the loss of a hard-won "white" identity, even if explicit mention of race is avoided.

Discussion

Examining discourses related to refugee deservingness reveals the implicit moral judgments that lie at the root of these assessments. While such judgments spring in part from personal convictions, they are also connected to extrinsic factors (Willen 2012), which in Ireland's case include its historic and contemporary location on the margins of Europe, the economic crisis, and transnational discourses about asylum seekers that circulate throughout the Global North.

Ireland's sense of marginality within a global community—fueled at first by a long history of colonization and subsequent underdevelopment and now by disciplinary austerity measures partly imposed by the EU—is related to competing moral assessments of asylum seekers. When assessing asylum seekers' deservingness for better living conditions and a permanent place in the nation, some pro-immigrant activists, including asylum seekers themselves, consider parallels between Ireland's status as a postcolonial, emigrant-sending country and the position of the Global South. Others draw on transnational discourses of human rights to oppose ill treatment by the state, for example by pointing to the violence of deportation. In both instances, deservingness is based on perceptions of close social proximity (Willen 2012), either by virtue of a similar past or a shared humanity.

On the other side of the debate, perceptions that a great social distance separates Irish from asylum seekers contribute to some stakeholders' assessments that the latter do not necessarily deserve better living conditions, much less the right to settle in Ireland. These moral assessments draw on older discourses originating during the economic boom, which framed asylum applicants as "bogus" in order to delegitimize their claims for protection and thus their juridical right to protection. Moreover, asylum seekers were posited as moral and economic threats to the nation through their childbearing, which—while legal prior to the referendum—was nonetheless deemed an abuse of Irish citizenship that also purportedly overburdened maternity hospitals. In post-referendum and post-boom Ireland, the focus is no longer childbearing but asylum seekers' supposed abuse of the appeals process, which leads to long stays in direct provision and again, presents an economic burden to Irish society. However, the degree of perceived economic threat is arguably higher today, given the current economic insecurity, widespread social suffering due to austerity measures, and large numbers of asylum seekers entering Europe from the Middle East. As a result, many contest what they see as limited resources going to undeserving outsiders while they struggle to pay bills—an illustration of the relational nature of deservingness assessments (Willen 2012) and a facet of right-wing "new nationalism" that combines anti-state sentiment with concerns over resource allocation (Delanty 2000 cited in Garner 2006: 264).

The 2004 citizenship referendum and continued concern over relatively few asylum seekers is a response to the newfound European modernity, which is characterized in part by low fertility, an aging population, and high inward migration (Lele 2008). As in other European contexts, the Irish state and electorate have identified migration as the "problem" to be solved, as the referendum starkly illustrated (ibid.). But when it comes to demographic changes in the Irish context, Elisa White (2012) suggests, there is more at stake than fears over "cultural loss," as right-wing activists often present it. Rather, given Ireland's history of colonization and emigration, and the processes of negative racialization they involved, such change can also signal a potential loss of a relatively new white Irish identity—a privileged but ultimately tenuous identity that racial discrimination and anti-immigrant rhetoric seek to reinforce. Ultimately, in the eyes of some, the only way to stem further change that undermines a white, Catholic pre-1990s Irish identity is to cut ties with a hegemonic EU, which has wreaked havoc on Ireland's ability to control its own affairs.

The ways in which refugee deservingness is reckoned in Ireland derive from local events but are also part of a larger nexus of practices and discourses found throughout Europe that vacillate between a "politics of pity and control" (Fassin 2013) when it comes to asylum seekers. Although Ireland may be understood as occupying a relatively powerless place in the EU in terms of its economic and political influence, it can no longer be characterized as a "pre-modern" place in Europe. Rather, it is squarely located within the global flow of capital and people, sharing with other European states and populaces a sense that certain newcomers—especially asylum seekers and Muslims—threaten national integrity, privileged identities based on "whiteness," and increasingly, national security. Drawing on Barker (1981), many write about the "new racism" in the West—particularly in Europe—and its effects on immigrants (Cole 1997; Silverstein 2005). In this configuration, racist rhetoric is masked by subtler objections to immigrants based on cultural incompatibility and the defense of law and order and local economic interests.

As Syrians and other displaced people cross European borders in greater numbers, they are variously constructed as "refugees," "illegals," "economic migrants," or would-be "terrorists." These labels and slippages between them are no trivial matter: they influence public, political, and scholarly discourse and have material impacts on the lives of immigrants, as I have shown here in the discussion of the direct provision system in Ireland. As part of a "burden sharing" scheme, over the next two years Ireland has agreed to take in four thousand Syrians who are currently in Greece and Italy. How long they will languish in direct provision centers and what sort of broader public welcome they will receive are yet unknown.

Shay Cannedy is Visiting Assistant Professor at the Department of Anthropology at Southern Methodist University, Dallas, TX (USA). Her research focuses on questions of forced migration, border securitization, and forms of migrant resistance. Her current project considers the implicit logics undergirding state and public perceptions of refugee deservingness in Ireland and how African migrants strategize for refugee recognition in an era of tightened borders.

Notes

1. I use pseudonyms throughout this chapter.
2. Although citizenship laws in Europe vary, generally Western, Central, and Northern European countries reckon citizenship through descent (*jus sanguinis*) rather than through birth on national soil (*jus soli*).
3. The seventeen private companies that run most of the direct provision centers together receive approximately €50 million per year (O'Brien 2014).
4. As permitted by the Lisbon Treaty, Ireland can opt out of EU asylum and immigration directives, as evidenced by its decision not to adopt the EU minimum standards of reception conditions for asylum seekers. These standards include a dignified standard of living, material reception conditions, and a limited right to work. The state chose not to adopt these minimum standards due to its policy of denying asylum seekers the right to work (Thornton 2014).
5. Prior to the enactment of the International Protection Act of 2015, new asylum applicants applied for subsidiary protection (a complementary protection status for those who do not meet the Refugee Convention standards but are deemed to be in need of protection) at the same time that they applied for refugee status. However, claims for subsidiary protection were only investigated when refugee status was denied. Applicants who were denied these statuses could apply for Leave to Remain, a humanitarian status granted at the discretion of the Minister for Justice. This process thus entailed examination and re-examination of cases, resulting in long delays and high costs for the government.

References

Arendt, H. 1966/1951. *The Origins of Totalitarianism*, 3rd ed. New York: Harcourt and Brace.
Barker, M. 1981. *The New Racism*. London: Junction.
Bhabha, H. 1994. *The Location of Culture*. London and New York: Routledge.
Blumer H. 1958. "Race Prejudice as a Sense of Group Position." *Pacific Sociological Review* 1(1): 3–7.
Bobo L. 1988. "Group Conflict, Prejudice, and the Paradox of Contemporary Racial Attitudes," in *Eliminating Racism: Profiles in Controversy*, ed. P. Katz and D. Taylor, 85–114. New York: Plenum Press.
Chonaill, Á. 2015. Interview by Vincent Brown. *Tonight with Vincent Browne*. TV3, 5 June.
Cole, J. 1997. *The New Racism in Europe*. Cambridge: Cambridge University Press.
Conlan, S., S. Waters, and K. Berg. 2014. *Difficult to Believe: The Assessment of Asylum Claims in Ireland*. Dublin: Irish Refugee Council.
Conway, B. 2006. "Who Do We Think We Are? Immigration and the Discursive Construction of National Identity in an Irish Daily Mainstream Newspaper, 1996–2004." *Translocations: The Irish Migration, Race and Social Transformation Review* 1(1): 76–93.
CSO (Central Statistics Office). n.d. Seasonally Adjusted Standardised Unemployment Rates (SUR). Retrieved 3 August 2015 from http://www.cso.ie/multiquicktables/quickTables.aspx?id=mum01.
Deegan, S. 2015. *RTE Prime Time*. Broadcast 2 July.
Delhey, J. 2001. "The Prospects of Catching up for New EU Members: Lessons for the Accession Countries to the European Union from Previous Enlargements." *Social Indictors Research* 56(2): 205–231.
Donovan, D., and A. Murphy. 2013. *The Fall of the Celtic Tiger: Ireland the Euro Debt Crisis*. Oxford: Oxford University Press.
Espenshade, T., and K. Hempstead. 1996. "Contemporary American Attitudes toward U.S. Immigration." *International Migration Review* 30(2): 535–570.
Fassin, D. 2013. "The Precarious Truth of Asylum." *Public Culture* 25(1): 39–63.
FLAC (Free Legal Advice Centres). 2003. Direct Discrimination? An Analysis of the Scheme of Direct Provision in Ireland. Dublin: FLAC.
Garner, S. 2004. *Racism in the Irish Experience*. Dublin: Pluto Press.
———. 2006. "The Uses of Whiteness: What Sociologists Working on Europe Can Draw from US Research on Whiteness." *Sociology* 40(2): 257–275.
———. 2007. "Ireland and Immigration: Explaining the Absence of the Far Right." *Patterns of Prejudice* 41(2): 109–130.

Garner, S., and A. Moran. 2009. "Asylum Seekers and the Nation-State: Putting the 'Order' back into 'Borders' in Australia and the Republic of Ireland," in *Race & State*, ed A. Lentin and R. Lentin, 103–118. Newcastle upon Tyne: Cambridge Scholars.

Gray, B. 2004. "Remembering a 'Multicultural' Future through a History of Emigration: Towards a Feminist Politics of Solidarity Across Difference." *Women's Studies International Forum* 27(4): 413–429.

Harrell-Bond, B. 1999. "The Experience of Refugees as Recipients of Aid," in *Refugees: Perspectives on the Experience of Forced Migration*, ed. A. Ager, 136–168. London and New York: Pinter.

Haynes, A., E. Devereux, and M. Breen. 2008. "Public Exercises in Othering: Irish Print Media Coverage of Asylum Seekers and Refugees," in *Facing the Other: Interdisciplinary Studies on Race, Gender, and Social Justice in Ireland*, ed. B. Faragó and M. Sullivan, 162–181. Newcastle upon Tyne: Cambridge Scholars.

Ignatiev, N. 1995. *How The Irish Became White*. London: Routledge.

IMF (International Monetary Fund). 2015, "Executive Board Concludes Third Post-Program Monitoring Discussions with Ireland." *IMF*, 22 June. Retrieved 31 July 2015 from http://www.imf.org/external/np/sec/pr/2015/pr15288.htm.

IRC (Irish Refugee Council). n.d. *Direct Provision and Dispersal: Is There an Alternative?* IRC: Dublin. Accessed 18 August 2015: http://www.irishrefugeecouncil.ie/direct-provision/direct-provision-ngo-forum.

———. 2012. *State Sanctioned Child Poverty and Exclusion*. Dublin: IRC.

Kenny, C. 2010. "Commentary: Finding a Voice or Fitting In? Migrants and Media in the New Ireland." *Media, Culture & Society* 32(2): 311–322.

Lele, V. 2008. "'Demographic Modernity' in Ireland: A Cultural Analysis of Citizenship, Migration, and Fertility." *Journal of the Society for the Anthropology of Europe* 8(1): 5–17.

Lentin, R. 2008. "From Racial State to Racist State? Racism and Immigration in Twenty First Century Ireland," in *Race & State*, ed. A. Lentin and R. Lentin, 187–206. Newcastle upon Tyne: Cambridge Scholars.

Lentin, R., and R. McVeigh. 2002. "Situated Racisms: A Theoretical Introduction," in *Racism and Anti-Racism in Ireland*, ed. R. Lentin and R. McVeigh, 5–56. Belfast: Beyond the Pale.

———. 2006. *After Optimism? Ireland, Racism and Globalisation*. Dublin: Metro Eireann.

Loftsdóttir, K. 2011. "Negotiating White Icelandic Identity: Multiculturalism and Colonial Identity Formations." *Social Identities* 17(1): 11–25.

Luibhéid, E. 2013. *Pregnant on Arrival: Making the Illegal Immigrant*. Minneapolis, MN: University of Minnesota Press.

Mac Cormaic, R. 2014. "High Court Facing 4½-year Asylum Case Backlog, Conference Hears." *Irish Times*, 21 June. Retrieved 23 July

2015 from http://www.irishtimes.com/news/crime-and-law/high-court-facing-4-year-asylum-case-backlog-conference-hears-1.1840426.

Malkki, Liisa. 1995. "Refugees and Exile: From 'Refugee Studies' to the National Order of Things." *Annual Review of Anthropology* 24: 495–523.

Mancini, J., and G. Finlay. 2008. "'Citizenship Matters': Lessons From the Irish Citizenship Referendum." *American Quarterly* 60(3): 575–599.

McVeigh, R. 1992. "The Specificity of Irish Racism." *Race and Class* 33(4): 31–45.

Mercille, J. 2014. "The Role of the Media in Fiscal Consolidation Programmes: The Case of Ireland." *Cambridge Journal of Economics* 38(2): 281–300.

Neville, T. 2015. Interview by Tom McGurk. *The Late Review with Tom McGurk*. TV3, 27 July. Retrieved 9 December 2015 from https://www.youtube.com/watch?v=5_bq8pbIe_E.

O'Brien, C. 2014. "How Direct Provision Became a Profitable Business." *Irish Times*, 9 December. Retrieved 3 September 2015 from http://www.irishtimes.com/news/social-affairs/how-direct-provision-became-a-profitable-business-1.2030519.

O'Doherty, I. 2014. "It's Time We Closed the Door on Our Failed Asylum Policy." *Independent.ie*, 17 September. Retrieved 23 September 2014 from http://www.independent.ie/opinion/columnists/ian-odoherty/its-time-we-closed-the-door-on-our-failed-asylum-policy-30592113.html.

O'Flynn, M., L. Monaghan, and M. Power. 2014. "Scapegoating During a Time of Crisis: A Critique of Post-Celtic Tiger Ireland." *Sociology* 48(5): 921–937.

O'Malley, E. 2008. "Why Is There No Radical Right Party in Ireland?" *West European Politics* 31(5): 960–977.

ORAC (Office of the Refugee Application Commissioner). 2014. Annual Report, ORAC. Retrieved 1 September 2015 from http://www.orac.ie/website/orac/oracwebsite.nsf/page/CRSE-9XQK2A15304722-en/$File/2014%20Annual%20Report.pdf.

RIA (Reception and Integration Agency). 2014. Annual Report. RIA. Retrieved 28 July 2015 from www.ria.gov.ie.

———. 2017. Monthly Report July. RIA. Retrieved 16 August 2017 from www.ria.gov.ie.

Rolston, B. 1999. "Are The Irish Black?" *Race and Class* 41(1–2): 95.

Silverstein, P. 2005. "Immigrant Racialization and the New Savage Slot: Race, Migration, and Immigration in the New Europe." *Annual Review of Anthropology* 34: 363–384.

Storey et.al. 2015. "More than 100 Irish Academics: Austerity Has Ravaged Both Ireland and Greece." *Analyze Greece! News and Left Politics*, 13 July. Retrieved 14 July 2015 from http://analyzegreece.gr/topics/greece-europe/item/292-more-than-100-irish-academics-usterity-has-ravaged-both-ireland-and-greece/.

Thornton, L. 2014. "The Rights of Others: Asylum Seekers and Direct Provision in Ireland." *Irish Community Development Law Journal* 3(2): 22–42.

Titley, G. 2012. "Asylum Seekers in Ireland Languish in the Magdalene Laundries of our Time." *The Guardian*, 3 October. Retrieved 15 October 2014 from http://www.theguardian.com/commentisfree/2012/oct/03/asylum-seekers-ireland-magdalene-laundries.

Tormey, A. 2007. "'Everyone with Eyes Can See the Problem': Moral Citizens and the Space of Irish Nationhood." *International Migration* 45(3): 69–100.

Turner, T., and C. Cross. 2015. "Do Attitudes to Immigrants Change in Hard Times? Ireland in a European Context." *European Societies* 17(3): 372–395.

Uchechukwu, H. n.d. *Parenting in Direct Provision: Parents' Perspectives Regarding Stresses and Supports*. Galway: NUI Galway.

White, E. 2012. *Modernity, Freedom, and the African Diaspora: Dublin, New Orleans, Paris*. Bloomington, IN: Indiana University Press.

Willen, S. 2012. "Migration, 'Illegality,' and Health: Mapping Embodied Vulnerability and Debating Health-Related Deservingness." *Social Science & Medicine* 74(6): 805–811.

5
What Is a Life?
On Poverty and Race in Humanitarian Italy

Andrea Muehlebach

In late spring 2013, when I was in Milan to conduct fieldwork, I wandered around the city's subway stations and was struck, again and again, by the figure of a child abstractly rendered in red and white, staring at me forlornly from a series of huge white posters plastered on the subway system's walls. The figure came in three versions, one girl and two boys, whose eyes pleaded with me—us, the commuters—insisting that we rise up against an "act of theft" that was robbing entire generations of Italian children of their future. Initiated by Italy's branch of Save the Children, the campaign, called Allarme Infanzia (Childhood Alarm), argued that Italy's crisis of austerity and "years of absence on the part of politics and the lack of interventions in favor of children and youth" had "ransacked" (*saccheggiato*) young people's perspectives and left Italy's children facing "lives without dignity" (AllarmeInfanzia Manifesto 2013). This campaign was organized around a manifesto stating that a third of all Italian children were at risk of poverty and that 18 percent had dropped out of school. It further claimed that 1.5 million children live in toxic environments and that the youth unemployment rate is at 40 percent. This meant that stakes were high. As the campaign put it in its press release, surveys that document child poverty put Italy at the tail end of European misery, with only Greece and Bulgaria worse off (AllarmeInfanzia Press Release 2013: 1).[1] Allarme Infanzia thus appealed to Italians to denounce the "serious deficit in futurity that young generations face" (*il gravissimo deficit di futuro delle giovani generazioni*), calling for a "massive mobilization on the part of public opinion" with the goal of having "public institutions reintroduce urgent and structural interventions in favor of minors and youths who are increasingly threatened in their right to a dignified life."

The posters were just one step in the Allarme Infanzia campaign, which further invited Italians to support the initiative by sharing the poster on their facebook pages or blogs, printing out banners and posting them on the walls of public buildings, holding demonstrations (the campaign reported that several "guerilla" interventions were held in sixteen Italian cities on the day the campaign was launched), and denouncing the dispossession that the phenomenon of child poverty represents. Accordingly, the campaign website features videotaped testimonials bearing witness to poverty in Italy. It is also populated with almost two thousand videos and written statements (what the website calls *denuncie* or "denunciations", the Italian term used when criminal charges are filed). Many Italians heeded the call and "screamed out their appeal for all the children of Italy," as one woman put it in a post on the website's "notice board" (AlarmeInfanzia Bulletin Board 2013).

At first glance, this Save the Children campaign seems to share many of the basic features of what we have come to recognize as "humanitarian reason" (Fassin 2012), which operates according to similar logics no matter the location—France, Africa, Indonesia (ibid.; Redfield 2008; Clarke 2010). The place where its gaze and practices settle is of little relevance to the functioning of its surface operations—its spectacularization of suffering; its representational

Figure 5.1 "They have robbed me of my future but no-one hears me. In Italy, 1 in 3 children are at risk of poverty." Image courtesy of Save the Children Italy (www.savethechildren.it).

techniques, which tend to congeal around abject figures such as the orphaned child (Bornstein 2011; Dahl 2014); its tendency to requalify the political as moral. Yet upon further examination this campaign shows that the humanitarian gaze may in fact exhibit an entirely different moral economy altogether once it loops back on itself. Even in its familiarity as a genre of humanitarian intervention, Allarme Infanzia offers insight into how global economies of compassion come to see, listen to, and act upon suffering in highly differentiated ways. What does it mean when the humanitarian gaze, which has so insistently made distant forms of suffering visible, returns to more proximate forms of crisis—the crisis of one's own children, their future, and thus "our future"? What does this campaign, organized around an Italian child's cry (Fig. 5.1), tell us about how economies of compassion operate differently when organized around different kinds of bodies and different kinds of injury?

Based on a visual and texual analysis of this Save the Children Italy campaign, this chapter argues that this distribution of emotion, suffering, and politics becomes especially clear when the figure of the Italian (i.e., always presumably "white") orphan is juxtaposed with the figure of the black orphan that is often so central to these campaigns. I thus use Save the Children's Italian campaign to think about the racial politics of humanitarian reason and to explore how black and white lives matter (or not) in a country that has been "brought to its knees" by austerity (Pipyrou 2014: 534). How and to whom is compassion extended to or withheld from when the horizons of rights-based citizenship have radically contracted—especially in the Italian South, which has long been wracked by poverty and haunted by enduring legacies of racial exclusion and stereotypes of African alterity (Schneider 1998; Pipyrou 2014)?

I argue that black and white bodies are situated at the two end points of a scale of what constitutes livable life—a scale first inaugurated by the anti-slavery campaigns that represent the historical core of humanitarian reason. I thus explore the place of race in humanitarian regimes and the often unstable and uncertain forms of difference they rely on. Drawing on work that has explored humanitarianism's racial impetus (Barnett 2011; Bystrom 2011; Fadlalla 2011; Haskell 1985; Loftsdóttir 2014; Martinez 2011), I also suggest that Allarme Infanzia offers insight into questions of tolerability. What forms of dispossession and injustice do Italians find tolerable when they play themselves out upon black bodies? What becomes intolerable when played out in seemingly more proximate, more recognizable, worthier white lives? Such questions pose themselves with great urgency, now that the shores of Europe have been transmuted into zones of unspeakable human tragedy.

The Allarme Infanzia campaign raises the question of threshold as well. At what point do what kinds of bodies enter the field of vision of the humanitarian regime? At what point is humanitarian crisis declared? How is the question of life and livable life differentially answered? As many scholars have well described, the threshold of the livability of black (and other racially marked) life has so radically contracted that it is set at the gates of death. Put another way, the humanitarian outcry occurs around "existence under threat" (Fassin 2012: 232). Emergencies are declared and assistance is offered "unconditionally" to those "whose life is at risk" (Bradol, cited in Fassin 2012: 233; see also Redfield 2008: 132).

This humanitarian right-to-life ethic, as one might call it, insists on "the persistence of life"—that "which remains to one who has nothing left" (Badiou 2006: 583). It insists on the worthiness of those whose lives are not even "worth a dollar," as Médicins Sans Frontières has put it (Fassin 2012: 232). In contrast, Allarme Infanzia displays a very different threshold at which crisis is declared. It refers not to physical survival or to the worthiness of life, biologically conceived, but to a different kind of life altogether. Here, life is declared to be unlivable much earlier, at the point where the rights of citizens and the kind of livable life that citizenship is supposed to guarantee come under threat. At stake is not the survival of starving individuals, but that of a long-abandoned Italian welfarist commitment—not the orphan's body per se, but the body of the caring nation as a whole. Here, humanitarian crisis is not declared at the threshold of physical death but at a point where the organism of the nation and its social reproduction are at stake.

Lives are thus arranged differently along a racialized scale of what humanitarian reason defines as life worth living: a "hierarchy of humanity" (Fassin 2012: 231) that insists on both the social rights of the Italian child whose forlorn figure Allarme Infanzia used to hail some iteration of the twentieth-century welfare state back into existence and, at the other end of the scale, a bare right to life reserved for Italian children's counterparts in the Global South. As Arendt (1966/1951) put it long ago, these are two qualitatively different kinds of lives organized around the incommensurable figures of the human and the citizen, the human being the remnant remaining when the right to citizenship has been lost or never granted. These figures emerge out of the two different ethical imperatives of common humanity and social solidarity (Lakoff 2010:

66); of biological survival versus a more generalized "flourishing" or well-being (Ticktin 2011: 214); of naked *zoe* versus the citizen's *bios* (Agamben 1998).

Such hierarchies of humanity have characterized humanitarian reason since its inception—perhaps precisely because it was born out of concern for the slave and was thus always already raced. The image of the tortured black body in chains was the image that enabled the "historic breaching of established categories of humanity … It was the first time that a large number of people became outraged, and stayed outraged for many years, over someone else's rights. And most startling of all, the rights of people of another color, on another continent" (Adam Hochschild, cited in Barnett 2011: 57). Already then, humanitarianism exhibited a racial logic that today plays itself out in Save the Children's Italian campaigns. The anti-slavery movement insisted that slaves, bodies scarred and chained, were to be guaranteed bodily integrity and granted the gift of freedom (Bornstein and Redfield 2011: 8). But this was freedom of a particular kind—limited in duration and circumscribed in its reach.

As Miriam Ticktin (2011) has described for France, those "who have their biology as primary resource" cannot ever hope to fully inhabit the *bios*. Broken bodies function as a kind of currency but do not translate into much more than "minimal social and political recognition" (ibid.: 215–216). The same was the case for the early nineteenth-century abolitionists who were outraged by slavery but "remarkably dispassionate" about the miseries of wage labor that slaves inevitably encountered in the "free market" (Barnett 2011: 9; Haskell 1985: 557). They called for the recognition of slaves as "men and brothers" even as they left racial categories, incipient theories of racial inferiority, and class inequalities intact (Barnett 2011: 60). Slaves could thus hope for a sort of freedom, but it would be a heavily stunted one that denied them full social and political recognition. Humanitarian reason, in short, emerged out of the eventfulness of the gift of freedom—out of the black body suddenly healed from the torture of slavery and liberated from its chains. It was never aimed at longer-term structural reform and never organized around rights and equality. The political potential of slave emancipation was instead subsumed under a paternalistic Christian mantle (ibid.: 58–60). Thus, even as humanitarian reason included all under the grand wings of the human family, it was already arranging humans along a scale of livable life, the tail end of which was inhabited by the slave for whom the gift of life and freedom was a momentary event. Their bodies' freedom mattered. But this was a freedom that was never meant to translate into long-term social solidarity or full inclusion in the body politic.

As I describe below, one finds these same logics in Save the Children Italy's Africa campaigns, where black bodies plead for a tiny bit more life—that is to say, for bodily integrity and freedom from imminent death. These logics are not operable in the case of Allarme Infanzia's campaign for Italy's white children. Allarme Infanzia instead represents a political (not a moral) plea for the life of a nation whose social contract has become undone. It urged Italy to move away from its brutal austerity regime and ensure an enduring freedom from want for its citizens. It also summoned Italians into collective outrage rather than individual sympathy. Race thus mediates not only what life and livability mean in the humanitarian imaginary, but also the way publics cohere around different kinds of affect depending on what kind of child is suffering in their midst.

Theft of the Future

As I sit writing this chapter, a UNICEF Canada catalogue lies on my desk. Featuring a black baby, naked and swaddled in a soft woolen blanket as if just born, its face turned toward the light, the cover reads, "Your 2013/2014 *SURVIVAL GIFTS* [bold and in cursive] catalogue has arrived." The back cover of the catalogue, which depicts a pair of muddy hiking boots and the words "No child too far" and "Keep a child alive, Help a child thrive," thus reveals how different lives are held sacred in different ways. Organized around a biopolitical ethic of survivalism, the catalogue mirrors other Save the Children campaigns as well. Take "Every One," an anti–infant mortality campaign launched globally by Save the Children in 2009 (Fig. 5.2). Its Italian version features "Mataya," who lives in a mud hut, barefoot and in a smudged white dress. She is gazing up toward an arch of colored balloons floating around her, seemingly delighting in the fact that we, the humanitarians, have just gifted her another birthday, an additional year and thus another lease on life. The stated goal of the campaign is not to guarantee Mataya a fully lived life, since our capacity to think beyond the next monthly donation is limited (see also Redfield 2012). Rather, the minimum we are called upon to do is to "give her one more birthday."

Mataya, sitting alone in her mud hut, illustrates the critique already made by others: that humanitarianism tends to display a right-to-life ethic that privileges punctuated, limited, incremental interventions, singular in focus and effect (Lakoff 2010; Redfield 2012). Its presentist temporal logics privilege immediate physical survival and "species-level needs and health" (Bornstein and Redfield 2011: 5-6). Mataya thus poignantly reveals the space-time compression that unfolds around the black body in the humanitarian regime—a body bared of futurity and devoid of a collectivity to attach itself to. This is what Guyer (2007: 409) means by a "presentist" temporal order, stunted in its minimalism and its lack of "reach of thought and imagination, of planning and hoping."

The campaign for Mataya starkly differs from Allarme Infanzia, which is organized entirely around an aspiration to a fullness of life through rights and futurity. Indeed, Allarme Infanzia devised a whole nomenclature of loss and deprivation and a series of maps and interactive graphs to help Italians diagnose the mechanisms through which futures had been stolen.[2] Theft had occurred on multiple levels, ranging from missing school meals and polluted environments to the fact that 21 percent of Italian fifteen-year olds can barely read, or that 18 percent of Italians never graduate from middle school. Children have been "robbed of the afterschool program" and "robbed of the job they had dreamed of." The effect, Allarme Infanzia argued, was a dizzying range of poverties: economic, cultural, educational, social, and spatial (see AllarmeInfanzia Manifesto 2013: 1–2). This was not Mataya's poverty, a poverty that appeared "abject because it puts men under the absolute dictate of their bodies" and that has nothing much more than the "rule of necessity" and the "urgency of the life process" to bring to bear on the scene of the political (Arendt 1966/1951: 54). Allarme Infanzia was not about *zoe* but about *bios*, not about bare life but about public and political flourishing, not

Figure 5.2 Save the Children campaign "Every One," Italy 2009. Image courtesy of Save the Children Italy (www.savethechildren.it).

about naked physiology but biography, not about individual necessity but collective growth. As a campaign organized around the figure of the Italian child with the inalienable right to rise above immediate necessity and to inhabit the future, Allarme Infanzia drew Italians into recognizing what they had lost: social rights, solidarity, and the welfare state.

To that end the campaign thus devised a series of interactive graphs that allowed Italians to become cognizant of this loss. At stake was what Jane Guyer has described as the "near future," namely the twentieth-century temporal order that, in Europe at least, had emerged out of institutional and governmental interventions in the form of "taxes, regulations, protections and redistributive subsidies" (Guyer 2007: 412). While achieved very late and only partially in Italy, twentieth-century Italian welfarism did include precisely the kinds of protections and forms of redistributive action that Allarme Infanzia demanded that the state reinstate. As Allarme Infanzia implies, this welfarism came with a temporal grid: five-year plans, benchmarked stages, institutional sequences, and the creation of cumulative effects [ibid.: 413], all of which allowed for incremental, sequenced near-future planning for individuals, families across generations, and nations, and for enduring horizons of anticipation and aspiration both individual and collective.

Strikingly, Allarme Infanzia differentiated between a variety of temporal dispossessions, that is, a variety of futures that could not be actualized in the present. Save the Children Italy's "Atlas of Childhood at Risk" lists different kinds of futures: the near future (*il futuro prossimo*), impaired by "unemployment, the aging of the population, [and] public debt"; the immediate future (*il futuro anteriore*), marred by "[electronic] hyperconnection and disconnection;" and the blocked future (*il futuro bloccato*). Given their abysmal levels of schooling, Italian children's "capacity to futurity" (*capacità di futuro*) is one of the lowest in Europe (Cederna 2012). The urgency with which Save the Children Italy launched its campaign over the loss of futurity revealed how tenuous Italy's hold over the near future had been from the start. Arriving late on the scene of European modernity, Italy had always had a highly self-reflexive relationship to its movement as a nation through time (Schneider 1998; Giordano 2014: 19); it always progressed too haltingly toward an imagined future of European civilization. In Italy, "futurity" and its loss resonate painfully, because possession of the near future was not always self-evident but always already precarious. For example, Italy has a long history of anxiety about its "illiterate masses" and thus its location within Europe. The illiteracy rate, which was 80 percent at the time of national unification in 1861, was halved by the 1920s, when primary education was made compulsory. Seventy years later, still only 90 percent of children were enrolled in primary school because many parents (especially in Italy's rural and southern regions) were simply not able to send their children to school. The specter of sliding "back" into such a state of misery thus resonates deeply with Italy's long history of marginality within the European context.

Italy's public expenditure peaked in the late 1970s—precisely at the historical moment when the "crisis" of welfare began to rear its head in Thatcherite Britain. No sooner were public services in the Italian welfare sector established than they were immediately constrained by the economic pressures and prevailing ideology of the last three decades of the twentieth century (Ginsborg 2001: 44). Thus, even as the campaign evoked specters of raced temporal horizons— Italian children *ought* to have access to an extended and enduring futurity that differed significantly from the mimimalist future reserved for Mataya—it was also haunted by the specter of this distinction's increased instability. The reality was that Mataya and the Italian child might not be so different after all, and that the Italian child's position on the scale of livable life was in fact increasingly precarious. This was "depressing," as Valerio Neri, the director general of Save the Children Italy, put it (Save the Children 2013). Allarme Infanzia insisted that the Italian child ought to live life as chronicity and near-future teleology. Life for the Italian child was not to be organized around the eventfulness of punctuated, compressed time ("let's give her one more birthday") but around a horizon of "dignified" long-term perspective. In this campaign, it hence was not the right to life but the right to futurity that was hailed back into existence to become a public demand.

In this way Allarme Infanzia was very much like but also fundamentally unlike humanitarian reason, in that instead of a moralizing appeal, it consisted of an eminently political call. Save the Children's crying child was supposed to generate not public sentimentality but a public politics. Here, suffering was not a matter "of individual psychology," political violence was not requalified as psychosomatic "trauma," and a political understanding of social situations was not displaced by emotional response. Emotions were marshaled, to be sure, but they were geared toward a collective denunciation of austerity, not toward depoliticized victims.

The campaign made clear that the presentist, punctuated, individualized commitments of the humanitarian regime were deemed unworthy of the Italian child and should therefore be refused. Allarme Infanzia transcended the realm of mere matter, that which remains to those who have else nothing left, and instead laid claim to futurity itself. The goal of the campaign was dignity defined not as bare survival, but as the assuredness that child-citizens ought to be embedded synchronically within a larger collective, protective, rights-based order, and diachronically within a set of institutions that allow for stability across time.

The point here is that this politics is raced, reserved only for that abstract outline of a child's figure on a poster in a subway in Milan. I have wondered about the Banksy-esque graphics of the poster and why it departs so radically from humanitarian organizations' hyperrealist "iconography" of suffering—the close-ups of big, fly-riddled brown eyes and extended bellies (Dahl 2014: 635). Perhaps it was unthinkable to represent Italian children through the visual pornographies of suffering that the Global North has become so accustomed to (and indeed demands) when it comes to extending sympathies to the abject poor of the Global South. Perhaps the imagery used by Allarme Infanzia signaled that Italian children—suffering enough to be made the subjects of an urgent humanitarian campaign—were not quite "African" yet. Perhaps the abstract graphics signaled that although Italian children had bare physical demands—school meals, clean environments—these demands were really just a symptom of privilege, that is to say, of a more abstract aspiration toward a futurity where all children are fully embedded within a national welfarist space-time that extends its social solidarity to all citizens.

Mataya, living on the other end of the world, matters quite differently in that it is matter that she is reduced to. She is, to use Franz Fanon's language, "epidermialized" within the global economy of compassion and care. Her body signifies little more than matter that must be saved. She is "fixed" (Fanon 1991: 116) in the sense that the system of signification within which she is a sign allows both literal and abstract mattering: Literal mattering for the black child; abstract mattering for the white child. Italian children matter not in terms of their mere bodies but as symbols of deep citizenship that the welfarist nation-state ought to help reproduce and maintain.

Guerilla Nation

Allarme Infanzia was not foregrounding the compassion and sympathy so central to the humanitarian regime, though these affects are, of course, also operable. Rather, it sought to intervene in and constitute the Italian public through popular outrage. The public that Allarme Infanzia tried to summon was therefore not primarily a sympathetic but an angry one that was supposed to rise up collectively to combat this national scandal. Allarme Infanzia thus used humanitarian registers to present humanitarian crisis with new meanings and stakes, moving from sympathy to anger, humanitarian to politicized discourse, and individual witnessing to collective denunciation. Italians were invited to stand not simply as individual witnesses but as collective judges as well. Allarme Infanzia, in short, was organized around a particular form of address: by inviting short voice recordings and written statements, it hailed outraged citizens into taking ownership of the campaign. As the campaign put it, addressing its audience with the intimate "tu," rather than the informal "Lei": "We need to be heard, and there's no-one better than you to sound the alarm for our children! Help us stop the theft of our children's future: register your appeal, either vocally or in written form." The affective publics that were here hailed into existence are clearly organized around racial difference. Within Italian humanitarian sensitivities, black suffering is lamentable and mournable but inevitable. White suffering, on the other hand, is unthinkable, unacceptable, criminal.

The appeal seemed to have had an effect. Apart from a series of video clips featuring Italian movie, TV, and radio stars, all denouncing the theft of Italian children's futures, Allarme Infanzia's website received more than two thousand written testimonials responding with indignation, and sometimes desperation, to the call of the campaign. Often, the testimonials mirror the language provided by the campaign itself, performatively reiterating the anger that Allarme Infanzia seemed to have wanted to generate. As one Valter Moretti put it on 21 May 2013, "one in three children is at risk of poverty. 18% drop out of school. 1.5 million live in poisoned environments. Where—in an ill-fated developing country? No, this is happing here, at home! So join this campaign!" (AllarmeInfanzia Bulletin Board 2013). Others are heartbreaking pleas of desperation: "Me and my wife have a daughter of two months, and the more I look at her, the more my heart cries. We want change, we are unemployed and I don't see a future, neither for us, nor our angel. Do something" (Marco Raiano, 22 May 2013). Visitors to the website were invited to vote on the most memorable appeals by "liking" them. Some received thousands of "likes" ("Closing a birthing station in a mountain town (Petralia Sottana) where the next closest is 80 kilometers away is a crime! Defend our rights!" Marco Macaluso, 20 May 2013;

3,880 likes); others, tens of thousands of "likes" ("Land, air, and aquifers are contaminated with toxic industrial waste just North of the Neapolitan periphery. The incidence of tumors is on the rise. They are mining the future of our children. Help us!" Raffaele Franzese, 27 May 2013; 40,034 likes). Others answered by accepting the website's invitation to vocalize their desperation in ten-second voice recordings. These range in tone from resigned whispers ("Give us at least a minimal possibility to prove ourselves and to give ourselves a future," Loris dall'Acqua, 20 May 2013) to urgent alarms ("Children! Children are our Future! We *are* the Children! Let's save the children! Let's save ourselves! Let's all save each other!" Giovanni Nicita, 31 May 2013), yet all are united in a chorus of anger and despair.

Because visitors to the website had the opportunity to "like" contributions, the campaign was a highly choreographed communicative act that sought to assemble the Italian public in a rhythm of call and response—a refrain that was supposed to reiterate not just care for Italy's children but a kind of intimacy and cohesion of the national body politic as well. It was as if Allarme Infanzia was attempting to catapult the national body that had provided the grounds for the twentieth-century welfare state into the austerity-ridden Italian public sphere of today. This was an attempt to momentarily reconstitute the national body through affect and even, it turns out, "guerilla" warfare.[3]

On the nights of 19 and 20 May 2013, hundreds of volunteers and staff of Save the Children Italy descended upon sixteen Italian cities. Armed with campaign posters, they plastered Allarme Infanzia images all over public buildings and walls, in front of schools, along parking lots, and at metro stations. The goal was for Italians to wake up in the morning, encounter the cry of the child, and respond to it—not simply through donations (though this was certainly also a goal), but through denunciation. The politics of the campaign lay not only in its aim to performatively reiterate a national body but also in its demand that citizens hold the implicit referent—the negligent, even criminal state and the hidden forces that seem to govern it—accountable.

These populist evocations of an "internal frontier" that pits "the people" against indeterminate elite powers were not merely rhetorical. As the director of Save the Children Italy's Programming, Raffaela Milano, put it, "we want to build maximal pressure until children once again become a priority for *political* action. Otherwise, the social damage will be irreparable, both for our children and for the nation." A "manifesto" on Allarme Infanzia's website elaborated on these kinds of statements, ending with a plea for "long-term" and "structural" public interventions. Allarme Infanzia, in short, was a highly politicized anti-austerity campaign in the guise of humanitarian sympathy. It ventriloquized the registers of humanitarianism while taking an unequivocally political stance.

Let us now return to Mataya, who does not accuse anyone of robbing her of her right to life. Unlike the children in Italy's Allarme Infanzia campaign, she does not hold specific political institutions and policies accountable—let alone the nation-state she lives in, somewhere in Africa. Instead, Mataya inhabits a humanitarian regime where responsibility is diffused and blame generalized. Allarme Infanzia, in contrast, not only hails the Italian citizenry but also summons the accountable Italian state back into being. Thus, while all children appearing in humanitarian campaigns plead for sympathy, the Italian children do much more. In these two cases—the call to accountability for random empathetic individuals, and the call to accountability vis-à-vis the thieving Italian state—both affect and the capacity to identify and hold addressees accountable are differentially distributed. Thus dignity, which was designated an essential component of human existence since the founding of the UN, in fact means very different things. For Mataya, dignity is located on the level of the body, a body whose dignity is (or is not) restored by an unnamed general global addressee. The Italian child's indignity is registered long before its body's dignity is even an issue; it is its transcendent futurity that must be restored by a state held explicitly accountable for the social contract it has broken.

Rights and the Not-Quite-Whites

Poverty in Italy is not distributed equally across the body politic but instead organized around a political geography of exclusion and impoverishment that has long pitted the country's North against its South. This North-South divide took shape in the late 1800s after the country's unification, when existing differences within Italy became not just reified but racialized as well (Schneider 1998: 3). The South was identified as a zone of abject squalor, home to "illiterate multitudes" suffering from their "colossal ignorance" (Pasquale Villari, cited in Moe 1998: 52), and soon also came to be seen as a site of racial deviance, especially with the founding of the "science" of criminology in the 1880s and 1890s. Southeners, in short, became Italy's not-quite-whites—carriers of "inferior Mediterranean-type genes"

(Schneider 1998: 10) derived from "African and Eastern elements" (Cesare Lombroso, cited in Gibson 1998: 101; Giordano 2014; Pipyrou 2014).

This highly racialized political geography has been enduring and efficacious, persisting well into the twenty-first century and intensifying as Northern regionalist movements drew on already existing stereotypes of Italian Southeners. The right-wing regionalist party, Lega Nord, has attacked the national government since the 1990s for overtaxing the productive economies of Northern Italy and overspending on welfarist infusions of capital and social services to the "African" South (Pipyrou 2014). It did so even as the national government (in 1992, in anticipation of entry into the European Monetary Union) terminated a large range of social welfare programs dating back to the 1950s (Schneider 1998: 1). Allarme Infanzia, while attempting to rehabilitate abstract national solidarity, was in fact haunted by the figure of enduring racialized Southern poverty.

Indeed, Allarme Infanzia inflected its nomenclature of poverties with specters of Southern deprivation. Under "educational poverty," for example, Allarme Infanzia's website provided viewers with a short video clip featuring a Southern Italian middle school principal overwhelmed by the challenges spawned by the radical depletion of the administrative and pedagogical staff at her school (Save the Children Blog 2013). "We are exhausted and overwhelmed" by problems due to overcrowding, school absenteeism, and unmotivated teachers, she said. The other project highlighted under "educational poverty" was *Fuoriclasse* ("Out of the Classroom"), dedicated to the growing problem of children's absenteeism from schools and similarly focused exclusively on the Southern Italian cities of Naples, Crotone, and Scalea. Under "cultural poverty," Allarme Infanzia pointed to the many children "disconnected" from recreational and cultural activities. A video illustrates a series of camps that in 2012 were offered to four thousand children "all over Italy." Yet the clip is narrated by a series of children's voices that almost without exception are inflected with Southern Italian accents (Save the Children Blog 2013).

Similarly, under "economic poverty," Allarme Infanzia lists projects that Save the Children organized for mothers in Bari (a city at the Southern heel of Italy) (Save the Children Manifesto 2013). It also features a video clip of "Paola," an unemployed single mother of three who lives with her mother and three brothers. Fighting back tears, her voice once again displaying the unmistakable Southern

Italian lilt, she insists that children are always the first to understand a parent's distress. Paola's narrative of suffering is accompanied by Allarme Infanzia's narrative, which adds that "she cries every day over the impossibility of giving her daughters a future, or even a present" (Save the Children Blog 2013).

Importantly, this anxiety over the future has a long history in Southern Italy; indeed, Italian scholars began using the currently widely circulating term "precarious economy" (*economia precaria*) in the 1970s (Labini 1970 and Cerase 1978, cited in Pipyrou 2014: 536). Here, life was about "working for the day, without any guarantee and prospect of improvement" (Cerase 1978: 117)—a misery (*miseria*) that was overcome for only a few decades when the North initiated a series of extraordinary welfarist interventions into the South in the 1950s. Many were terminated in the early 2000s.

The cry uttered from subway posters in Italy's cities was thus unmistakably Southern. Italy's "Southern question," as Gramsci (1926) called it long ago, haunted the campaign like a ghost. Thus the question posed on the posters was not "Will we hear the Italian child's cry?" but "Will we hear the Southern Italian child's cry?" Put differently, the question of tolerability—of whether injustice and dispossession would move the nation to action when implicitly articulated through the figure of the not-quite-white Southern Italian child—revealed itself in its frailty as well. After all, all forms of public address are fragile and uncertain. They are aspirational in that the speaker must "abandon the security of its positive, given audience" and instead postulate a "circulatory field of estrangement that it must then struggle to capture as an addressable entity" (Warner 2002: 113). The addressable entity to be captured by the Allarme Infanzia campaign was thus one that was deeply fractured in its very foundation: a national entity that had once sought to overcome the North-South divide through national welfarist solidarity but that since the 1990s had largely replaced these large-scale ambitions with provincialized, often overtly racist regionalist politics (Holmes 2000). The outraged national public that Allarme Infanzia sought to summon thus revealed itself to be recursively organized around various shades of "Europeanness" versus "Africanness" that color the body politic from Italy's North to South. The humanitarian gaze, folded back in on itself, thus never quite gazes at itself but at the estranged other in its midst. The capture of Italy, the addressable entity that was supposed to cohere around the figure of the child abandoned by its nation, was thus an undertaking that was never guaranteed at all but always already precarious.

Meanwhile, an audience seemed to have been captured, at least to a small degree. In 2014, an already ongoing social experiment called Support for Active Inclusion (Sostegno per l'Inclusione Attiva) was extended to all of Southern Italy and hailed by the current Italian minister of labor and social politics as the largest poverty reduction initiative that the country had ever seen. Heavy-handedly wedding economic support for poor families to obligations to seek work, care for disabled family members, send children to school, and periodically visit pediatricians, the goal was to align Italy and especially its impoverished Southern regions with Europe. These interventions do not quite match Save the Children Italy's demand that Italy "return to the future" through major interventions into public education (Save the Children 2013). But Save the Children Italy's director of programming nevertheless noted with some satisfaction that Allarme Infanzia and its previous campaigns to end child poverty had contributed to the "activation" of the Italian government. In 2014, €167 million were transferred to the Italian South, followed by an additional €27 million in 2015. However, strong critiques continue to point out that there is "no structural plan" for the Italian South (Monga 2015: 5) and that apart from a few token gestures, the South has been "abandoned" (Di Fiore 2015: 26).

Mataya in Italy

I want to end by posing a question about the insanity unfolding on Italy's coastal borders—that is, the innumerable refugees desperately trying to reach its shores. How are the state and its citizens to respond to this ongoing humanitarian crisis, in which the Italian coast guard rescued 140,000 people from the Mediterranean in 2014, a year in which 3,200 people drowned after armed human traffickers pushed them onto tiny rubber dinghies and forced them to sail out onto dangerous seas? As Graham-Harrison and Scammell (2015) have reported, by January 2015 the number of new arrivals had risen by two-thirds compared with the same month in 2014. This predates the unspeakable misery of the Syrian refugee crisis. Almost 12,000 of the immigrants who arrived in Italy in the first nine months of 2014 were unaccompanied minors (mostly boys between the ages of eleven and seventeen) from Somalia, Eritrea, Syria, Bangladesh, and Afghanistan. Adults are usually interned in one of Italy's eleven detention centers, "cruel" prison-like camps to which humanitarian associations such as the Italian Doctors for Human Rights have been denied access because of violent tensions inside (Povoledo 2013). In Lampedusa, the tiny island that is Italy's southernmost landing point for arriving immigrants, the overcrowding has gotten so bad that "supplies of clothing, food and water for new arrivals have run out. The latest migrants to arrive were sleeping in the open air around the buildings and still wearing clothes soaked with sea water from their voyage" (Graham-Harrison and Schammell 2015; see also Sorge in this volume). These camps are, once again, located at the very tail end of a scaled humanitarianism that moves between immediate bodily needs (which currently are not even minimally provided for, as images of desperate Syrian refugees in Greece show) and futurity—between necessity and dignity.

Having arrived in Italy, unaccompanied minors are separated from adults and offered community-based housing, regular meals, education, and a little spending money until the age of eighteen. But instead, as the *Toronto Star* reported (Simmie 2014), many "grab food every morning at a Catholic charity and sleep on cardboard at the bus station a few blocks away." Italy, for them, is far from the promised land; rather, it is simply "a place where African boys arrive, not a model country," as Italian Prime Minister Matteo Renzi recently said (Renzi 2015: 6). Their goal is to move on to wealthier countries like Germany and Sweden and make money to send home to their families. Some might succeed in doing so. "Of the 12,164 minors who arrived in Italy in the first nine months of 2014, 3,163 are now off the radar. Gone" (Simmie 2014). What drives more than three thousand minors to leave behind the gifts of accommodation, food, and pocket money? What drives them to live on the sidewalks of Rome and Milan, hawking cheap trinkets, hauling crates of produce through narrow streets, or picking vegetables in fields? As one young refugee called Mohammoud put it, "I want to go to Sweden. My mission is not done yet" (ibid.). This mission consists of sending money back home so that indebted parents can find relief and attempts can be made to meet faint promises of futurity. It turns out that the Italian child's counterpart—those Matayas for whom humanitarianism offers quick fixes like additional birthdays and whose brothers have appeared en masse on Italian shores—are just as desperate for the futurity and stability that the Italian nation claims for its own children. They are so desperate, in fact, that many of them forgo incremental safeties such as room, food, and a few years of education in order to make that future happen, now.

Acknowledgments

I warmly thank Kristín Loftsdóttir, Andrea L. Smith, and Brigitte Hipfl for initiating this important conversation on crisis and whiteness in contemporary Europe. Thank you also to Andrew Gilbert, Claudio Sopranzetti, and especially Ramah McKay for their insightful readings of the text.

Andrea Muehlebach is Associate Professor of Anthropology at the University of Toronto and the author of *The Moral Neoliberal: Welfare and Citizenship in Italy* (2012). Her research interests include welfare, citizenship, labor and affect, and most recently the politics of water privatization, financialization, and re-municipalization in austerity-ridden Europe.

Notes

1. Save the Children reports in its press release (AllarmeInfanzia Press Release 2013) that when it comes to "poverty of futurity" (povertà di futuro), Italy occupies one of the lowest rungs on the European ladder. This narrative was mirrored in a 2013 Oxfam study that reported that Italy had already been economically fragile when the 2010 sovereign debt crisis swept across the Eurozone, and that the country's brutal austerity measures "far from reversed this trend" (Oxfam 2013: 3). In 2011, Mario Monti, an economics professor and former member of the European Commission, had formed an "emergency government" in response to Italy's $2.6 trillion debt—the highest in the Eurozone after Greece, and one of the highest in the world. Monti's goal was to "save Italy from the precipice" (Donadio and Povoledo 2011) by increasing household taxation to 44.7% of gross income, introducing a new property tax that many Italians who own property cannot pay because they have no monthly income or pension, and radically cutting social spending (from 2008 to 2013, social services were slashed by a stunning 75%). Austerity, in short, exacts "high social costs," especially from children (Oxfam 2013: 3).
2. Allarme Infanzia's Press Release (2013) writes about three "principle and most consequential thefts" that have been committed vis-à-vis "our young human capital." They are, first, cuts in funding for minors and families. Italy ranks 18th of twenty-seven European countries when it comes to social spending on minors and families. This means that "indispensible resources for a dignified life" have been withdrawn. Almost

29% of children under the age of six—950,000 children—live on the edge of poverty. Italy ranks 21st in Europe with regard to children being at risk of poverty and social exclusion, and almost 28% live in a state of "material deprivation." Second, there also exist a "theft of education" and, third, the "theft of work." The number of youth who neither work nor study has reached three million, putting Italy in 25th place out of the twenty-seven European countries.

3. The term "guerilla" was used without quotation marks by Save the Children's Allarme Infanzia campaign.

References

Agamben, G. 1998. *Homo Sacer: Sovereign Power and Bare Life.* Stanford, CA: Stanford University Press.

AllarmeInfanzia Manifesto. 2013. Retrieved 17 August 2017 from https://www.allarmeinfanzia.it/manifesto/.

AllarmeInfanzia Communicato Stampa [Press Release]. 2013: 1–2. Retrieved 17 August 2017 from http://www.allarmeinfanzia.it/wp-content/uploads/2013/05/comunicato-stampa.pdf.

AllarmeInfanzia Bacheca [Bulletin Board]. 2013. Retrieved 17 August 2017 from https://www.allarmeinfanzia.it/bacheca/.

Arendt, H. 1966/1951. *The Origins of Totalitarianism*, 3rd ed. New York: Harcourt and Brace.

Badiou, A. 2006. *Les Logiques des Mondes: L'être et l'événement, 2.* Paris: Seuil.

Barnett, M. 2011. *Empire of Humanity: A History of Humanitarianism.* Ithaca, NY: Cornell University Press.

Bornstein, E. 2011. "The Value of Orphans," in *Forces of Compassion: Humanitarianism between Ethics and Politics*, ed. E. Bornstein and P. Redfield. 123–147. Santa Fe, NM: SAR Press.

Bornstein, E., and P. Redfield, eds. 2011. *Forces of Compassion: Humanitarianism between Ethics and Politics.* Santa Fe, NM: SAR Press.

Bystrom, K. 2011. "On Humanitarian Adoption (Madonna in Malawi)." *Humanity: An International Journal of Human Rights, Humanitarianism, and Development* 2(2): 213–231.

Cerase, F. 1978. "Economia precaria ed emigrazione" [Precarious economy and emigration], in *Un secolo di emigrazione italiana (1876–1976)*, ed. G. Rosoli, 117–150. Milan: Feltrinelli.

Cederna, G. 2012. "Mappe Per (Ri)Connetersi al #Futuro: Atlante dell'Infanzia (A Rischio)." [Maps to (Re)Connect with the #Future: An Atlas of Children (At Risk)]. Save the Children Italy. Rome: Arti Grafiche Agostini. Retrieved 17 August 2017 from https://www.savethechildren.it/atlante-dell-infanzia-rischio.

Clarke, K. 2010. "New Spheres of Transnational Formations: Mobilizations of Humanitarian Diasporas." *Transforming Anthropology* 18(1): 48–65.Dahl, B. 2014. "'Too fat to be an orphan': The Moral Semiotics of Food Aid in Botswana." *Cultural Anthropology* 29(4): 626–647.

Di Fiore, G. 2015. "Morte alla Sanità, Pd in piazza, il sindaco: sciacallaggio politico" [Death in the Sanità, PD in the streets, and the major: political profiteering]. *Il Mattino*, 8 September, 26.

Donadio, R., and E. Povoledo. 2011. "Facing Crisis, Technocrats Take Charge in Italy." *New York Times*, 16 November. Retrieved 11 December 2015 from http://www.nytimes.com/2011/11/17/world/europe/monti-forms-new-italian-government.html?_r=0.

Fadlalla, A. 2011. "State of Vulnerability and Humanitarian Visibility on the Verge of Sudan's Secession: Lubna's Pants and Transnational Politics of Rights and Dissent." *Signs* (37): 159–184.

Fanon. F. 1991/1952. *Black Skins, White Masks*, trans. R. Philcox. New York: Grove Press.

Fassin, D. 2012. *Humanitarian Reason: A Moral History of the Present.* Berkeley, CA: University of California Press.

Gibson, M. 1998. "Biology or Environment? Race and Southern 'Deviancy' in the Writings of Italian Criminologists 1880–1920," in *Italy's Southern Question: Orientalism in One Country*, ed. J. Schneider. 99–115. New York: Bloomsbury Academic.

Ginsborg, P. 2001. *Italy and Its Discontents: Family, Civil Society, and State 1980–2001.* London: Penguin Books.

Giordano, C. 2014. *Migrants in Translation: Caring and the Logics of Difference in Contemporary Italy.* Berkeley, CA: University of California Press.

Graham-Harrison, E., and R. Scammell. 2015. "Surge in Number of migrants Trying to Reach Italy from Libya." *Guardian*, 18 February. Retrieved 22 November 2015 from http://www.theguardian.com/world/2015/feb/18/thousands-of-migrants-nearly-die-in-a-week-trying-to-reach-italy-from-libya.

Gramsci, A. 1926. *Some Aspects of the Southern Question.* Unfinished manuscript. Retrieved 22 November 2015 from http://www.uky.edu/~tmute2/geography_methods/readingPDFs/gramsci-southern-question1926.pdf.

Guyer, J. 2007. "Prophecy and the Near Future: Thoughts on Macroeconomic, Evangelical, and Punctuated Time." *American Ethnologist* 34(3): 409–421.

Haskell, T. 1985. "Capitalism and the Origins of the Humanitarian Sensibility, Part 2." *American Historical Review* 90(3): 547–566.

Holmes, D. 2000. *Integral Europe: Fast-Capitalism, Multiculturalism, Neofascism.* Princeton, NJ: Princeton University Press.

Labini, P. 1970. *Problemi dello sviluppo economico.* Bari: Laterza.

Lakoff, A. 2010. "Two Regimes of Global Health." *Humanity: An International Journal of Human Rights, Humanitarianism, and Development* 1(1): 59–79.

Loftsdóttir, K. 2014. "Within a 'White' Affective Space: Racialization in Iceland and Development Discourses." *Social Identities* 20(6): 452–470.

Martinez, S. 2011. "Taking Better Account: Contemporary Slavery, Gendered Narratives, and the Feminization of Struggle." *Humanity* 2: 277–303.

Moe, N. 1998. "The Emergence of the Southern Question in Villari, Franchetti, and Sonnino," in *Italy's Southern Question: Orientalism in One Country*, ed. J. Schneider. 51–77. New York: Bloomsbury Academic.

Monga, F. 2015. "Sud, non vedo un piano strutturato" [The South: I don't see a structural plan], *Il Mattino*, 8 September, 5.

Oxfam. 2013. "The True Cost of Austerity and Inequality: Italy Case Study." *Oxfam*. Retrieved 22 November 2015 from https://www.oxfam.org/sites/www.oxfam.org/files/cs-true-cost-austerity-inequality-italy-120913-en.pdf.

Pipyrou, S. 2014. "Cutting *bella figura*: Irony, Crisis, and Secondhand Clothing in Southern Italy." *American Ethnologist* 41(3): 532–546.

Povoledo, E. 2013. "Italy's Migrant Detention Centers are Cruel, Rights Groups Say." *New York Times*, 5 June. Retrieved 11 December 2015 from http://www.nytimes.com/2013/06/05/world/europe/italys-migrant-detention-centers-are-cruel-rights-groups-say.html?_r=0.

Redfield, P. 2008. "Doctors Without Borders and the Moral Economy of Pharmaceuticals," in *Human Rights in Crisis*, ed. A. Bullard, 129–144. Aldershot, UK: Ashgate.

———. 2012. "Bioexpectations: Life Technologies as Humanitarian Goods." *Public Culture* 21(1): 157–184.

Renzi, M. 2015. "L'Italia che non si arrende" [The Italy that will not surrender]. *L'Unità*, 7 September, 1 and 4–9. Save the Children. 2013. "Italia agli ultimi posti in Europa per 'povertà di futuro' di bambini ed Adolescent" [Italy finds itself at the lowest rungs in Europe when it comes to the "poverty of futurity" among children and adolescents]. 13 May 2013. Retrieved 17 August 2017 from https://www.savethechildren.it/press/italia-agli-ultimi-posti-europa-%E2%80%9Cpovert%C3%A0-di-futuro%E2%80%9D-di-bambini-e-adolescenti.

Save the Children Blog. 2013. "La povertà economica delle famiglie" [The economic poverty of families]. Retrieved September 14, 2016, at http://www.savethechildren.it/informati/blog/la_poverta_economica_delle_famiglie

Schneider, J. 1998. "Introduction: The Dynamics of Neo-Orientalism in Italy: 1848–1995," in *Italy's Southern Question: Orientalism in One Country*, ed. J. Schneider. 1–23. New York: Bloomsbury Academic.

Simmie, S. 2014. "Young and Alone, with an Uncertain Future." *Toronto Star*, 11 July 2014. Retrieved 11 December 2015 from http://www.

thestar.com/news/world/2014/11/07/young_and_alone_with_an_uncertain_future.html.

Ticktin, M. 2011. *Casualties of Care: Immigration and the Politics of Humanitarianism in France.* Berkeley, CA: University of California Press.

Warner, M. 2002. *Publics and Countepublics.* Cambridge: Zone Books.

6

Policing Crisis in Austrian Crime Fiction

Brigitte Hipfl

What is it about crime fiction that makes it so popular? Not only does this genre dominate the book market in the Western world; it has also captured television, which airs crime and police series around the clock. Why is crime fiction set in Germany the fictional TV genre of choice for those aged fourteen and older, ranking third after news and local information programs (Statista 2015)? Why were episodes of the police detective series *Tatort* the top four most watched Austrian TV films in 2014 and the top two in 2015 (ORF Medienforschung 2014; Medienforschung 2015)? In this chapter I offer answers based on an understanding of crime fiction as a cultural means of perpetual expression and containment of crisis. I will analyze one highly acclaimed Austrian TV crime show to explicate the ways in which crisis is represented and expressed, and how this relates to the wider contemporary context.

The fascination for crime and detective stories is not confined to Germany and Austria, but pervades the entire Western world. "Ours is a culture fascinated by crime," as Thompson (1993: 1) characterizes the United States. For Lee (2004: 81), television crime drama is a "forum for working through the trauma of living in a violent culture." Obviously, there are different traditions and regional specificities in crime drama. For example, the booming Scandinavian crime fiction that has become such a familiar brand is characterized by a particular bleakness that, according to Peacock (2014: 3), reflects a specific historical moment (see also Arvas and Nestingen 2011: 1). Peacock (2014: 3) points to the genre's potential by claiming that crime drama "can tap more than any other genre" into "a certain strand of Scandinavian sensibility." Australian scholar Ian Buchanan

(2012), who organized a conference on crime fiction in Wollongong, Australia, in 2012, makes a similar argument:

> ... today it is only crime fiction that is capable of telling the truth about our society. Only crime fiction has the grit needed to bring to light both the dark underbelly of society and the malfeasance and inequities that hide in plain sight. It is in this sense that crime fiction can be understood as national allegory ... because the truths it has to tell are ultimately all truths about the state of the nation.

In this respect, it seems to come as no surprise that almost every Western nation has crime fiction authors and TV series that address and express specific social issues, moods, and collective feelings. An analysis of crime fiction can give us deep insights into the concerns and worries at stake, or to phrase it differently, into how various scenarios of crisis in specific sociopolitical contexts are addressed and made palatable.

In this chapter, I make the claim that crime fiction and TV police series in particular, are not only continuous repetitions of crisis scenarios, but also more or less successful attempts to both police societal crises and offer ways to come to terms with them. I start by arguing that crime fiction can be considered a way of educating the public as it copes with crises, because the genre has the potential to express the affective cartography that characterizes contemporary conditions as they impact the public. Following Deleuze's (1992) claim that the modulation of affect has become one of the key means of sustaining power relations in contemporary so-called "control societies," I understand media as one of the main institutions, players, and performers of "affective work." With its focus on the production and modulation of affects as the currently dominant form of capitalism, "affective work" also connotes the emergence of new forms of labor as well as the so-called "affective turn" in the humanities and social sciences that emphasizes body and sensation, that is, the forces of encounter that produce new assemblages (see, e.g., Clough 2007; Gregg and Seigworth 2010; Timm Knudsen and Stage 2015; Sharma and Tygstrup 2015).

From a media and cultural studies perspective that takes into account the "affective turn" and critical race studies, I will analyze an award-winning episode of *Tatort*, Austria's most popular TV crime series. By pointing out how societal crisis is discursively addressed in this particular episode, and what kinds of "structures of feeling" (as worked out by Raymond Williams 1977: 131) are expressed, I wish to illustrate the "affective work" crime fiction performs. On the one hand, I identify the othering, gendering, and racialization of societal crisis in the example presented here; on the other, I argue that this crime fiction is communicating both a crisis of precarity and a crisis of the police. In brief, the state of crisis will be explored as a crisis of the state together with what are offered as ways to cope with it. The chapter concludes with a discussion of the expression of anger as a response to this crisis, pointing to the potential openings that paradoxically become available with crisis.

Crime Fiction as Perpetual Expression and Containment of Crisis

The fascination with crime fiction is not a recent phenomenon. Writers' and intellectuals' interest in this genre goes back a long time. The modern form of crime fiction is usually traced to short stories authored by Edgar Allan Poe in the 1840s. Since then, alongside countless crime-based books and films, scholarly reflections on the subject have filled the bookshelves. In early twentieth-century Germany, for public figures like Krakauer, Brecht, Benjamin, and Bloch, crime fiction "offered a means of understanding modernity as a period of perpetual crisis and undecidability" (Herzog 2009: 15). In their view, the essential modernist experience of isolation and strangeness that, like the impenetrability of the city, results from processes of industrialization and urbanization, was converted through detective stories and crime fiction into mystery, thus offering a way, according to Raymond Williams (quoted in Herzog 2009: 17), to penetrate these conditions of modernity and make them understandable. In effect, the genre's ability to expose and reflect on social structures, power relations and forms of domination, exclusion, and marginalization endures to this day. Through representations of mundane everyday struggles of ordinary people, we get insights into the state of a nation, which, as I will develop in more detail later, is currently in a state of crisis.

One explanation for the huge success of televised crime fiction derives from its capacity to excel in what characterizes television in general, namely its capacity to "respond to real events, changes in social structure and organization, and to shifts in attitude and value" (Newcomb and Hirsch 1983: 563). Detective and police TV shows give viewers access to what it feels like to live under historic-specific conditions by expressing what Raymond Williams (1977) called "structures of feeling." Williams intended this concept to put the focus on the beliefs and values of a specific society or social group, and to point out in particular how these beliefs and values are "actively lived and felt, and the relations between these and formal and systematic beliefs" (ibid.: 132). With the focus on lived experiences, Williams refers to "elements of impulse, restraint, and tone; specifically affective elements of consciousness and relationships" (ibid.). His interest is in how these elements are connected, so he defines them as a *structure* and highlights their *social*—not private or idiosyncratic—dimension (ibid.: 132). Structures of feeling direct us to a third layer in addition to the social and material infrastructure: "that of affective infrastructure" (Sharma and Tygstrup 2015: 2).

In times of crisis, TV crime fiction offers appealing modes of addressing and working through crisis. Charlotte Brunsdon (1998: 223) observed that the proliferation of crime-based fiction in the 1980s and 1990s in Great Britain "speaks very directly to the concerns of a Great Britain in decline under a radical Conservative government with a strong rhetoric of law and order." She argued that television crime fiction "has been a privileged site for the staging of the trauma of the breakup of the post-war settlement" (Brunsdon 1998: 223). Brunsdon is not referring to a literal representation of society in the crime series on TV (ibid.: 224–225); rather, she sees these episodes working with and through the anxieties and exclusions of contemporary citizenship. For her, the genre "stages the drama of the responsible citizen caught in the embrace of what increasingly seems an irresponsible State" (Brunsdon 1998: 225).

Indeed, this is precisely the task of this genre: to address the tensions that manifest themselves between the state's protection of its citizens and the contemporary precariousness of life. Since solving the crime is a key formula of crime fiction, tensions and crises not only become palatable but also are contained. In TV crime series in particular, the police detectives who are the mainstays from one episode to the next embody the containment of crises. This containment of crises is one of the key characteristics differentiating crime fiction from other genres that also deal with crisis, such as post-apocalyptic fiction. In the latter case, the audience is confronted with the consequences of an ultimate crisis, a catastrophe or an apocalypse, and ways of surviving and then building something anew. In the police genre, it is the detective him- or herself who resolves the immediate crisis, thus giving the impression that everything is under control.

Tatort: Educating the Public in Coping with Crisis

Tatort, the most popular TV crime series in the German-speaking context, has been on air since 1970 with almost one thousand episodes produced by July 2015. It is based on a concept that was unique at the time and has now become well known through examples like *CSI: Miami, CSI: New York,* and *CSI: Las Vegas*; that is, a TV crime series jointly created and produced by different regional broadcasters. In the case of *Tatort*, Germany's regional public broadcasters produced their own *Tatort* episodes starring their own idiosyncratic police detectives, accentuating the local color of the region. Now that Austrian and Swiss public broadcasting has joined in, a total of twenty-one television police teams are currently operating in German cities like Munich, Berlin, Leipzig, Cologne, and Frankfurt, as well as in Vienna and Zurich. Each episode is located in one of these cities, though at times the detectives operate in more rural areas. The use of regional diversity is one of the reasons for the extraordinary success of *Tatort*. Every episode offers both a narrative about a crime event, which comes to a closure, and an ongoing narrative that focuses on the lives and problems of the detectives themselves.

The cultural significance of *Tatort* is indicated by the series' traditional Sunday evening prime-time slot on the main public TV channels in Austria, Germany, and Switzerland. Watching *Tatort* has become a ritual for many viewers of all age groups and social backgrounds, and is one of the few examples of trans-generational TV experiences. Public viewing of *Tatort* in bars and pubs on Sunday evenings has also become popular recently.

Tatort is the jewel in the crown of ARD (Arbeitsgemeinschaft der öffentlich-rechtlichen Rundfunkanstalten der Bundesrepublik Deutschland), the consortium of public broadcasters in Germany. By meeting one of the key requirements of public television in Germany and Austria— addressing issues of social relevance and making them accessible to as many citizens as possible[1]— *Tatort* serves as a cultural forum, as described by Newcomb and Hirsch (1983: 566). It addresses social and cultural issues, and comments on ideological problems that are in contemporary circulation. In his analysis of *Tatort*, Buhl (2013: 19–20) pinpoints how the series contributes to public opinion, thus aiming to facilitate social integration of the national population.

Conceptualized from the very beginning as realistic social criticism with an educational intent (Witte 1994, quoted in Ortner 2007: 53; Hißnauer 2014: 4), *Tatort* is regarded as an "archive of contemporary history," a "popular memory of contemporary culture" (Wenzel 2000), a "seismograph of German sensitivities and mentality" (Gräf 2010: 8), and even an "unconscious historiography" of Germany (Wenzel 2000). One could also describe the sociopolitical function of *Tatort* as public education through popular media. Cop shows in general, according to Sabin et al. (2015: 1), "transmit and reflect the politics of the moment." The way *Tatort* addresses and deals with specific kinds of problems represents what is considered to be shared cultural knowledge of specific historic moments (Gräf 2010; Buhl 2013). The different episodes (re)construct what can be considered the sociopolitical consensus. Hence, Buhl (2013: 304) sees the *Tatort* series as a "consensus machine" that enunciates and cements moral principles, values, and social rules, and delimits what is sayable and knowable under specific sociopolitical conditions. As Buhl observes, *Tatort* generally revisits issues that have already been publicly discussed and rarely addresses a totally new topic, instead working through a topic that is already well known, if often contested. For him, this is an effect of the institutional background of *Tatort*, which, as already argued, offers containment of crises and seldom allows unsettling and disturbing provocative dramatizations that cannot be easily resolved.

Grasping the political and cultural relevance of crime fiction requires attention not only to the work it does on the level of knowledge and discourse, but also to the ways in which it sensualizes the audience by making it feel the complex social issues that are usually discussed in theoretical and abstract ways in public discourse. This point was also emphasized by Gansel and Gast (2007: 43), as well as by Buhl (2013: 304), in their analyses of *Tatort*. Though not explicitly using Williams's concept of structures of feeling, they describe the characteristics of *Tatort* as the "felt sense of the quality of life at a particular place and time," which, according to Williams (1963: 47), emerges from the historical and social relations of culture. Similarly, Pribram's (2013: 92) analysis of crime fiction and what she calls the justice genres in US television points out that the "structure of feeling" accounts for "the emotional repercussions … of what it means to live in a particular time and place." She convincingly illustrates how different TV crime series focus on different, coexisting structures of feeling in the contemporary United States. For example, *CSI*'s sense of speed, efficacy, and rationality supports a belief in a world we can still control and an overall feeling of reassurance; *The Wire*'s focus on inequality and imbalance of power produces a sense of frustration; meanwhile, in the case of *Cold Case*, an overall feeling of loss emerges.[2]

In this chapter, I am interested in the ways in which crisis is addressed in one episode of *Tatort*, and in the structures of feeling related to it. I will make the argument that this *Tatort* episode deploys crisis in two entangled ways. First, it focuses on one specific problem: that of human trafficking, presented to the audience as a practice transported into Austria by the East European other and thereby reproducing stereotypical images of migrants from Eastern Europe. Second, it portrays the helplessness of the police and the limits of their agency in encounters with the criminal element, indicating a "crisis of the state" as elucidated by Bauman and Bordoni (2014), among others.

Angezählt: Crisis Imported by the Migrant Other

Sabine Derflinger, the director of the *Tatort* episode *Angezählt*,[3] wanted to make the cruel, inhuman business of trafficking and forced prostitution in Vienna accessible to a broader public. The director's intention was to let the audience feel with Bibi, the female police officer, what it is like to live in that kind of reality, and what violence against women means (Priesching 2013: 1–2). The episode, broadcast on 15 September 2013, opens with a scene of Vienna's most famous and highly celebrated space of multicultural encounter, the Naschmarkt, an inner-city market that is constantly crowded and busy. A young boy with dark hair, dark eyes, and slightly dark skin—clearly marked as Eastern European—is riding his bike. Next, we see a bowling café where a male is harassing a waitress, who seems disturbed. She tries to call somebody on her cell phone and then goes outside for a smoke. This scene is interspersed with cuts to another scene in which a young woman pushes a young boy out of a shabby apartment where she works as a prostitute. Viewers then see the boy circle around the waitress, raise his toy water gun and spray her. Instead of water, however, it holds gasoline. Her cigarette ignites her clothes, and she is severely burned and later dies in the hospital.

The waitress, Yulia Bakalova, turns out to be a former prostitute who was victimized by a Bulgarian trafficking ring and then testified in court against the pimp, who received jail time. The female police detective Bibi Fellner has been working with Yulia and promised her protection. Bibi is devastated to learn that Yulia called her just after being harassed by her former pimp, now released from prison. The pimp had hired the boy to spray gas on her body. Later in the episode, we find out why the young boy (Ivo) complied—he was attempting to rescue his mom from a life of forced prostitution. The same pimp's illusory promises had enticed her to leave their Bulgarian village for Vienna.

How does this episode address forced prostitution, and how is such prostitution related to particular "structures of feeling" that characterize contemporary Austrian society? I will claim that the overall feeling expressed in this episode is one of *precariousness* clearly exemplified by the migrants in this episode, particularly migrant women. Feelings of insecurity and despair are not confined to them alone; they are also transferred to the police officer, Bibi. I take this structure as indicating a tendency toward what can be called the *normalization of precarity* in Austrian society.

Trafficking in prostitution, as depicted in this episode, is an organized crime that is often discussed, both legally and academically, in the European context. Scholars disagree over whether the key players are large transnational syndicates, small criminal groups, or corrupt individuals (Andrijasevic 2010: 7–8). What is common to all of these practices is that they approach young women in Eastern Europe who find themselves in situations defined by poverty and lack of perspective, and seduce them with false promises or force them to leave their country of origin. In the episode of *Tatort* discussed here, two young women from Bulgaria are presented as victims of involuntary prostitution. A fellow countryman who has "made it" in the West brutally forces them into prostitution to work off what they supposedly owe him for the journey and rent for their apartment. One of these women is Yulia, the waitress who is killed in revenge for having cooperated with the police and pressed charges against the Bulgarian pimp. The second woman is Nora, the mother of the boy who was hired by the pimp to spray gas onto Yulia. In the episode, the audience is confronted with the exploitative conditions of forced sex work—in a context clearly marked as culturally segregated. This cultural distancing can be seen in the director's choice of setting: Turkish teahouses, where clients approach prostitutes who then take the johns to their apartments to perform sex work.

By presenting such sex work as a separate world almost devoid of native Austrians, the episode resonates with elements of "parallel societies," a problematic German discourse of racialization and othering that assumes there exists a homogenous mainstream German culture. Immigrants, originating particularly from Turkey, have been accused of not properly integrating into German society. Instead of adjusting to German "Leitkultur," they supposedly create parallel worlds based on their own ethnic values and cultural practices, thereby representing a threat to the nation (see, e.g., the critical discussion of the concept by Bukow et al. 2007). The world of forced prostitution confronting the audience in *Angezählt* is a world defined by patriarchal structures, violence, and criminality, all of which the Bulgarian expatriate pimp expresses through exaggerated performances of masculinity and interactions aimed at humiliating the prostitutes and the police.

This is also a world in which the economic crisis seems to harm women in particular. Women's attempts to escape from their economically disadvantaged countries of origin end up in violence, forced prostitution, and even death. Men, however, as exemplified in this case by the pimp, seem to find ways to start businesses, albeit by exploiting and oppressing women. In addition, the immigrant other from the East is sexualized in this episode. The two immigrant women Yulia and Nora are represented as sex workers, confirming Austrian statistical data. As Boidi (2015) states, most of the sex workers currently in Vienna are from new European Union member states like Romania and Bulgaria. Immigrant men in this episode, on the other hand, are presented as either bosses in the sex business or clients. Male clients in this episode are marked as immigrant men (e.g., the client wrongly accused of the murder is identified as Iraqi), suggesting a sustained demand for prostitution because of the sex drive of male migrants. Consequently, the whole problem of forced prostitution is presented as a problem "caused" by immigrants who have brought it to Austria.

Crisis, then, is located elsewhere; in this case it emerges from poverty found in Bulgaria. In this way the episode reproduces what has become the dominant European narrative of human trafficking: young women from Eastern Europe are taken advantage of by others who prey on their hopes for a better life in one of the more affluent Western European countries (Andrijasevic 2010). Compared to the rest of Europe, patriarchal structures are more deeply rooted in new Eastern European member states like Bulgaria, and the status of their women is more devalued, in this particular episode. Here we find echoes of the colonial imaginary of Austria's Habsburg past. Even though the monarchy had no colonies and its official policy was "unity in diversity," processes of so-called inner colonization nevertheless took place, especially during the late nineteenth-century occupation of Bosnia-Herzegovina (see Ruthner 2002; Donia 2007). These particular processes were fueled by the mission to civilize and modernize the eastern and southeastern parts of the empire that were considered backward. The cultural politics of the Double Monarchy was defined by a hierarchy that prioritized German-speaking culture, which represented the progress and civilization of Western Europe over the eastern and southeastern peripheries of the empire, inhabited by "uncivilized" Slavic cultures (see also Hipfl and Gronold 2011: 30–31).

This episode of *Tatort* clearly positions the two migrant prostitutes as victims of patriarchal oppression and domination. They are not given any agency in their capacity to make decisions regarding their lives. When one prostitute cooperates with the police by testifying about the violence and abuse she has experienced at the hands of the pimp, the result is a revenge killing. Despite assurances to protect her, the police officer, Bibi, is unable to prevent the prostitute's death. With its focus on trafficking, the episode resonates with "measures, such as anti-trafficking-campaigns, that mobilise a stereotypical gendered representation of 'Other' women as victims and men as criminals" (Andrijasevic 2010: 131).

Additionally, this episode addresses illegal prostitution as a problem that an understaffed police department cannot handle properly. This was confirmed by a police spokesperson who, immediately after the episode was aired, issued a public statement asserting that six officers were not enough to deal with the more than six thousand illegal sex workers in Vienna. I will return to this aspect later in more detail. For now, I want to show how this mirrors Austria's contradictory position on sex work. On the one hand, prostitution is perceived as a threat to Austrian morality, national health, and public order that is connected to worries about increased migration and trafficking. On the other hand, prostitution is legal and thus a source of state income through taxes (Boidi, El-Nagashi, and Karner 2009: 15).[4] One effect of this double standard, according to Boidi (2015), is that instead of being protected by the police, sex workers are subject to control. In a similar vein, Marjan Wijers, former president of the European Commission's Expert Group on Trafficking in Human Beings, regrets having pushed the term "trafficking" as a political issue because "trafficking" is a term that "is predominantly used by states to legitimise repressive measures against migrants and sex workers rather than to protect them from abuse and secure their rights" (Wijers in Andrijasevic 2010: 142).

Angezählt exposes the slavery-like conditions endured by migrant women forced into illegal prostitution. The police officer Bibi Fellner, for her part, embodies and expresses anger, despair, and feelings of hopelessness when confronted with the attack on Yulia. Bibi's emotional outbursts—her tears over the death of Yulia, her attempt to physically attack the pimp—allow viewers to feel the desperation and helplessness of prostitutes at the mercy of pimps. Bibi's compassionate response is also a model for the audience, showing the kind of emotion that is appropriate to feel and alluding to a humanitarian discourse of collective global compassion that emerged as the media increasingly depicted the suffering of distant strangers (see Höijer 2004).[5] Bibi sides with the prostitutes. She wants to do everything in her power to help them escape from their prisoner- and slave-like existence. Yet she does not specifically address the ways in which employment and immigration regulations intersect with the exploitation and abuse of migrant women, as pointed out by Andrijasevic (2010: 142).

The female detective's strong emotional reactions support the overall impression that this episode deploys an "othering" of crisis, as well as a gendered embodiment of crisis. Crisis is located elsewhere and is transported into Austria via migration and trafficking. This resonates with fears that emerged with the European Union's expansion to include Eastern European countries like Slovakia, Romania, and Poland in 2004. Public discussion in Austria was rife with apprehension that this would result in increased crime and attract people who would abuse social support while trying to work the system.[6] The criminal elements in the *Tatort* episode are men who are clearly marked as migrants from the East: the Bulgarian trafficker and pimp cooperates with the Turk who runs the place of solicitation where the prostitutes meet their clients. These clients too are marked as having an Eastern ethnic background, as exemplified by the Iraqi who was wrongly accused of the murder. The problematic, dark, inhuman side of forced prostitution seems to belong only to immigrants. Implicitly, this association of immigrants with prostitution fuels cultural racism (Balibar 1991), where migrant cultures are seen as different in the sense of being less civilized. An ascribed patriarchal structure defined by male dominance and victimized women is one of the key elements used to denote a civilizational status inferior to that of Western Europe.

In *Angezählt*, the "bad-guy pimp" is depicted in such a way that his criminal acts and malpractices are the outcome of his personality, rather than the result of fateful coincidences or external forces as is predominantly the case in other episodes in which non-migrant criminals are represented. The ruthless Bulgarian pimp stops at nothing. He even abets a child to become complicit in murder. This is a racialized construction, in that the "bad guy's" actions are associated with his cultural background—something quite common for foreign wrongdoers, not just in the *Tatort* series (Buhl 2013) but in news reports as well (Lünenborg 2009). This construction feeds a structure of feeling that helps to create anxiety connected to an image of Europe as a "fortress" threatened by unwanted elements like the pimp, forcing their way in. This structure of feeling is also rooted in gender differences in the representation of migrants from the East, where the active dimension of migration is connected with assertiveness, aggression, violence, and criminality as represented by males, and its passive side by suffering, victimized females. The images of oppressed, victimized women in need of help trigger sentiments of compassion, producing an additional structure of feeling.

As Lauren Berlant (2004: 10–11) contends, as much as emotional responses to suffering are socially needed and appreciated as humane reactions, there is always the danger that they are an expression of, and at the same time a reinforcement of, the privileged situation of their audiences, who are able to decide whose claims to suffering are compelling and worthy of redress. Berlant also alerts us to the danger that compassion, often connected to the respondent's desire to "feel good," is confined to an expression of empathy with the sufferer, remaining in the personal realm and leaving the social and political conditions that produce precarity, injustice, and inequality unexplored. In the next section, I will focus on another structure of feeling expressed in *Angezählt*: precarity, as embodied by the female migrants.

Female Migrant Sex Workers as the Embodiment of Precarity

Focused as it is on the criminal and violent pimp, the *Tatort* episode *Angezählt* avoids addressing the fact that sex work is a preferred entry occupation for immigrants because no requirements are needed, earnings are immediate, and it allows for high mobility (Wagenaar, Altink, and Amesberger 2013: 11). This kind of "cash economy that operates in the shadows" (ibid.) makes sex workers vulnerable to exploitation. According to Andrijasevic (2010: 127), the political changes after 1989 "were decisive for the entry of 'central' and 'eastern' European migrants in large numbers into 'west' Europe's sex industry." Currently, more than 90 percent of female sex workers in Austria are immigrants (Wagenaar, Altink, and Amesberger 2013: 11). The situation of migrant sex workers is precarious because of Austrian immigration legislation. The Austrian "immigration package" of 2006 made it more difficult for non-EU migrant sex workers to remain in the country. Earlier they were issued so-called "prostitution visas" (residence permits allowing self-employed individuals to work in prostitution), but now only short-term residence permits with a maximum stay of six months are issued for temporary or seasonal work.[7] Initial applications and applications for extensions can only be made from abroad. Denied a long-term stay and always in fear of expulsion and deportation if caught working in Austria without a permit, non-EU sex workers must remain constantly mobile, moving in zones of illegality, which then makes them more dependent (Boidi, El-Nagashi, and Karner 2009: 71). Even sex workers who have worked, lived, and paid taxes in Austria for several years do not have the same rights as other residents (Wagenaar, Altink, and Amesberger 2013: 11).

The migrant prostitutes in this *Tatort* episode exemplify the precariousness of life and the political dimension of precarity as conceptually developed by Judith Butler (2004), Isabell Lorey (2010), and Butler and Athanasiou (2013). These scholars understand precariousness as an existential condition of vulnerability based on the fact that all bodies rely on other bodies and depend on supportive social relations for survival. Yet precarity, in the words of Athanasiou (in Butler and Athanasiou 2013: 19), is "the politically induced condition in which certain people and groups of people become differently exposed to injury, violence, poverty, indebtedness, and death," a condition that is related to "socially assigned disposability … as well as to various modalities of valuelessness." The episode portrays both female characters who migrated from Bulgaria to Austria as subjected to male violence and abuse and forced into prostitution by their fellow countryman. Prostitution is the only way to work off the "debts" they had accrued, that is, the journey to Austria and rent for their apartment there. In Austria, they are also devalued as "prostitutes," as the conversation between police officers in the episode illustrates when it is discovered that the victim of the crime was a former prostitute. Tellingly, Yulia literally becomes a disposable body after she has done her duty and cooperated with police to put the pimp behind bars for forced prostitution. Only the female officer, Bibi, is outraged to find that the police have not lived up to their promise to protect the woman.

These two migrant bodies exemplify the insecurity and desperation that come with precarity. In *Angezählt*, this sense of insecurity and desperation is not restricted to the migrants but is also expressed in the investigating policewoman's rageful response. I make the claim that this episode is but one example in Austrian media where precariousness is attached to the bodies of (female) migrants, even as these migrants generate a structure of feeling that is more widespread. Precariousness is no longer something ascribed to the other but has become normalized under neoliberal conditions. As Butler observes, "the differential ways of allocating precarity, of assigning disposability, are clearly aims and effects of neoliberal forms of social and economic life" (Butler in Butler and Athanasiou 2013: 20–21). Similarly, Lorey (2010) argues that with the massive reduction of permanent employment contracts and the dismantling of social security systems all over Europe, precarization is no longer a phenomenon confined to social groups at the margins: "Precarization is currently in a process of normalization" (ibid.: 3). Temporary jobs with no social benefits and the necessity of high mobility and flexibility are, for her, indications that precarization has become a neoliberal instrument of governance: "Neoliberal societies are now governed internally through social insecurity, which means providing the minimum possible social security" (ibid.). Butler describes the affective registers of precarization as the "lived feeling of precariousness, which can be articulated with a damaged sense of future and a heightened sense of anxiety" (Butler in Butler and Athanasiou 2013: 43). The *Tatort* episode *Angezählt* addresses and expresses this feeling of precariousness, and can thus be seen as one of the ways in which a population becomes acclimatized to insecurity.

However, the topic of forced sex work among migrant women, as articulated in *Angezählt*, refers to "broader transformations of borders, labour, and citizenship in Europe," indicating "a rupture of the state and its territory and of the citizen-worker dyad on which are based the logic of inside and outside" (Andrijasevic 2010: 143). While *Angezählt* deploys an othering of crisis, it also presents a crisis of the state for the viewer. The failure of the police is evident: they are not containing the crisis in this episode. They are not able to get criminal activities under control or protect forced migrant sex workers. These are indications of what Zygmunt Bauman characterizes as the present crisis: a waning of the state's capability to manage social realities within its territorial boundaries (Bauman and Bordoni 2014: 12).

Police in Crisis: The State in Crisis

The episode of *Tatort* discussed here addresses some of the ways in which globalization, and especially the continuous flows of people and the challenges related to such movement, affects the nation-state.

As Bauman and Bordoni (2014) observe, under contemporary conditions—in which current challenges and problems are globally produced—nation-states lack the instruments necessary to deal properly with such effects. Crises of territorial sovereignty (Bauman and Bordoni 2014: 22), as diagnosed by Bauman and exemplified in *Angezählt*, manifest themselves in the debilitated competency of state institutions like the police. Police in this episode are unconvincing in both their handling of the case of the pimp with a Bulgarian background and their dealings with him personally. The disrespect the pimp shows to female and male police officers alike clearly embodies the crisis of the state. Following Bordoni, this situation is characteristic of current conditions, which he describes as a constant state of crisis involving the modern state, "whose structure, functionality, effectiveness … are no longer suited to the times in which we live" (Bauman and Bordoni 2014: 27).

Neoliberalism, as the old-new game in town—a central tenet of which is the transfer of responsibility from the state to the individual—illustrates very well the waning of state competency that goes hand in hand with the waning of trust in state institutions. Based on the rhetoric that everybody forges their own destiny by "making the right choices," it is the individual subject who becomes responsible for the successes and failures that occur.

Interestingly, in *Angezählt* the "bad-guy pimp" embodies the neoliberal subject who acts according to this principle in an exaggerated fashion, illustrating what can go awry when self-interest and self-serving become the only criteria for organizing one's life. Following his own rules, the pimp seeks revenge for being exposed to the police by Yulia and takes action to have her killed. He represents the dark side of individual responsibility in neoliberalism's "free choice" society, where individuals take their duty to the extreme, defining their own laws and acting accordingly. In his presumptuous conversation with the police officers, the pimp positions himself as a successful entrepreneur who, by virtue of owning an expensive car and a number of apartments in Vienna, has "made it," and owns much more than they do. He fits perfectly into what, according to Athena Athanasiou, constitutes the political imaginary of (post)colonial capitalist Western modernity, where "being and having are constituted as ontologically akin to each other; being is defined as having; having is constructed as an essential prerequisite of proper human being" (Butler and Athanasiou 2013: 12–13).

In this chapter, I suggest that "state of crisis" and "crisis of the state" can be used synonymously following Bauman and Bordoni

(2014), who convincingly pinpoint this entanglement. As Bauman stresses, "our problems are globally produced, whereas the instruments of political action bequeathed by builders of nation-states were reduced to the scale of services *territorial* nation-states required; they prove therefore singularly unfit when it comes to handling global, *extraterritorial* challenges" (Bauman and Bordoni 2014: 21–22; emphasis in original). The inadequacy of the police in *Angezählt* mirrors what Bauman describes as the demotion of formally sovereign units "to the rank of local police precincts struggling to secure a modicum of law and order necessary for the traffic whose comings and goings they neither intend, nor are able to control" (Bauman and Bordoni 2014: 22). Bauman's diagnosis needs to be supplemented with an argument from Chakrabarty (2012: 7), who makes the point that the state's failures with respect to economic, political, demographic, and environmental factors also produce refugees, asylum seekers, and illegal workers as the new subalterns of the global economy.

As this chapter is being written, in the summer of 2015, the Austrian state is challenged by what is publicly discussed as Europe's "migrant crisis": hundreds of thousands of people fleeing war and persecution in Syria and other parts of the world. One of the routes followed by the refugees and asylum seekers goes to and through Austria. In August 2015, the asylum reception center in Traiskirchen, Austria, intended to house 1,000 inhabitants, was overcrowded with 4,800 plus people living in conditions that Amnesty International declared inhuman and shameful (Southam 2015). In response, Austria's public discourse has a dual focus. On the one hand are the problems the state faces in managing the incoming asylum seekers. Statements issued by government representatives problematize the unequal distribution of asylum seekers within Europe, where a few states, Austria among them, carry the biggest burdens. Austrian Justice Minister Wolfgang Brandstetter even threatened to bring a charge against the European Commission if no measures were taken to distribute asylum seekers more fairly within Europe. On the other hand is the public discourse concerning the so-called "migrant crisis," characterized by a juxtaposition of the rhetoric of the political right (fueling fears of a mass influx of people, arguing for "Fortress Europe," devaluing asylum seekers as "economic refugees" who just want to take advantage of state support) with approaches that have taken on responsibility, mostly through humanitarian rhetoric generated by NGOs and private initiatives that have organized support for these asylum seekers. I now turn to this latter approach—what I refer to as responsiveness to crisis situations—in the final part of this chapter.

Responsiveness: An Ethical Approach to Crisis

Coming back to *Angezählt*, and specifically Bibi's outrage, her "unprofessional" conduct when she physically attacks and reviles the pimp, and later her criticism of her colleagues' handling of the case, I suggest that we view her behavior as an ethical reaction to the crisis of the state/state of crisis. My argument draws on feminist research that has found that expression of anger is a source of empowerment and a step towards change. Audre Lorde (1997: 283) states that her response to racism is anger, and that "anger has eaten clefts into my living only when it remained unspoken." She points out that every woman "has a well-stocked arsenal of anger potentially useful against … oppressions, personal and institutional, which brought that anger into being. Focused with precision it can become a powerful source of energy serving progress and change" (ibid.: 280). However, Lorde continues, women in general have been raised to avoid the anger of others and, particularly tellingly, have not learned to express anger among peers. Bibi is furious when she finds out about the circumstances that led to Yulia's death. Using Athanasiou's terminology, Bibi "bears responsibility" in the sense that she addresses the power relations that are responsible for the situation she is facing. She not only rakes the pimp "over the coals," but she also confronts her police partner by addressing the underlying patriarchal social structures and the involvement of men in general (including policemen) in the exploitation of prostitutes.

Following Athanasiou (Butler and Athanasiou 2013: 105), Bibi's responsiveness can be described as a "disposition toward others"; that is, as a responsibility toward others that is to be differentiated from "responsibilization" (Butler and Athanasiou 2013: 106). Responsibilization is the key element of neoliberalism's focus on personal responsibility defined by self-interest and mastery of one's individual risks. Such is the character of the pimp, who embodies an entrepreneurial, presumptuous attitude and whose actions to safeguard his business are defined by self-centeredness. In comparison, Bibi is portrayed as vulnerable—the episode's opening scene shows her working through her sad and troubled childhood in a session with her psychotherapist—and thus embodies what for Butler and Athanasiou (2013) is the condition of "dispossession." By that they mean we are not self-sufficient but relational beings, as experiences of grief and loss often dramatically illustrate. At the same time, this condition of dispossession is also the source of responsiveness and responsibility to others (Athanasiou in Butler and Athanasiou 2013: 104–105).

Bibi's anger and fury differ from both the humanitarian approach defined by discourses of victimization and charity, which lacks political claims and confrontations, and from the sentimental humanism in the form of compassion that has become central to the moral economies of neoliberalism (Athanasiou in Butler and Athanasiou 2013: 113–114). Anger and outrage, as expressed by Bibi, are ways to avoid what Spelman (quoted in Woodward 2004: 70) sees as the seduction of the tender feeling of compassion, which "[serves] to seal a short circuit of feeling, confining it to the individual," and what Berlant (2004) problematizes as the effects of sentimental narratives, where empathetic identification confines the audience to their private worlds. Bibi's reaction to the misery of the two female immigrants in this episode is emphatic, but it does not reduce them to mere victims. Rather, her outrage indicates a mode of gaining insights into hegemonic power relations and inequalities by naming and criticizing the violent oppressor and the institutionalized processes of marginalization and precarization. Bibi addresses violence and injustice through her anger and performs what Spelman (1989: 266, quoted in Bargetz 2012: 188) calls "acts of insubordination" that, by countering racialized and sexualized normative regimes, can be politically mobilizing.

Conclusion

The affective work of the *Tatort* episode discussed in this chapter is ambivalent. On the one hand, the structure of feeling that runs through the narrative reiterates an othering and racialization of crisis. Migrants from Eastern Europe are blamed for bringing crisis into Austria's "safe haven" by transferring not only themselves but also the problems from their country of origin. Through the topos of trafficking, Eastern European migrants are represented in stereotypically gendered ways. The male villain exemplifies the fears that repeatedly emerge in public discourse about immigrants from the East—namely criminal and misogynist conduct—while the female migrants are victimized. This is connected with a European social imaginary of a "Fortress Europe" threatened by unwanted elements forcing their way in, and accompanied by feelings of compassion towards the disadvantaged women from Eastern Europe.

On the other hand, this crime fiction episode appears to reject us-them binaries and gives the audience hints of a broader social understanding of crisis as precarity—the unequal distribution of insecurity based on global and structural relations. By illustrating failures in policing the crisis, the episode does more than show that crisis always means a crisis of the state: it also indicates that precarity is not confined to marginal groups like migrants from the East, but is on its way to becoming normalized as an everyday state of affairs.

Brigitte Hipfl is a retired Ao. Professor in the Department of Media and Communication Studies at the University of Klagenfurt, Austria. She works on media and gender, subject formations, the affective labor of media, and postcolonial Europe, and is currently exploring migration in Austrian cinema and TV. Her publications include *Teaching "Race" with a Gendered Edge* (2012) co-edited with Kristín Loftsdóttir and *Wir und die Anderen. Visuelle Kultur zwischen Aneignung und Ausgrenzung. (We and the Other. Issues of Appropriation and Exclusion in Visual Culture)* Herbert von Halem Verlag, 2021 (co-edited with Anna Schober).

Notes

1. In Europe, a public broadcasting service, deeply rooted in the respective national culture of television and opposed to commercial broadcasting, is supposed to serve the public by providing independent, diverse information as well as quality entertainment (Collins 2004).
2. *CSI: Crime Scene Investigation*, the first series in the *CSI* franchise, is a US TV show that began airing on CBS in October 2000. It ended in 2016, after fifteen seasons. *CSI* focuses on the work of forensic investigators who solve criminal cases by collecting and scientifically examining evidence like blood, saliva, and skin. *The Wire* (a title referring to the wiretapping of suspects' phones) was first broadcast in 2002 by the US cable network HBO; it ended after five seasons, in 2005. Lauded for its realistic portrayal of urban life, *The Wire* presents a bleak picture of the post-industrial United States. *Cold Case*, another US crime series broadcast on CBS, ran for seven season from 2003 to 2010, specializing in new evidence in past murder cases.
3. *Angezählt*, which means "counting," refers to the moment the referee starts counting when a boxer is unable to continue fighting.
4. Prostitution is tolerated and legalized in Austria, but sex work is still considered "against good morals" (Boidi, El-Nagashi and Karner 2009:

70). Legally, prostitution is regulated differently throughout Austria's nine provinces by way of either the "brothel model," which prohibits prostitution unless it is exercised and solicited in licensed brothels, or the "prohibited zone model" applied in Vienna, which allows prostitution anywhere outside designated prohibited zones like school neighborhoods and residential areas. Registration with the local authorities is compulsory for sex workers, who must undergo mandatory health checks and are taxed as self-employed workers (ibid.: 70).
5. See also the elaborate discussion of humanitarian reason's relation to distant suffering by Andrea Muehlebach in this volume.
6. See also the emergence of similar sentiments toward immigrants in Ireland and Great Britain as respectively discussed by Cannedy and Garner in this volume.
7. Legal approaches to sex work and immigration in Europe vary. A good overview and comparison can be found in Boidi, El-Nagashi, and Karner (2009). Under Austria's "self-employment" regulation of 2003, only self-employed persons or employed "key professionals" are allowed to immigrate to Austria for the purpose of gainful employment. Prostitutes are defined as self-employed persons.

References

Andrijasevic, R. 2010. *Migration, Agency and Citizenship in Sex Trafficking*. New York: Palgrave Macmillan.
Arvas, P., and A. Nestingen. 2011. "Introduction: Contemporary Scandinavian Crime Fiction," in *Scandinavian Crime Fiction*, ed. A. Nestingen and P. Arvas, 1–17. Cardiff: University of Wales Press.
Balibar, E. 1991. "'Is there a 'Neo-Racism'?" in *Race, Nation and Class: Ambiguous Identities*, ed. E. Balibar and I. Wallerstein, 17–28. London: Verso.
Bargetz, B. 2012. "Zum Verhältnis von Politik, Emotionen und Geschlecht," in *E-Motions: Transformationsprozesse in der Gegenwartskultur*, ed. E. Mixa and P. Vogl, 176–188. Vienna and Berlin: Turia + Kant.
Bauman, Z. and C. Bordoni. 2014. *State of Crisis*. Cambridge and Malden, MA: Polity.
Berlant, L. 2004. "Introduction: Compassion (and Withholding)," in *Compassion: The Culture and Politics of an Emotion*, ed. L. Berlant, 1–13. New York and London: Routledge.
Boidi, M. 2015. *Sex Work in Austria*. Online video. Retrieved 15 November 2015 from <https://vimeo.com/134195949?utm_source=email&utm_medium=clip-transcode_complete-finished-20120100&utm_campaign=7701&email_id=Y2xpcF90cmFuc2NvZGVkfDMyOTY3OG

M0NjJlOThhMTFhMTU0OGNlODFjMmRiYTIyMTQ1fDQyMjI3M
zY2fDE0Mzc1NzYyODV8NzcwMQ%3D%3D>.
Boidi, M., F. El-Nagashi, and B. Karner. 2009. *Sex Work, Migration, Health: A Report on the Intersections of Legislation and Policies Regarding Sex Work, Migration and Health in Europe.* Hamburg: Mottendruck.
Brunsdon, C. 1998. "Structure of Anxiety: Recent British Television Crime Fiction," *Screen* 39(3): 223–243.
Buchanan, I. 2012. "Telling Truths: Crime Fiction and National Allegory." Conference for Readers, Writers and Critics, Wollongong, 6–8 December 2012. Wollongong: University of Wollongong. Retrieved 15 November 2015 from http://lha.uow.edu.au/hsi/istr/UOW121005.html.
Buhl, H. 2013. *Tatort. Gesellschaftspolitische Themen in der Krimireihe.* Constance and Munich: UVK.
Bukow, W., et al. 2007. "Was heißt hier Parallelgesellschaft? Zum Umgang mit Differenzen," in *Was heißt hier Parallelgesellschaft? Zum Umgang mit Differenzen*, ed. W.-D. Bukow, C. Nikodem, E. Schulze, and E. Yildiz, 11–26. Wiesbaden: VS Verlag für Sozialwissenschaften.
Butler, J. 2004. *Precarious Life: The Powers of Mourning and Violence.* London and New York: Verso.
Butler, J., and A. Athanasiou. 2013. *Dispossession: The Performative in the Political.* Cambridge and Malden, MA: Polity.
Chakrabarty, D. 2012. "Postcolonial Studies and the Challenge of Climate Change." *New Literary History* 43(1): 1–18.
Clough, P.T. ed. 2007. *The Affective Turn: Theorizing the Social.* Durham, NC and London: Duke University Press.
Collins, R. 2004. "'Ises' and 'Oughts': Public Service Broadcasting in Europe," in *The Television Studies Reader*, ed. R. Allen and A. Hill, 33–50. London and New York: Routledge.
Deleuze, G. 1992. "Postscript on the Societies of Control." *October* 59(Winter): 3–7.
Donia, R. J. 2007. "The Proximate Colony: Bosnia-Herzegovina under Austro-Hungarian Rule; Kakanien Revisited." Retrieved 4 September 2016 from http://www.kakanien-revisited.at/beitr/fallstudie/rdonia1.pdf.
Gansel, C., and W. Gast. 2007. "Krimi und Agenda-Pushing: Der deutsche TV-Krimi zwischen Unterhaltung und politisch-gesellschaftlichem Diskurs." *merz: medien + erziehung. Zeitschrift für Medienpädagogik* 4: 38–46.
Gräf, D. 2010. *TATORT. Ein populäres Medium als kultureller Speicher.* Marburg: Schüren.
Gregg, M. and G. Seigworth, eds. 2010. *The Affect Theory Reader.* Durham, NC and London: Duke University Press.
Herzog, T. 2009. *Crime Stories: Criminalistic Fantasy and the Culture of Crisis in Weimar Germany.* New York and Oxford: Berghahn Books.

Hipfl, B., and G. Gronold. 2011. "Asylum Seekers as Austria's Other: The Re-emergence of Austria's Colonial Past in a State-of-Exception." *Social Identities* 17(1): 27–40.
Hißnauer, C. 2014. "'Vergangenheitsbewältigung' im *Tatort*? NS-Bezüge in der ARD-Krimireihe." *Repositorium Medienkulturforschung* 3: 7–49. Retrieved 16 November 2015 from http://repositorium.medienkulturforschung.de/rmkfwordpress/wp-content/uploads/2014/04/2014_04_08_RMKF_7_Hi%C3%9Fnauer_Tatort.pdf.
Höijer, B. 2004. "The Discourse of Global Compassion: The Audience and Media Reporting of Human Suffering." *Media, Culture & Society* 26(4): 513–531.
Lee, S. 2004. "'These are our stories': Trauma, Form, and the Screen Phenomenon." *Discourse* 25(1–2): 81–97.
Lorde, A. 1997. "The Uses of Anger." *Women's Studies Quarterly* 25(1–2): 278–285.
Lorey, I. 2010. "Becoming Common: Precarization as Political Constituting." *e-flux* (June–September). Retrieved 16 November 2015 from http://www.e-flux.com/journal/becoming-common-precarization-as-political-constituting/.
Lünenborg, M. 2009. *Migrantinnen in den Medien. Eine systematische Literaturanalyse*. Herausgegeben vom Ministerium für Generationen, Familie, Frauen und Integration des Landes Nordrhein-Westfalen. Duisburg: WAZ.
Newcomb, H., and P. Hirsch. 1983. "Television as a Cultural Forum." *Quarterly Review of Film Studies* 8(3): 561–573.
ORF Medienforschung. 2014. *Die meistgesehenen Sendungen im Jahr 2014*. Retrieved 16 November 2015 from http://mediaresearch.orf.at/index2.htm?fernsehen/fernsehen_hitliste.htm.
———. 2015. *Die meistgesehenen Sendungen im Jahr 2015*. Retrieved 13 March 2016 from http://mediaresearch.orf.at/index2.htm?fernsehen/fernsehen_hitliste.htm.
Ortner, C. 2007. *Migration im tatort, Das Thema Einwanderung im beliebtesten deutschen TV-Krimi*. Marburg: Tectum.
Peacock, S. 2014. *Swedish Crime Fiction: Novel, Film Television*. Manchester and New York: Manchester University Press.
Pribram, D. 2013. *Emotions, Genre, Justice in Film and Television*. New York and London: Routledge.
Priesching, D. 2013. "Sabine Derflinger: 'Für Männer ist es leider toll, Frauen zu kaufen.'" *DerStandard.at*., 6 September. Retrieved 16 November 2015 from http://derstandard.at/1378248365736/Derflinger-Fuer-Maenner-ist-es-leider-toll-Frauen-zu-kaufen.
Ruthner, C. 2002. "Central Europe goes Postcolonial: New Approaches to the Habsburg Empire around 1900." *Cultural Studies* 16(6): 877–883.
Sabin, R., et al. 2015. *Cop Shows: A Critical History of Police Dramas on Television*. Jefferson, NC: McFarland.

Sharma, D., and F. Tygstrup. 2015. "Introduction," in *Structures of Feeling: Affectivity and the Study of Culture*, ed. D. Sharma and F. Tygstrup, 1–19. Berlin, Munich, and Boston, MA: De Gruyter.

Southam, H. 2015. "How Austria Has Become Central to Europe's Migration Crisis." *Guardian*, 28 August. Retrieved 15 November 2015 from http://www.theguardian.com/world/2015/aug/27/austria-western-europes-migration-crisis-starts-here.

Statista. 2015. *Beliebteste Fernsehformate in Deutschland in den Jahren 2014 und 2015*. Retrieved 16 November 2015 from http://de.statista.com/statistik/daten/studie/171208/umfrage/beliebteste-fernsehformate/.

Thompson, J. 1993. *Fiction, Crime, and Empire: Clues to Modernity and Postmodernism*. Urbana and Chicago, IL: University of Illinois Press.

Timm Knudsen, H., and C. Stage, eds. 2015. *Affective Methodologies: Developing Cultural Research Strategies for the Study of Affect*. Houndmills and New York: Palgrave Macmillan.

Wagenaar, H., S. Altink, and H. Amesberger. 2013. *Final Report of the International Comparative Study of Prostitution Policy: Austria and the Netherlands*. The Hague: Platform 31. Retrieved 16 November 2015 from http://kks.verdus.nl/upload/documents/P31_prostitution_policy_report.pdf.

Wenzel. E. 2000. *Ermittlungen in Sachen Tatort: Recherchen und Verhöre, Protokolle und Beweisfotos*. Berlin: Bertz und Fischer.

Williams, R. 1963. *Culture and Society*. Harmondsworth: Penguin.

———. 1977. *Marxism and Literature*. Oxford: Oxford University Press.

Woodward, K. 2004. "Calculating Compassion," in *Compassion: The Culture and Politics of an Emotion*, ed. L. Berlant. New York and London: Routledge, pp. 59–86.

7

Crisis France

Covert Racialization and the Gens du Voyage

Andrea L. Smith

Introduction

In the summer of 2010, during France's worst recession since World War II (Bowd 2013: 93), violence against the police rocked the country. French President Nicolas Sarkozy responded with a new "anti-crime" initiative that culminated in the expulsion of nearly ten thousand Roma that year.[1] Sarkozy's initiative caused tremendous backlash in France as well as among European Union (EU) officials and Roma activists in a period some call Sarkozy's "summer of shame" (About 2012). This chapter takes a close look at this moment of state crisis and the media firestorm that followed to discuss what it reveals about the construction of difference in contemporary France.

Times of economic collapse are often moments of race talk, when politicians are tempted to resurrect worn "us-versus-them" tropes in their efforts to mobilize a frayed national unity. Sarkozy's actions targeting foreign Roma appear to fall into such a pattern, as they occurred when anti-Romany populist politics were on the rise across the European continent (Stewart 2012). In European contexts, discussions of crisis and difference often raise concerns about a rise of "Europism" (Essed 1995: 45), an inward-looking, defensive construction of a "pure Europe" that can manifest itself differently in different settings, sometimes buttressed by or intersecting with gender, racial, or religious distinctions, as the chapters in this volume elucidate. In this chapter, I raise another key marker of difference, place-making practices. Distinctions made between ideal and what are deemed aberrant relationships between people and place can harden into enduring social categories; hence, talking about peoples' relationship to place can be a covert way of talking about race. Pan-European ideologies play out differently in each national setting, and anti-Romany sentiment is no exception.

Exploring difference—racial, ethnic or otherwise—in France presents its own unique challenges. While the country appears breathtakingly diverse to outsiders, its residents find the use of such concepts as race or ethnicity inappropriate or downright divisive.[2] While the country's colonial heritage has very much shaped its present circumstances, including the distinction of having the largest Muslim population of any country in Europe, at the same time, there is a longstanding French state tradition of *not* recognizing distinct ethnic, racial, or other subgroups within the national body, and racializing language has been tabooed by anti-racist movements that date to the era of decolonization (Noiriel 2009). And yet there is abundant evidence that race matters (Constant 2009). This raises two sets of questions. First, how are discriminating, racializing, or ethnocentric ideologies learned and disseminated in a place where the language of race and ethnicity is highly censured? Second, how do scholars theorize questions of difference making, and which terms should we use? Are such concepts as "racialization" appropriately applied to the French context?

In answering these questions, it is my positionality as an *American* scholar of French colonial racisms that poses the most challenges: since what I explore here are legal texts and official discourse, my positionality as a white woman is a less immediate issue, however, as an American I must take care not to fall into the classic pattern of American scholars imposing their race-sensitive framework onto French society (Peabody and Stovall 2003: 5). Beth Epstein (2011: 10), facing similar challenges in her interpretation of life in a French *banlieue*, writes that "as an observer of French life I have had to take into consideration what many French people maintain is a particularly American tendency to insist on the relevance of race and ethnicity in contexts where, they say, they simply do not apply."

In what follows, I explore Sarkozy's anti-Roma agenda, highlighting especially the language he used in presenting it to the public during this moment of state crisis. Because I am interested in the missives of state officials, the coded language used in them, and their public reception, I employ methods influenced by linguistic anthropology and the anthropology of the state. Based on my prior ethnographic fieldwork conducted in southern France (A. Smith 2006, 2013), and informed by insights drawn from theory on covert racialization, indexicality, and place-making processes, I scrutinize public discourse and the press's reaction, and examine what can be viewed as missteps in official discourse that allowed the public a glimpse behind the mask of the state. I will show how a politician's attempt at decisive action inadvertently revealed much about state officials' ways of conceptualizing the social field. The firestorm that followed permits an unusual glimpse into the French management of difference, a story that, notably, starts in the metropole.

Crisis France

The 2008 economic crash was experienced variously across Europe. In contrast to Iceland, for instance (see Loftsdóttir's chapter in this volume), France experienced it less as a singular calamity and more as one in a long series of crises. In fact, by some accounts, the country has been in near-perpetual crisis since World War II; it is difficult to find moments when the country has *not* been embroiled in "crisis talk."[3] Some interpret the 2008 crisis as "a new chapter in an ongoing story of national decline" (Waters 2013: 335). Nicolas Sarkozy faced these economic perturbations when he was entering the second year of his presidency (2007–2012). He had pursued a neoliberal agenda,[4] but when the economic collapse occurred he shifted his approach, declaring "laissez-faire capitalism" to be over and attempting a new version of French *dirigisme* (see Murphy 2017: 201-202). These strategies were ineffective, and after his party's crushing defeat in the March 2010 regional elections, he returned to neoliberal initiatives with vigor.

The new crisis appeared in the midst of these difficulties. After police killed a French Gens du voyage man of Romany descent at a traffic stop in mid July that same year, some forty Gens du voyage retaliated by attacking a police station in the town of Saint-Aignan-sur-Cher on 17 July (Cornevin 2010). That same day, an attack on a casino in Grenoble left a man of North African descent dead and a policeman wounded (About 2012: 95), sparking three days of rioting in that city. Both incidents received tremendous media coverage, and President Sarkozy responded quickly. On 21 July he issued a "Declaration on Security" in which he announced a "real war on crime" (*véritable guerre à la criminalité*):

> Extremely grave events have occurred recently in the Isère and the Loir-et-Cher, marking an escalation of violence, in particular against the

forces of order. These events are unacceptable. The rule of law must be respected on the national territory ... The government has launched a real war against crime. It is a real war that we will mount against traffickers and delinquents. (Translation by the author)

In his speech, as reported the next day in *Le Monde,* Sarkozy noted that the recent incidents "underline the problems caused by the behavior of some of the Gens du voyage and Roma" (Bordenave and Leparmentier 2010) suggesting that foreign Roma and French Gens du voyage were threatening the national order. By Roma, he meant Travellers or Gypsies, who had been arriving in France from Romania and Bulgaria in increasing numbers since these countries joined the EU in 2007. Gens du voyage, on the other hand, is an internal French administrative category created in 1969 to designate French citizens who live in mobile homes. While some Gens du voyage have Roma ancestry, this is not explicitly denoted by their official label. Sarkozy called for holding a meeting of high-level ministers the next week, adding that their deliberations would culminate in the "expulsion of all irregular camps" (ibid).

Sarkozy's strongly worded speech two days later in Grenoble linked Gens du voyage, Roma immigrants, and French citizens of "foreign origin" with rising criminality and announced an accelerated evacuation of illegal camps (Leparmentier 2010: 8). He discussed the need to "reestablish the Republican order" that was threatened by attacks on the police and by "unplanned, illegal Roma settlements" (Bărbulescu 2012: 284). As he framed it, the recent crime wave was the result "of a profound contempt towards the fundamental values of our society" (ibid.: 285).

These statements constructed the recent violence as a problem brought to the nation by outsiders living in ways distinct from mainstream French society (i.e., in "irregular camps") and described the perpetrators as culturally alien, claiming they showed "contempt toward the fundamental values of (French) society." Absent in his addresses was any connection between the social unrest and sharp economic decline in France or beyond.

Reaction and Response

Despite national and international outcry, Sarkozy and his ministers brazenly carried out the planned destruction of "irregular" Roma encampments throughout the summer of 2010. These actions were widely covered in the media; in fact, mediatization of the activities was apparently an integral part of Sarkozy's strategy (Gould 2014: 30), as if the expulsions themselves were in part a demonstrative public performance of assertive, decisive leadership.

The counter-response from Roma and human rights activists was immediate. Vice-President of the European Commission and Commissioner for Justice, Fundamental Rights and Citizenship Viviane Reding made a public statement accusing France of undertaking "ethnically-based Nazi-style deportations," adding that "the Commission will have no choice but to initiate infringement action against France" (cited in Gould 2014: 31). The European Parliament issued a critical resolution. Roma deportations were criticized not only on moral grounds, but also as violating EU law protecting the free movement of citizens. As EU citizens, Roma from Bulgaria and Romania should be able to move and reside freely within the territory of any member state for three months, after which time they must prove they are not an "unreasonable burden."[5] Furthermore, EU directives allow states to deport individuals for security reasons, but only on a case-by-case basis; France's blanket attack on whole communities of Roma defied that regulation.

Critics also challenged France's imposition of additional residency requirements for Romanians and Bulgarians if they wished to stay longer than three months (O'Nions 2011: 368). These included criteria that many Roma were hard pressed to meet—being professionally employed, having economic resources to care for oneself and family, or being a student (Bessone et al. 2013: 190)—criteria not required of nationals of other EU member states (CNCDH 2012: 169; Bessone 2013: 190). France's "voluntary return program" was also scrutinized. As part of this program, individuals were granted a resettlement sum of €300 per adult and €100 per child. Some have called this practice "expulsion in disguise" (Bessone 2013: 190) and noted that it was applied almost exclusively to Roma populations. In fact, the government's decision to double the resettlement sum (from €150 to €300) had the unforeseen effect of attracting to France impoverished Roma who had never traveled there before (Nacu 2012: 1325).

Sarkozy and his administrators responded to these critiques by claiming that they were not singling out Roma specifically. This position was undermined when a series of government circulars were released to the press explicitly targeting Roma camps, and even establishing expulsion quotas: "in each administrative zone of France there should be at a minimum one clearing, dismantling or expulsion operation per week" (Gould 2014: 30). The Roma expulsions led to outrage and mass protests in France. But although they represent an extreme treatment of difference, these expulsions are not my focus here. Instead, I am interested in the furor over Sarkozy's framing of the situation: what alarmed many French observers was that Sarkozy's anti-Roma proclamations and initiatives targeted both foreign Roma and French citizens, the Gens du voyage, referencing both social categories in the same sentence. As *Le Monde* reported on 21 July (Caro 2010), he was quickly accused of their *"amalgamation"* — of lumping them together. In other words, at a moment of immediate crisis Sarkozy slipped into language that many in France found reprehensible, with unforeseen consequences.

The national reaction to this language and its implications was widespread. Stéphane Lévêque, director of the National Federation of Associations in Solidarity with Gypsies and Gens du voyage, said, "On the one hand, there are Roma, who are foreign EU citizens, and on the other, Gens du voyage, who are entirely French (*Français à part entier*), and have been so longer than Bretons or the Savoyards" (Caro 2010). Some accused Sarkozy of unleashing the phantom of race and fostering ethnic conflict. Representatives of the League for the Rights of Man argued that the president was stigmatizing these ethnic groups by organizing a meeting on the criminality of these two populations. Alain Daumas, president of the French Union of Gypsy Associations, stated more pointedly in a *Le Monde* article of 28 July 2010 ("Reunion controversée") that Sarkozy's initiative revealed a "racial politics" (*une politique de nature raciale*). In an editorial entitled "No to the Ethnic Partition of the Republic," Alain Jakubowicz, president of the International League Against Racism and Anti-Semitism, characterized Sarkozy's language as marking a "severe break in the republican social pact" (*Le Monde*, 13 August 2010, 14). How might we understand these particular critiques? Was Sarkozy indeed treating the Gens du voyage in defiance of republican law, as critics were arguing? Was he participating in their racialization or "ethnicization"? To grapple with these questions, we must turn to French approaches to difference.

Republican Universalism and Race Talk in France

According to the principle of republican universalism, the French state does not recognizes any distinct racial or ethnic groups within its polity. Instead, a multitude of individual citizens are imagined as having a direct, unmediated relationship to the state. Article 1 of the

French Constitution underscores this point, maintaining that the Republic is "indivisible" and "ensures equality before the law of all citizens regardless of origin, race or religion." This ideal continues to animate everyday life in contemporary France. As the anthropologist Epstein (2011: 12) writes, "More than a mere abstraction, the republican ideal is hotly debated as a part of everyday politics in France; in order to understand how it functions, it is also necessary to grasp the passions, in current-day France, that these debates can enflame."

Republican universalism influences how the state addresses difference through official statements and legal texts. As a result of the application of this principle, race and ethnicity were never codified in France as official categories and do not appear in the national census,[6] which is thereby distinguished from practice in many other European countries and the United States. In fact, in France, the collection of data relative to ethnic or racial origins has been strictly forbidden since 1978.[7]

It is difficult to assess the degree to which the absence of racial and ethnic census categories has influenced how people discuss difference in everyday discourse. Historian Gérard Noiriel (2009: 173–174) points out that many staunch republicans such as Paul Broca were early promoters of a racialized vision of humanity. He dates the general repugnance toward the word "race" among republican elites to the 1930s, when the left constructed its political project around denunciations of anti-Semitism and racism, a project that would evolve into a critique of colonialism; a similar fight against racism would help unite the left in the 1970s. Today, belonging to the nation is associated with a "commitment to the common interest" (Epstein 2011: 12), and the grounds of difference that are given prominence include such categories as occupation, education, or social class (ibid.: 14). "Ethnic communities" are viewed as nonexistent, superfluous, or potentially divisive (ibid.: 9–10; see also Simon 2008: 7), and there has been a "disqualification of 'race' as a descriptive category altogether" (Fassin 2009: 27–28; Sabbagh and Peer 2008: 2; Epstein 2011: 91). As Beriss (2004: 126) noted, culture became a "gloss for something that 'looks' like race," what Balibar (1991: 21) described as a "racism without races."

And yet, as black activists have made clear, race matters in France. As Fred Constant reports, "color blind in theory, it has always been color-coded in practice" (Constant 2009: 146). By the summer of 2010, a public sensitization to difference was growing and being articulated in the public and official spheres. Always a diverse population (Noiriel 1988), the French saw their diversity expanded by the settlement of millions of former colonial subjects after World War II. Following the activism of young North African youth in the 1980s and their call for a *droit à la différence*, recognition of the persistent social, spatial, and economic marginalization of French people of colonial ancestry grew (Fassin 2002: 404). The "fight against discrimination" became a primary focus in the 1990s and took on a new sense of urgency after the 2005 riots, leading to the recent establishment of a robust set of laws against direct and indirect discrimination and a new agency, the French High Authority against Discrimination and for Equality, to oversee progress in this regard (see Simon 2008: 23).

Yet it has been hard to document the contours of discrimination and exclusion, let alone address them, because of the state's official color-blind policies. This stance has posed a conundrum: without clear data, the documentation of racist, ethnocentric or Islamophobic practices is difficult at best. For this reason, some scholars and activists called on the state to gather *"statistiques ethniques"* (ethnic statistics, or data on ethnicity, race, and other social characteristics), unleashing dramatic, contentious public debates that have endured for decades.[8] It is hard to overstate the degree to which this discussion has embroiled French scholars, activists, and now the general public. Positions fall into roughly two camps. Some scholars and activists press for data to help reveal the contours of discrimination. Contrariwise, the "republican" position vehemently opposes such a tack, partly due to fear that the society will descend into a conflict-ridden, American-style *communautarisme* (see Tin 2008). At the same time, there has been an increased self-racialization by French blacks who strategically and intentionally deploy the "taboo-ridden nomenclature 'Noir'" to self-identify (Keaton, Sharpley-Whiting, and Stovall 2012: 1–2).

It was within this social field that the president of the republic engaged in what seemed to many to be "ethnicizing" or racializing language. He identified the Roma, certainly an ethnic group, along with a whole category of French citizens, the Gens du voyage, as threats to the nation, implying an underlying connection. His linking of the two groups and connecting them to social disorder (when in fact, foreign Roma were not involved in either instance of anti-police violence in 2010) led observers to claim that state officials were following an underlying *ethnic* script, targeting Romany people regardless of nationality, which is illegal under French law and anathema to republican ideals. And Sarkozy was not the only one in his administration to link these two groups. In the days leading up to his famous 30 July speech, his interior minister, Brice Hortefeux, claimed on national television that, "The situation isn't the same, but in the three cases, Roma, sedentary and non-sedentary Gens du voyages, the consequence is the same: an increase in delinquency."

Even after government officials denied targeting these populations as members of ethnic groups, leaked circulars alluded to an "ethnic database" in which people of Roma background were identified by name (Johannès 2010). This file (known as MENS, an abbreviation of "non-sedentary ethnic minorities") was kept by the Central Office for the Fight against Itinerant Delinquency. Although the gendarmerie and minister of the interior claimed not to know of it, Gens du voyages associations eventually found it on the Internet. The website displayed a map of France; when a user selected a region, the website revealed the names of specific families along with their purported "specialties," such as jewelry theft, stealing cars, or money laundering. Even the foreigners so enumerated were identified as Roma first, and then classified by nationality. As journalist Franck Johannès explained, "it isn't Hungarians or Georgians who might be Roma, but Roma who are Hungarian or Georgian." That is, the database privileged ethnic background over nationality in direct violation of French law (Johannès 2010).[9]

Thus the president and his administration regularly linked Roma and Gens du voyage in their speech and actions. The meaning behind the *gens du voyage* label was consequently called into question as some suggested it was a clever yet technically legal way to identify, target, and manage a distinct ethnic group, French Travellers or *Tsiganes*, using coded euphemistic language. At the very moment when activists were complaining that the state had no clear figures on the number of black French—leading a private association, the Representative Council of Black Associations, to carry out its own "census" (Tin 2008: 36)—the public was reminded that the state had been gathering such statistics for Gens du voyage, and had been doing so for over a century. Suddenly, scholars and the press returned to the Gens du voyage to further explore just who these people were, with consequences Sarkozy probably never imagined.

Regulating Gypsies in France

To understand the racializing nature of a purportedly non-ethnic social label, we must first consider its origins. Traveling groups in France have been subject to a distinct administrative regime for centuries due to their different place-making practices. By most accounts, different groups known alternatively as *Bohémiens*, *Romanichels*, *Manouches*, or *Tsiganes* arrived from the East by the fourteenth and fifteenth centuries[10] and soon encountered varying forms of suspicion and discrimination. By the seventeenth century, their mere presence on French territory could make them subject to banishment, hanging, galley service, and corporal punishment (Liégeois 2007: 109).

Nomadic populations came under further scrutiny after the mid-nineteenth century, when agricultural and economic upheaval led whole families to "take to the road" in search of work (T. Smith 1999: 825). At this time the figure of the "vagabond" emerged as a threat to national order, and local regulations were designed to follow the movement of musicians, circus performers, peddlers, and vagrants (About 2012: 101). By 1864, the Ministry of Interior noted that there was no legal framework for the Gypsy population, and a circular requested police surveillance of all "*Bohémiens*." State officials hoped to encourage them to settle down, stating that by assigning "each of them with a distinct and compulsory place of residence, the government will be able to disseminate them, thus breaking apart these criminal conspiracies" (ibid.: 101–102).

In the early years of the Third Republic (1870), the Ministry of the Interior developed regulations to strengthen surveillance of Gypsies on a national scale (ibid.: 102). In March 1895, a census of all "nomads, bohemians and vagrants" was mandated (Filhol 2012: 322). In 1907 a new policing unit, the *Brigades Mobiles*, was created and ordered to "photograph and identify vagrants, nomads, Gypsies, whether alone or in groups"; nearly eight thousand so-called "nomads" were documented in this way (About 2012: 104).

Finally, a 16 July 1912 law regulated all mobile populations (*ambulants*) in France.[11] It is important to note that the legal texts related to this law did not mention racial and ethnic qualities; instead, the law was designed to encompass everyone with aberrant place-making (i.e., nomadic) lifestyles. Reading between the lines, however, we see disproportionately numerous restrictions directed at people of Roma heritage. The law noted three kinds of *ambulants*: traveling merchants, people who work in traveling fairs (*forains*), and nomads (*nomades*). Merchants of foreign or French nationality could hold a "mobile profession" and had only to make an official statement to this effect at the prefecture where they resided (Hubert 1999: 24). Fair workers with no fixed address were henceforth required to carry an identity card with their photograph (Article 2). Filhol points out (2012: 336) that the law distinguished *forains* and *nomades* in part because the former did not want to be taken for Gypsies or become subject to similarly rigorous identification procedures. The final category included "those nomads whatever their nationality, all individuals circulating in France without home or fixed residence and not falling into the categories mentioned above, even if they have resources or seem to have a profession" (Article 3). The law's promulgators called this group *nomades* because they could not agree on a definition for *Tsiganes*; hence, the labels "Romanichels, Bohemians, and other Tsiganes" were dropped from the final law (Hubert 1999: 25).

One could argue that the 1912 law, by focusing on all itinerant people, followed republican principles because it did not specify a particular ethnic or racial group. However, it is clear from discussions leading up to the law that Gypsies, or *"nomades proprement dits,"* were lawmakers' primary focus. They also made little distinction between foreign and French nomads, calling French nomads *"malfaisants"* (troublemakers) and asking rhetorically, "Why should we watch them? Because they don't have a home, no civil status, they don't work, and they live off theft" (in Filhol 2012: 325). In his exposition of the goals of this law, its promoter, Senator Flandin, presented the "nomads" as a conquering population terrorizing the countryside.[12] With the passage of the 1912 law, people designated as nomads faced a whole new level of scrutiny: they were henceforth required to carry a *Carnet anthropométrique de l'identité* (see Noiriel 1988: 89)—a notebook with photographs and clear physical descriptions of each individual. These *Carnets* enabled close monitoring of French nomads. "Nomads" had to present them to local authorities when arriving at or departing from any municipality, and at least four agencies were involved in their registration and surveillance in the early years. The *Carnets* remained in force until 1969 and gained considerable notoriety following revelations of their use to place *nomades* in camps during the Vichy regime.[13] They were finally abolished in 1969 and replaced with new policies quite similar in spirit.

From *"Nomades"* to *"Gens du voyage"*

In the 1950s, humanitarian activists working with French traveling populations began to lobby for improvement in their living conditions and against the stigmatizing *Carnet anthropométrique*. They were concerned that local municipalities were forcing "nomads" to move or relegating them to unhealthy locations (Reyniers and

Williams 1990: 93). These activities culminated in new legislation in 1969,[14] which coined the term *gens du voyage*, designed as an improvement over the then derogatory label *nomade*. As a neologism, it carried no negative associations.

Critics have since argued that the new legislation was founded on the same principles as its predecessor: a desire to preserve the public order for the *sedentary* population, based on a presumption that nomadic people are a dangerous class that must be identified and disciplined (ibid.: 92). Although the *Carnet anthropométrique* was abandoned, it was replaced with the *livret de circulation*, and the idea of a *commune de rattachement* was introduced as an administrative site to play the role of domicile for those without one (ibid.). Now, in order to receive a *livret*, applicants were required to find such a "commune." But individuals could not freely select a commune, for they could identify only communes where the population without a fixed residence did not exceed 3 percent of the population. Starting at age sixteen, most holders of these cards were required to present themselves to a commissariat every three months to explain where they were living. Moreover, to vote, the *livret* holder had to demonstrate his or her attachment to the same municipality for three consecutive years (for everyone else, the wait time was six months) (Liégeois 2009: 58). And whereas sedentary French men and women with itinerant professions were required to meet with the authorities only every ten years, Gens du voyage "without fixed residence" were checked every six months, or 120 times more often than itinerant workers (Liégeois 2009: 61).

France's neoliberal turn over the past several decades has led to further confinement of the Gens du voyage, turning them into a kind of a migratory prison population. The "Besson Law" of 5 July 2000 was designed to encourage French cities to build more campsites. Its author, Louis Besson, member of the Socialist Party, noted in an interview with Elise Vincent in *Le Monde* on 18 September ("Louis Besson," 2010) that he had devised the law after noticing a reduction in the amount of land available for Gens du voyage campsites. When he was mayor in 1965, most towns still had a fairground at their entrance where Gens du voyage camped, allowing them to engage in commerce with local populations. As Besson explained, "with the arrival of the throwaway society and accelerated urbanization, these lands disappeared." One of the law's main goals, he stated, was to allow "nomads the chance to come and go freely" and to live in "decent conditions." However, there was a stick with this carrot: the law also banned the installation of illicit camps, which, as Besson explained, "exasperate elected officials and neighbors." French communes have been extremely slow to establish the campsites mandated by the Besson Law. In 2002, the estimated 30,000–35,000 caravans circulating in the country had access to only 5,000–10,000 legal campsites. Moreover, established sites were often unhealthy or outright dangerous due to their proximity to incinerators, dumps, highways, or railway lines.

Article 19 of then Interior Minister Sarkozy's March 2003 law on domestic security was the final blow. It banned all unofficial nomad encampments, punishing offenders with six months in prison, a fine of €3,750, and the possible revocation of drivers' licenses and impoundment of vehicles. The people it targeted perceived it as turning their very mode of life into a crime[15] while also criminalizing their place-making practices, given the dearth of legal campsites. Since as a result, migratory families often must gather illegally, conflicts occur regularly across the country, a situation that was ongoing during the summer of 2010 (Vincent 2010a, 2010b).

Race and Racialization in France

How might Sarkozy's discourse be viewed as "racializing"? US scholarship long viewed difference largely in terms of ethnic groups and ethnicities—as in the ethnicity paradigm of the 1920s and 1930s, in which race "was but one of a number of determinants of ethnic group identity" (Omi and Winant 1994: 15)—but now the tide has shifted the focus, not to race per se, but to *racialization*, the process by which race becomes meaningful in a particular context (Garner 2010: 19). As Hilary Dick (2011: E40) writes, "ethnicizing practices mark actors by casting cultural difference as 'colorful,'" that is, other, but nonthreatening; in contrast, "racializing practices mark actors as non-normative by dehumanizing them, representing them as undifferentiated, immoral, dangerous." Racializing discourse is that which sorts some people, things, places, and practices into "social categories marked as inherently dangerous and Other" (Dick and Wirtz 2011: E2).

Since race science was discredited following World War II, "race talk" has become more coded in both the United States and France. In her work on white racism in the United States, Jane Hill (2008: 14) writes that while "stereotypes and slurs are visible as 'racist' to most people ... other kinds of talk and text that are not visible ... may be just as important in reproducing the culturally shared ideas that underpin racism." Covert forms may in fact be even more important "because they do their work while passing unnoticed," communicating by absence and silence (ibid.), in language that is not "denotationally explicit about race" (see also Dick and Wirtz 2011).

Given France's long history of the state *not* "talking" about race, and a wider popular consensus against even using racial categories in everyday speech, France would seem a particularly fruitful site for a study of covert racialization, as scholars of terms such as "immigré" have demonstrated (Silverman 1992). Covert racialization can be achieved through indexicality, when a linguistic structure (such as a word or way of speaking) becomes "ideologically associated with an attitude, set of assumptions, [or] personality type" (Modan 2007: 106). Once such a linguistic structure comes to signal or "index" the attitude or set of assumptions, race can be alluded to and communicated without ever being mentioned. The regular association of people with specific places and place-making practices is often key in speaking indirectly about whole populations and placing them in a hierarchical relationship to some normative standard (Smith and Eisenstein 2013, 2016). As Gabrielle Modan (2007: 319) writes in her research on a Washington DC neighborhood, talking about geography is a remarkably common way to set up a "moral and deictic center and then distance other people from that center." The people she studied shared an understanding of a web of ideological distinctions between "suburb" and "city." Characteristics linked to "the suburb"— whiteness, quiet, clean language, and so forth—were used in conversation to index each other, the suburbs, a suburban identity, or race (ibid.: 107), as in "her neighborhood is so quiet" (meaning the individual is white). In this way someone can communicate the perceived racial identity of an individual without ever using overtly racial or ethnic terms.

Similar speech patterns are common in France. People may avoid overtly racializing or ethnicizing speech, but they can still communicate about social distinctions indirectly through place-based indexicality. The *banlieue*, for instance, is weighted with rich associations, and the term can be used to index its residents, people of certain class backgrounds, ancestry, phenotype, certain aesthetics, ambience, danger, and so forth (Epstein 2011: 1–2; see also Nacu 2012: 1326), clearly communicating without ever directly mentioning the ethnic or racial origins of the people thus indexed.

Turning to the Gens du voyage, we can see their very separation from the rest of French society, albeit under a "race-neutral" social label, as a racializing move. We could argue that a moral evaluation of different "spatial practices" has been implied by French legislation targeting nomadic populations since the earliest years of singling out this way of life. That it is treated as suspect and dangerous is evident in the array of special legislation designed for non-sedentary peoples, legislation that has persisted almost unbroken since before the modern French state. Different administrative regimes were designed for different place-making practices, and a hierarchy of peoples was created, in which nomadic citizens were deemed different and lesser.

How might we understand the French official assertion that "Gens du voyage" is an empty administrative category with no ethnic content? Such a label, while expressly not about race or ethnicity, but people with distinct place-making practices, acts as a euphemism, a way to talk about social categories without using ethnic or racial languages. Furthermore, theory about social labels suggests we investigate their indexical functions. In her book *White by Definition*, Virginia Domínguez argues that social identities are meaningful only in relation to other identities. Social identities are conceptions of the self that are constructed in opposition to other such selves, and as social identities evolve, so too do the boundaries between them (Domínguez 1986: 10). Social labels, then, are signs used "in thinking and communicating" and convey messages both referentially and indexically (ibid.: 11); their meaning is tied to the context of usage (ibid.). Labels reflect "both a larger body of 'knowledge' and the context of experience of those for whom the labels become meaningful" (ibid.: 267). Through usage, then, labels gather new associations, making their full meaning context-dependent. For this reason, a new label given to a stigmatized population will gather these stigmatized associations over time, leading highly stigmatized social groups to adopt new terminology as a result.[16] We can see this process with the terms *nomades* and Gens du voyage. The label *nomade* was generated at the turn of the century as politicians grappled with the problem of disparate vagabond populations.[17] Despite politicians' clear concern with Gypsies, the text of the 1912 law concerned *ambulant professions* and did not overtly identify any groups according to their ethnic or racial heritage. Even "nomad" is not necessarily a racial category. As it became associated with negative content, however, it became a derogatory term. *Gens du voyage*, designed to address the stigma associated with the "nomad" label, was neutral at the time of its codification in the 1969 law, however over time it too has become weighted with negative associations.

When a social label designates a population that is treated by the state as distinct, subject to discriminatory regulations, or forced to live in designated locations, that label will become imbued with associations stemming from this context, which it will eventually index. In the French press, one sees "Gens du voyage" associated today with "invasion," "infiltration," "vandalism" "filth," "expulsion," "illegal encampment," and "no fixed address." A process of deixis is underway: these people come "from elsewhere," they "storm" the field, they "infiltrate," they are "expelled." They are described as pests invading the social body. They are thoroughly French, yet because they are described as continually coming from somewhere else, they are discussed as if they were perpetual outsiders. The final straw was the way the president of the republic talked about them in connection with the foreign Roma, dragging into public view this whole chain of indexical associations with all their implications and triggering a firestorm of critique.

Aftermath

In their recent book, *State of Crisis*, Bauman and Bordoni link Europe's 2008 economic crisis with a crisis of the state, noting the state's experience of a loss of sovereignty due to the machinations of global capitalism. At such moments of state crisis, leaders often experience what they term a "crisis of agency" (Bauman and Bordoni 2014: 21). We can see such a crisis in the example at hand. Faced with systemic economic decline and an immediate circumstance of violent disruption, the French president was in a bind. Caught between the electors, who can put him out of office, and his inability to carry out effective change on the wider economic domain, yet wanting to demonstrate decisive action, he framed the immediate crisis as a problem from without and began to expel some of the poorest people on the European continent, even though Roma were not involved in the two violent attacks to begin with. His initiative backfired, however, when he included the Gens du voyage in his discourse, as this brought their whole history and special state treatment to national attention.

It is common for leaders of a nation under threat to rally around traditional values or mores. What is striking in this case is the way Sarkozy did so almost accidentally. While many French expressed horror at the treatment of the foreign Roma, what became the primary concern was Sarkozy's mixing of Gens du voyage and Roma in his proclamations and initiatives, and thus his breach of the fundamental principles of republican universalism. Ironically, then, he helped build national consensus and reinforce key national values at a moment of crisis, but not at all in the way he probably wished, for he did so by unwittingly positioning *himself* as the primary threat to the nation.

That a new consensus has been forged is clear from the state's actions regarding the Gens du voyage since the summer of 2010. Politicians and activists have turned their attention to the discriminatory regulations and the internal contradictions in state policy that they reveal, which some term "the upside" of this crisis (About 2012: 114). In October 2012, the French Council on the Constitution determined that distinguishing between different types of ambulatory licenses based on resources was unconstitutional and repealed the requirement of uninterrupted residence in the same commune in order to vote (Roger and Rollot 2012). The council also ruled that the *titre de circulation* requirement was not contrary to the Constitution, but in June 2015, the deputies nevertheless voted to abolish the law of 1969 requiring the *livret de circulation* (Molodtzoff 2015), and it appears that further change is underway.

At the same time, though, policies toward foreign Roma have remained largely unchanged or even hardened. Despite uproar, France expelled almost 10,000 Roma in 2010 and nearly the same number (8,455) in the following year. The subsequent administration of François Hollande, if anything, accelerated the practice, evicting nearly 20,000 Roma in 2013 (Sayare 2014) and even took a populist anti-Roma position during his electoral campaign.

In times of crisis in Europe, tensions often emerge between attachments to the nation, to the EU, and to more amorphous constructions of "Europeanness." Sometimes they lead to a stronger relationship between race and nation, or to articulations of whiteness. The chapters in this volume show that post-2008 "crisis talk" has often elicited strong affective connections to the nation and less so to the EU, and France is no exception. Despite the swift reaction to the racism implied in Sarkozy's targeting of the Roma, these evictions continue. At the same time, the *national* compact has been strengthened, and state officials have made many efforts to smooth out what suddenly appeared to be an anachronistic relationship between the state and the Gens du voyage. The "others within" are being incorporated into the national circle, at least officially, while the "others without" continue to be expelled. At a moment of tension between EU policy and French interests, national interests prevailed.

This does not mean that the Gens du voyage no longer experience discrimination. As scholars of race in France and elsewhere know well, official denial of difference does not mean it has evaporated from public life. While now struggling to update regulations, French officials continue to grapple with the nature of the label itself. In a parliamentary report presented to the National Assembly in March 2011, Deputy Didier Quentin stated (2011: 11), "it is absolutely essential to specify that the administrative category 'Gens du voyage' is not an ethnic category." Regular statements of this kind suggest a long-standing discomfort and seem an awkward attempt to balance universalist principles with a continued desire to maintain some means of singling out this population in particular. According to the social labeling theory mentioned above, until the unequal treatment associated with the official distinctions made between people based on place-making practices is eliminated, a covert racialization associated with this—or any other such label—will likely persist.

Conclusion: Crisis, Anti-Romany Sentiment, and the Colonial Past

At the present moment, the migration of Syrian and other refugees overshadows the "Gypsy panic" that was intensifying earlier in the second decade of the twenty-first century (Stewart 2012). This is a dramatic state of affairs, and only time will tell if it spurs on the ugly populist politics that was emerging in relation to the Roma. As Stewart writes, in the context of "looming economic catastrophe … vigilance about violence directed against minority groups is even more essential" (ibid.: x).

"Europeanness" is positioned in opposition to Roma in some countries, asylum seekers in others, and Islam in yet others. As I have tried to argue here, each country grapples with others in its own unique ways, depending on its particular history (Loftsdóttir 2012). In this example, the scapegoating of Eastern European Roma following crimes committed by other populations inspired an unpredicted consciousness-raising effect with regard to the Gens du voyage. Other countries coping with anti-Romany initiatives, whether popular or state-sanctioned, will find them carried out in wholly different swirls of distinctions, associations, and rationales.

Discussions of difference in France today are often dominated by explorations of the country's colonial past and the perpetuation of colonial-era ideologies (Blanchard et al. 2014). I certainly do not wish to deny the existence of the colonial legacy in French constructions of difference (on this, see A. Smith 2006), but what makes this discussion so important is its presentation of a case that is decidedly *not* colonial in origins and thus demonstrates how racializing logic and discourse may precede (if not inform) colonial practice. In the example addressed here, the establishment of a hierarchy of populations rooted in cultural difference—in this case, distinct place-making practices—predated most French colonial contexts by hundreds of years.[18] Of course, discriminatory measures targeting the *nomade* would be further elaborated in Algeria, where they were used in massive land expropriations (Ageron 1968; Ruedy 1967), and would also emerge in the Kabyle Myth and the differential treatment of "settled" versus "nomadic" indigenous Algerians (Lorcin 1995; Silverstein 2004). Linkages between colony and metropole cannot be automatically assumed but require careful scrutiny (Saada 2012: 250), and as this chapter has shown, special vigilance about the *direction* of influences is warranted. As I have demonstrated, we need not turn to France's colonies or its treatment of its citizens with ancestry in the former colonies to explore the question of French racialization, or to "demythologize republican memory" (Silverman 2007: 630).

Finally, this example shows that we must remain vigilant with respect to language, as both politicians and the public may communicate covertly about social diversity, touching on deep-rooted themes and images to communicate distinctions between self and other, and thus engaging in processes of dichotomization. Scholars of race may find the discourse of state officials in crisis to be most revealing. Despite France's official position on ethnicity and race, Sarkozy blundered by trying to rally the nation around a facile constructions of self and other, with consequences that are ongoing today.

Andrea L. Smith is Professor of Anthropology at the Department of Anthropology and Sociology at Lafayette College, Easton, PA (USA). Her research interests include postcolonial European social memory and silencing; French settler colonialism in Algeria; and race, ethnicity and place-making. Publications include the edited volume *Europe's Invisible Migrants* (2003), *Colonial Memory in Postcolonial Europe: Maltese Settlers from Algeria in France* (2006) and the co-authored work *Rebuilding Shattered Worlds: Creating Community by Voicing the Past* (2016).

Notes

1. "Roma," "Travelers," and "Gypsies" comprise a mosaic of diverse groups of varying relationship across Europe. Terminology has evolved over the past thirty years. In 2011 the Council of Europe and the European Union adopted the label "Roma" (CNCDH 2012: 159), the term used in this essay.
2. The literature on race and France is voluminous; good reviews can be found in Fassin and Fassin (2009) and Keaton et al. (2014). French citizens of African descent have reported macro- and micro-aggressions for years; some argue that France's colorblind discourse serves to buttress a racial order (Léonard 2014: 84).
3. Crises tied to Vichy, the wars of independence, and the collapse of the Fourth Republic were followed by those associated with the waves of immigration that accompanied decolonization. The *bidonville* housing crisis, May '68, the 1973 oil crisis, crises of integration and assimilation, the riots of 2005, and concerns about endemic discrimination followed in quick succession. The decline of French industry and the weakening of both labor and the labor movement have aggravated an employment crisis that only grows with each passing year (Epstein 2011: 76).
4. He reduced the workweek and capped taxes for the rich. See Murphy 2017: 201–202 for a succinct summary of Sarkozy's response to the 2008 crisis.
5. According to European directive 2004/58/EC on the rights of citizens.
6. Notable exceptions include their use in colonial records and in the registration of Jews undertaken during the Vichy regime (Simon 2008: 9).
7. Article 8-1 of the law no. 78-17 of the Law of 6 January 1978 on information, databases, and equality forbids the collection of such statistics unless there are exceptional reasons to do so.
8. Good English-language summaries of these debates can be found in the 2008 special issue of *French Politics, Culture & Society* 26(1).
9. This is punishable by five years in prison and a €300,000 fine.
10. It is hard to know whether the earliest references to Gypsies reflect their earliest presence in a given location (Liégeois 2007: 17).
11. The full title of the 16 July 1912 law is "La loi sur l'exercice des professions ambulantes et la réglementation de la circulation des nomads."
12. Senate hearing, 10 March 1911, in Liégeois (2007: 45).
13. Between three and six thousand French Gypsies were placed in some forty concentration camps at the request of Nazi officials. None were sent directly from France to Germany, however. See Fogg (2008: 350).
14. The law is "loi 69-3 du 3 janvier 1969 relative à l'exercice des activités ambulantes et au régime applicable aux personnes circulant en France, sans domicile ni residence fixe."
15. On 9 November 2002, *Le Figaro* noted that representatives of the Association Sociale Nationale Internationale Tzigane met with Sarkozy.

16. Note, e.g., the United States' regular rejuvenation of terminology to designate African-Americans. As new labels became associated with negative qualities, activists created new ones (Baugh 1991: 133; Smitherman 1991: 118–124).
17. Liégeois (2007: 34) points out that ethnonyms and autonyms do not necessarily correspond; moreover, the names different Roma use to self-identify are very context-dependent (ibid.: 52).
18. The ways anti-nomadic policies are inherent in state formation are articulated by Scott (1998).

References

About, I. 2012. "Underclass Gypsies: An Historical Approach on Categorisation and Exclusion in France in the Nineteenth and Twentieth Centuries," in *The Gypsy Menace: Populism and the New Anti-Gypsy Politics*, ed. M. Stewart, 95–114. New York: Columbia University Press.

Ageron, C. 1968. *Les Algériens musulmans et la France (1871–1919)*. Paris: Presses Universitaires de France.

Balibar, E. 1991. "'Is There a 'Neo-Racism?'" in *Race, Nation, Class: Ambiguous Identities*, ed. E. Balibar and I. Wallerstein, 17–28. New York: Verso.

Bārbulescu, H. 2012. "Constructing the Roma People as a Societal Threat: The Roma Expulsions from France." *European Journal of Science and Theology* 8(1): 279–289.

Baugh, J. 1991. "The Politicization of Changing Terms of Self-Reference Among American Slave Descendants." *American Speech* 66(2): 133–146.

Bauman, Z., and C. Bordoni. 2014. *State of Crisis*. London: Polity.

Beriss, D. 2004. *Black Skins, French Voices: Caribbean Ethnicity and Activism in Urban France*. Boulder, CO: Westview.

Bessone, M., et al. 2013. "Integrating or Segregating Roma Migrants in France in the Name of Respect: A Spatial Analysis of the *Villages d'Insertion*." *Journal of Urban Affairs* 36(2): 182–196.

Blanchard, P., et al. 2014. *Colonial Culture in France since the Revolution*. Bloomington, IN: Indiana University Press.

Bordenave, Y. and A. Leparmentier. 2010. "Des policiers de confiance autour de Nicolas Sarkozy." *Le Monde*, 22 July. Retrieved 3 September 2017 from http://www.lemonde.fr/politique/article/2010/07/22/des-policiers-de-confiance-autour-de-nicolas-sarkozy_1390963_823448.html?xtmc=gens_du_voyage_les_amalgames&xtcr=19.

Bowd, Gavin. 2013. "In France, Will Change Be Now or Never?" *Soundings: A Journal of Politics and Culture* 53: 93–102.

CNCDH (Commission Nationale Consulatative des Droits de l'Homme). 2012. *Avis sur les Statistiques 'Ethniques'*. 22 March 2012.

Caro, Ilan. 2010. "Gens du voyage: les amalgames du gouvernement." *Le Monde*, 21 July. Retrieved 3 September 2017 from http://www.lemonde.fr/societe/article/2010/07/21/gens-du-voyage-les-amalgames-du-gouvernement_1390710_3224.html.

Constant, F. 2009. "Talking Race in Color-Blind France: Equality Denied, 'Blackness' Reclaimed," in *Black Europe and the African Diaspora*, ed. D. Hine, T. Keaton and S. Small, 145–160. Urbana, IL: University of Illinois Press.

Cornevin, C. 2010. "Violence: la vallée du Cher en état d'alerte." *Le Figaro*, 20 July, 8.

Dick, H. 2011. "Making Immigrants Illegal in Small-Town USA." *Journal of Linguistic Anthropology* 21(S1): E35–E55.

Dick, H., and K. Wirtz. 2011. "Racializing Discourses." *Journal of Linguistic Anthropology* 21(S1): E2–E10.

Domínguez, V. 1986. *White by Definition: Social Classification in Creole Louisiana*. New Brunswick, NJ: Rutgers University Press.

Epstein, B. 2011. *Collective Terms: Race, Culture, and Community in a State-Planned City in France*. New York and Oxford: Berghahn Books.

Essed, P. 1995. "Gender, Migration, and Cross-Ethnic Coalition Building," in *Crossfires: Nationalism, Racism and Gender in Europe*, ed. H. Lutz, A. Phoenix, and N. Yuval-Davis, 48–64. London: Pluto.

Fassin, D. 2002. "L'invention Française de la Discrimination." *Revue Française de Sciences Politics* 52(4): 402–423.

———. 2009. "Nommer, interpréter. Le sens commun de la question raciale," in *De la question sociale à la question raciale: Représenter la société française*, ed. D. Fassin, and E. Fassin, 27–44. Paris: La Découverte.

Fassin, D. and E. Fassin, eds. 2009. *De la question sociale à la question raciale. Représenter la société française*. Paris: La Découverte.

Filhol, E. 2012. "Le contrôle des Tsiganes en Europe de la fin du XIXe siècle aux années trente." *Canadian Journal of History* 47: 317–354.

Fogg, S. 2008. "'They are Undesirables': Local and National Responses to Gypsies during World War II." *French Historical Studies* 31(2): 327–358.

Garner, S. 2010. *Racisms: An Introduction*. London: Sage.

Gould, R. 2014. "Roma Rights and Roma Expulsions in France: Official Discourse and EU Responses." *Critical Social Policy* 35(1): 24–44.

Hill, J. 2008. *The Everyday Language of White Racism*. Malden, MA: Wiley-Blackwell.

Hubert, M. 1999. "Les Réglemantations anti-Tsiganes en France et en Allemagne, Avant et pendant l'Occupation." *Revue d'Histoire de la Shoah* 167: 20–52.

Johannès, F. 2010. "La gendarmerie utilize un fichier illégal qui vise les Roms et les Gens du voyage." *Le Monde*, 8 October, 1.

Keaton, T., T. Sharpley-Whiting, and T. Stovall. 2012. "Blackness Matters, Blackness Made to Matter," in *Black France/France Noire*, ed. T.

Keaton, T. Sharpley-Whiting and T. Stovall, 1–14. Durham, NC: Duke University Press.
Léonard, M. 2014. "Census and Racial Categorization in France: Invisible Categories and Colorblind Politics." *Humanity & Society* 38(1): 67–88.
Leparmentier, Arnaud. 2010. "Gens du voyage et Roms; L'Elysée veut démanteler 300 campements illégaux." *Le Monde*, 30 July, 8.
———. 2009. *Roms et Tsiganes*. Clamecy, France: Collection Repères.
Loftsdóttir, Kristín. 2012. "Colonialism at the Margins: Politics of Difference in Europe as Seen through Two Icelandic Crises." *Identities: Global Studies in Culture and Power* 19(5): 597–615.
Lorcin, P. 1995. *Imperial Identities: Stereotyping, Prejudice, and Race in Colonial Algeria*. London: I.B. Tauris.
"Louis Besson: 'Cette loi n'est pas un traitement de faveur." 2010. *Le Monde*, 18 September. Retrieved 3 September 2017 from http://www.lemonde.fr/a-la-une/article/2010/09/14/louis-besson-cette-loi-n-est-pas-un-traitement-de-faveur_1410949_3208.html?xtmc=entretien_avec_louis_besson&xtcr=7.
Modan, G. 2007. *Turf Wars: Discourse, Diversity and the Politics of Place*. Malden, MA: Blackwell.
Molodtzoff, E. 2015. "Gens du Voyage: Fin d'une mesure discriminatoire." *France 3 Lorraine*, 15 June.
Murphy, J. 2017. *Yearning to Labor: Youth, Unemployment, and Social Destiny in Urban France*. Lincoln, NE: University of Nebraska Press.
Nacu, A. 2012. "From Silent Marginality to Spotlight Scapegoating? A Brief Case Study of France's Policy Towards the Roma." *Journal of Ethnic and Migration Studies* 38(8): 1323–1328.
Noiriel, G. 1988. *Le Creuset Français: Histoire de l'immigration XIXe–XX siècles*. Paris: Seuil.
———. 2009. "'Color blindness' et construction des identités dans l'espace public français," in *De la question sociale à la question raciale: Représenter la société française*, ed. D. Fassin, and E. Fassin, 166–182. Paris: La Découverte.
Omi, M., and H. Winant. 1994. *Racial Formation in the United States from the 1960s to the 1990s*. New York: Routledge.
O'Nions, H. 2011. "Roma Expulsions and Discrimination: The Elephant in Brussels." *European Journal of Migration and Law* 13(4): 361–388.
Peabody, S., and T. Stovall, eds. 2003. *The Color of Liberty: Histories of Race in France*. Durham, NC: Duke University Press.
Quentin, D. 2011. *Rapport d'information déposé par la Commission des lois constitutionnelles, de la législation et de l'administration générale de la République, en conclusion des travaux d'une mission d'information sur le bilan et l'adaptation de la législation relative à l'accueil et l'habitat des Gens du voyage*. Assemblée nationale, 13th legislature.
"Reunion controversée à l'Elysée sur les Roms et les gens du voyage." 2010. *Le Monde*, 28 July. Retrieved 3 September 2017 from http://www.lemonde.fr/societe/article/2010/07/28/reunion-controversee-a-l-elysee-

sur-les-roms-et-les-gens-du-voyage_1392787_3224.html?xtmc=reunion_controversee_gens_du_voyage&xtcr=5.

Reyniers, A., and P. Williams. 1990. "Permanence tsigane et politique de sédentarisation dans la France de l'après-guerre." *Etudes Rurales* 120: 89–106.

Roger, P., and C. Rollot. 2012. "Les 'sages' censurent a minima le statut des gens de voyage." *Le Monde*, 6 October, 9.

Ruedy, J. 1967. *Land Policy in Colonial Algeria*. Berkeley: University of California Press.

Saada, E. 2012. *Empire's Children: Race, Filiation, and Citizenship in the French Colonies*. Chicago, IL: Chicago University Press.

Sabbagh, D., and S. Peer. 2008. "French Color Blindness in Perspective: The Controversy over 'Statistiques Ethniques.'" *French Politics, Culture & Society* 26(1): 1–6.

Sayare, Scott. 2014. "France: Roma Evictions Increase." *New York Times*, 6.

Scott, J. 1998. *Seeing Like a State*. New Haven, CT: Yale University Press.

Silverman, M. 1992. *Deconstructing the Nation: Immigration, Racism and Citizenship in Modern France*. London: Routledge.

———. 2007. "The French Republic Unveiled." *Ethnic and Racial Studies* 39(4): 628–642.

Silverstein, P. 2004. *Algeria in France*. Bloomington, IN: Indiana University Press.

Simon, P. 2008. "The Choice of Ignorance: The Debate on Ethnic and Racial Statistics in France." *French Politics, Culture & Society* 26(1): 7–31.

Smith, A. 2006. *Colonial Memory and Postcolonial Europe: Maltese Settlers in Algeria and France*. Bloomington, IN: Indiana University Press.

———. "Settler Sites of Memory and the Work of Mourning." *French Politics, Culture, Society* 31(3): 65–92.

Smith, A., and A. Eisenstein. 2013. "Thoroughly Mixed Yet Thoroughly Ethnic: Indexing Class with Ethnonyms." *Journal of Linguistic Anthropology* 23(2): E1–22.

———. 2016. *Rebuilding Shattered Worlds: Creating Community by Voicing the Past*. Lincoln, NE: University of Nebraska Press.

Smith, T. 1999. "Assistance and Repression: Rural Exodus, Vagabondage and Social Crisis in France, 1880–1914." *Journal of Social History* 32(4): 821–846.

Smitherman, G. 1991. "'What Is Africa to Me?': Language, Ideology, and African American." *American Speech* 66(2): 115–132.

Stewart, M. 2012. "New Forms of Anti-Gypsy Politics: A Challenge for Europe," in *The Gypsy Menace: Populism and the New Anti-Gypsy Politics*, ed. M. Stewart. New York: Columbia University Press, pp. xiii–xxxviii.

Tin, L. 2008. "Who Is Afraid of Blacks in France? The Black Question: The Name Taboo, the Number Taboo." *French Politics, Culture & Society* 26(1): 32–44.

Vincent, E. 2010a. "Décodage: Pourquoi n'y a-t-il assez d'aires pour les Gens du voyage?" *Le Monde*, 15 September, 12.
———. 2010b. "Zoom: Un statut juridique à part." *Le Monde*, 15 September, 12.
Waters, S. 2013. "The 2008 Economic Crisis and the French Narrative of National Decline: *Une causalité diabolique.*" *Modern and Contemporary France* 21(3): 335–354.

8

Navigating the Mediterranean Refugee "Crisis"

Alter-Globalization Activism and the Sediments of History on Lampedusa

Antonio Sorge

Introduction

Beginning in late 2010, a series of political upheavals throughout North Africa popularly dubbed the "Arab Spring" generated a sudden influx of undocumented migrants north across the Mediterranean Sea into Europe. The tiny Italian island of Lampedusa was, and has remained, a prime destination for these new arrivals, largely because of its proximity to illegal ports of exit in Libya and Tunisia. In early 2011, unexpected numbers of boat people temporarily overwhelmed the island. Local authorities' unofficial estimates suggested that around five thousand forced migrants were present on Lampedusa during any single day throughout February and March of that year, marking an apparent high point in the refugee crisis—which nonetheless would intensify considerably in subsequent years, especially from 2013 onward. All but left to their own devices, these disoriented new arrivals wandered the streets of town, slept on benches, and camped on beaches and in makeshift tents on the rocky bluffs overlooking the port. National and international media swarmed to Lampedusa for the scoop, inevitably presenting images of a bucolic Italian island apparently besieged by *clandestini* ("clandestine" migrants), a term that obliquely condemns newcomers alleged to have no legitimate claims to asylum.[1]

"The invasion of Lampedusa" became a popular meme in political discourse throughout Italy and helped to precipitate a decline in tourist activity on the island for the summer of 2011. During this period, local expressions of anxiety about the presence of newcomers were not hard to come by and in several instances evidenced a style of fearmongering that relied on the mobilization of explicitly racialist categories of thinking.

This chapter examines how refugee arrivals were judged and perceived on Lampedusa from 2011 onwards, as well as permutations in local attitudes that followed the blossoming of a tourism industry on the island in the 1990s. I argue that the arrival of asylum seekers today is interpreted at the local level according to divergent sets of schemata, each speaking to contradictory visions of the island's place within the Mediterranean as refracted through the lens of a protracted international crisis. On the one hand, locally based alter-globalization activists' understandings cast Lampedusa as a site of peaceful encounter between Europe and Africa, Christian and Muslim, and attribute great historical depth to this vision. On the other, the narratives that inform many locals' views of the issues are more conflicted, frequently resting on a belief in the incommensurability of European Christian with Arabic Muslim and African cultures that represent a perspective against which activists must position themselves. These two images and their accompanying assumptions lie at two ends of a continuum and are by-products of Lampedusa's peculiar burden of history. Namely, the island is sited within a geographically liminal zone of encounter between Europe and Africa. The analysis that follows notes the centrality of this fact and proceeds on an assumption that there is a need to focus research on activism and social movements on the localized contexts in which they play out. On Lampedusa, this entails examination of local responses to the sudden arrival of asylum seekers in 2011, as well as reactions to activists' agendas and programs.

A review of local history is followed by discussion of the two visions of Lampedusa's place within the Mediterranean and of their respective proponents. I argue that the sedimented history of Lampedusa is a resource employed in the creation of a charter for the present, but how that history is construed, and by whom, can result in irreconcilable perspectives. This sociological approach to history asks how people orient themselves in the here-and-now with reference to an imagined past, and in turn generate constructs that reflect their political positioning in the present (Macdonald 2012: 234–235), offering insight into how contemporary events might be navigated.

The ethnographic montage I provide here is thus of a place of encounter where bewilderment, confusion, and uncertainty structure and define perceptions of what has come to be defined locally as a crisis of international proportions. From a methodological point of view, the ethnographic approach allowed a situated perspective frequently bypassed in migration studies: the view from the locality. The insights in this chapter are derived from research conducted over three months from May to July 2011, which I continued thereafter via electronic means, following developments on the island via social media sites, notably Facebook but also national, regional, and local independent media based on Lampedusa. The techniques of participant observation and unstructured interviews envisioned the site of investigation as an open social field and gradually helped to bring the contours of local life into focus, permitting unfiltered, first-hand access to debates and perspectives on current events.[2]

Changing Visions of the Mediterranean

Most of the five thousand more or less permanent residents of Lampedusa trace their ancestry to original mid-nineteenth century colonists from Western Sicily (Fragapane 1993: 393–432), while others are descendants of later arrivals in the late nineteenth and early twentieth centuries. A minority are seasonal residents who live most of the year on Sicily or mainland Italy, coming to the island only to pursue business interests related to tourism. Mass tourism on Lampedusa is a recent phenomenon dating to the 1990s, prior to which time the island economy was based on fishing, canning, and sponge diving. Throughout the early 2000s, the EU disbursed funds to encourage local fishers to relinquish their commercial fishing licenses with the stated intent of mitigating the effects of overfishing in the Mediterranean basin, but, according to other interpretations, this served to promote neoliberal market expansion (see Connolly 2013: 21). Locals invested these funds in various ways, renovating residential structures to transform them into summer lodging for vacationers, or retrofitting fishing vessels as pleasure craft, all in the hope of partaking in the expected bonanza of a bourgeoning tourism economy. The island today is significantly given over to seasonal mass tourism, and according to some local voices, the pursuit of tourist dollars has resulted in increased social atomization, greater competition, a lessening of community spirit among islanders, and an artificially enhanced perception of the dangers that forced migration poses for the island that is manifested in a range of previously uncommon hostile attitudes toward migrants (see Orsini 2014).

Looking to the past—three generations ago and earlier—Lampedusans were a mobile folk participant in a regional cosmopolitanism that crossed cultural divides. Navigating down to the North African coasts, fishers took up temporary residency in various Tunisian port cities, where small communities of Lampedusans lived year-round. This phase of Lampedusan history is well within living memory of elderly people on the island. Fishing and trade relations bridged long distances throughout the Mediterranean basin (Friese 2010: 330–331), but following World War II and the eventual expulsion of Italians from Tunisia, Algeria, and Libya, and the later extension of European borders to North African territorial waters, this intercultural communication based in a hybrid *ecumene* spanning the southern Mediterranean Sea ceased to exist. In this we see an affirmation of Jeremy Boissevain's (2013: 20) claim that in the past the Mediterranean was more fully integrated across civilizational boundaries than it is today. Island fishers now ply only the narrow coastal waters, and sell their catches to local hotels and restaurants during the high season. A highly mobile seafaring people have been rendered dependent in their subaltern role to a form of economic development adapted from the center (see Cassano 2012: 2). Not only do they stand helpless before a series of economic changes that have altered their ways of life, but now they must also confront the challenges posed by an unabated transnational population flow, the politics of which they are powerless to influence.

Due in part to increased media attention to undocumented migration to Lampedusa over the past decade, a new cosmopolitan category of people has arisen there. They are predominantly outsiders, an artistic/creative class of expatriates coming from across Italy, some of them full-time activists, including musicians, filmmakers, environmentalists, and students who live there seasonally. In 2009, a group of politically engaged youth formed the Associazione Culturale Askavusa (hereafter, Askavusa),[3] an alter-globalist and anti-capitalist association that has sought to raise awareness of, among other things, the experiences of undocumented migrants and of the militarization of the island that accompanies the enforcement of EU boundaries. Askavusa's core values imagine an upheaval of the extant social, political, and economic order, the abolishment of all national borders, and significantly, the end of Western hegemony over the Global South. Askavusa's vision of Lampedusa is that of an island defined by its centrality in the flux and flow of movement across the Mediterranean throughout history. Their convictions are not simply affirmed by its members, but regularly put into action, most prominently in early 2011 when Askavusa, in conjunction with the efforts of the local parish association, assisted in the orchestration of a grassroots effort to assist migrants in need. At this critical juncture, Lampedusans came out in large numbers to offer aid to desperate newcomers. But as we will see below, local goodwill seemingly evaporated at various points throughout the course of the 2011 crisis.

Askavusa bears the mark of a concern with the subaltern experience and an opposition to authority in all its guises, especially that of the nation-state. They are opposed to present-day programs of border enforcement that have restricted the arrival of non-EU migrants to Italy via progressively draconian legislation that has facilitated detention and deportation. In early 2014, as a counterpoint to official policy and by extension to what De Genova (2013) calls "the border spectacle"[4]—wherein a militaristic brand of humanitarianism sets the tone of the state's relationship to outsiders excluded from the rights of citizenship—Askavusa, in conjunction with over a dozen civil society groups and activists from across Italy, drafted the *Carta di Lampedusa* (Charter of Lampedusa 2014).[5] An online document translated into English, French, German and Spanish, this charter calls for the wholesale dismantling of the nation-state system and the global capitalist order along with it. Among its most noteworthy sections are those that affirm the values of anti-racism, the right to live and work in any national jurisdiction independent of presumed legality or illegality and regardless of existing labor market needs; abolishment of visas and immigration quotas; demilitarization and dismantling of borders; and the universal right to education, healthcare, welfare, access to public resources, and funds for the preservation of culture.

As a declaration, the charter clearly sees an opportunity for radical change within the current moment of crisis, and effectively distills the ethos of a style of activism concerned with precipitating the demise of the current liberal democratic global order. In its stead is to emerge a new system, one that does not stultify humanity's potential but rather is premised on and recognizes the inherent dignity of all, regardless of age, sex, race, or religion. Charles Lindholm and José Zuquete (2010) diagnose such styles of activist thought as representing what they call "aurora movements," which envision a "new dawn" that presents an alternative to the current neoliberal moment with its clear winners and losers. Aurora movements represent a dissident animus against the dominant extant order, and believe that the fate of the twenty-first century will be determined by a contest between two very different visions of the future, namely, one defined by a homogeneity of a singular market civilization, versus one defined by a diversity of civilizations, all on an equal footing with one another (Lindholm and Zuquete 2010: 8). Their members see radical activism as constituting an identity-forming process that enables self-empowerment and self-realization, and like the activists organized within what Manuel Castells (2012) calls "networks of outrage and hope," they are connected and Internet-savvy. In sum, the conditions that facilitate the emergence of such movements are found in the social and cultural dislocations, precarities, and uncertainties that mark late modernity.

Clearly, the ethic of cosmopolitanism exemplified by Askavusa and its members is not of the demotic or popular variety, characteristic of fishers from an earlier time who ranged far and wide and possessed a worldly grounding in salty realities, but rather of a more formal, even formalized, kind. It champions the ideal of global citizenship and is defined by internationalist political discourses. At the same time, it has little direct connection to the lives of everyday Lampedusans, be they of the older generation with its knowledge and perspectives of toiling with their hands and enduring hardship and uncertainty, or a younger generation forced to adapt to altogether new conditions of uncertainty in the present. Yet Askavusa activists have mastered an appreciation of island history and deftly tapped into some local currents and images of the island, most specifically its image as a symbol of peaceful encounters and refuge within the southern reaches of the Mediterranean Sea. By representing Lampedusa as the center of a boundless sea of difference, these activists' imaginings subvert narratives that conceive of the inner sea as a place of borders and boundaries, of insiders and outsiders. Their idealized set of schemata casts Lampedusa as an important center within a wider multicultural and multi-confessional pluriverse that they deem to have been characteristic of the Mediterranean Sea in ages gone by, and therefore as an extinguished civilizational arcadia compromised by the emergence of the nation-state system.

The Sediments of History

The source on which Askavusa's cosmopolitan imaginings of Lampedusa are based consists in part of an account contained in an obscure early seventeenth-century document, namely a diary of travels across the Mediterranean Sea authored by the English courtier and diplomat Sir Kenelm Digby, titled *Journey of a Voyage into the Mediterranean* and published in 1628. Within a short passage of this book, the reader is informed that Lampedusa is uninhabited, yet widely used as a site of refuge by Christian and Muslim seafarers during inclement weather (Digby 1628: 72). On an isolated coastal inlet (today called Cala Madonna), Digby suggests the presence of an hermitage at which Christian and Muslim mariners leave offerings of bread and oil, and that the site offers refuge to the travel-weary. Additional sources (see Fragapane 1993: 487–493) corroborate Digby's account, adding that the site, which was in a shallow cave, contained both a shrine to the Virgin and the remains of a Turkish marabout, and was thus of some religious importance. In the words of one interlocutor—a young activist associated with Askavusa who advocates locally for the provision of services to undocumented migrants—the significance of this holy site was that it was the focal point of an island where mariners could land and expect a suspension of all hostilities—a politically autonomous and liminal zone where all arms could be laid down in anticipation of peaceful recuperation from the arduous life of the sea. Thus, evidently, Lampedusa is, or

Figure 8.1 Cave at Cala Madonna, a purported sacred site presided over by a syncretic recluse in the early seventeeth century. Photo by Author.

at least holds the potential to be, a place of peaceful coexistence and non-violence, and even an ecumenical space.

Much can be made of this story, and its utility to cosmopolitan yearnings is clear, but despite its history as part of a wider Mediterranean *ecumene*, Lampedusa today is fully incorporated into a much more exclusionary pan-European formation. The hardened attitudes arising out of these vastly changed circumstances can be observed locally, through the lens of current events surrounding the steady arrival of asylum seekers from North Africa. To be brief, the new, small-scale, tourist-sector entrepreneurs experience potentially severe financial hardship in a bad tourism season, and refugee flows are not good for tourism. Gone are many Lampedusans' social memory of long-standing ties with Tunisia, Algeria, and Libya only a few decades ago (cf. Orsini 2014), and in its place an exclusionary form of Euro-Italian nativism has flourished. In this context, the members of Askavusa present themselves as harbingers of a return to the earlier, idealized, symbolic meanings of the little island, and their perception of some locals' attitudes is tinged with regret. They regard Lampedusans as having forsaken their true transnational Mediterranean essence in exchange for the ethically questionable proceeds of mass tourism. According to one Askvusa member, Enzo, Lampedusans are perennially unhappy, prone to lamenting their own circumstances but frequently indifferent to the plight of others who truly are in dire circumstances. "If you ask me", he told me, "I think there is another reality to understand, and it is more important than the proceeds of a tourist season. The fact is that the mass tourism economy has made Lampedusans intolerant and racist, and why? Because refugees eat into tourism revenues." He continued, revealingly: "But you know Lampedusa has always been a place of African and European contact. What we see now is nothing new. Have you been to the cave at Cala Madonna? That's the history of Lampedusa. It has always been a place of flux and movement of all peoples. Lampedusa belongs to Africa, too".

As an active member of Askavusa, Enzo has contributed to the establishment of Porto M, the local museum of migration, which exhibits objects scavenged from the "boat graveyard," a large field where migrants' boats are sequestered by government authorities for eventual disposal. The displayed items constitute a record of crossings made by irregular migrants, the majority of them refugees fleeing catastrophic circumstances, and stand as a testimony to the hardships of people who arrive on Lampedusa's shores only to be denied a voice by the bureaucratic apparatus that processes their claims. Assembled into installations of various kinds, the objects are intended to serve as a reminder of the borderlessness of the Mediterranean, itself a metaphor for the alternatives to contemporary forms of exclusionary politics. This is what Enzo tells me, and when I ask him how, fundamentally, these efforts are received locally, he hesitates and notes that much of the work he and his colleagues do is best appreciated by outsiders, such as myself:

> This museum spreads awareness among tourists who might want to know more about migration to Lampedusa. There aren't many, but still … As for Lampedusans, they have become closed. Not all of them, certainly, but … they have no patience, and are afraid that migration is tarnishing the island's image, and they feel this way because they have been seduced by the promise of tourism revenues. But for us, the root of all evil is always the same: the capitalist system, the love of money, imperialism, and the tyranny of the banks and of high finance. Migrants who come to these shores are the victims of the same types of processes that are making Italians suffer as well [see also Muehlebach, this volume].

Enzo says this as a Lampedusan. His proclamations as to the cause of ills and misfortunes near and far coincide with his deeply humane

Figure 8.2 Seized migrant vessels deposited in the "boat graveyard" for eventual disposal. Photo by Author.

perspectives. In his efforts he is accompanied by several associates, including a group of energetic organizers who in 2009 inaugurated Lampedusa's annual film festival, LampedusaInFestival, which engages themes of migration and incorporates an amateur film competition. Entrants' films engage migration themes within a framework of intercultural dialogue. The event is sponsored by the local administration and also receives funds from a number of NGOs, themselves registered recipients of UNESCO monies, as well as a number of local businesses—restaurants, hotels, and tourist shops—that view the festival as a potential attraction for summer tourists. Indeed, according to Enzo, attracting visitors to the island to spend money is one of the intended beneficial effects of the festival, and he is keenly aware of the spin-off benefits to the wider community. After all, the sense of precarity inherent to the tourism sector, where success is subject to the vagaries of wider regional developments, is at the root of local hostility toward migrants in the first place.

The opening ceremony for the 2011 edition of this festival was held in a locality just outside town near an iconic sculpture called *The Door of Europe* (*La porta dell'Europa*), an impressive stylized arch built by Sicilian sculptor Mimmo Paladino that, though erected only in 2008, is already in a state of disrepair as a result of wear caused by salt spray and petty acts of vandalism committed by local youth. A few meters away, an interpretive dance troupe presented a performance titled *Lettere dal Mare* ("Letters from the Sea"), consisting of several dance sets executed on a large stage upon which the bow of a migrant boat wreck was arranged as a backdrop. These were set to compositions by musician Antoine Michel, a Franco-Tunisian artist noted for a brand of multicultural music that bridges the northern and southern shore of the Mediterranean through hybrid sounds evoking the spirit of dialogue. One especially poignant performance in *Lettere dal Mare* evoked the lives and sufferings of late nineteenth- and early twentieth-century Italian immigrants to the Americas. Performers in period costumes danced a narrative of suffering and hope as a storyteller recited lyrical prose contained in letters sent from across the sea, conveying the dreams and desires of those many Italians who ventured a long way from home in search of a better life. This artistic rendering of the Italian immigrant experience was neatly juxtaposed to current developments on the island, and its purpose could not be clearer.

This dance performance was followed up with a folk music concert by a local singer-songwriter staged on top of a World War

II Italian naval bunker located in the vicinity. The ceremony was intended to open up a space of reflection on the Mediterranean as a place of cultural understanding, of openness toward the other, and of the possibilities of human enrichment that this entails. Gianmarco, one of the directors of the festival, concisely detailed for me what he wanted to accomplish: "through the festival we are trying to create a different Lampedusa, a more welcoming one, where people are willing to undertake a more critical view of migration policy, and in the end hopefully what will prevail is a new, more open, understanding of this island's place in the world." At the end of the opening events, the first scheduled item on the program took place in a local dance hall. It and consisted of a series of film screenings followed by public lectures delivered by special guests invited by Askavusa and the festival organizers. Apparently, the municipal council made no contributions to the festival, and the mayor Bernardino de Rubeis and local councilors were conspicuously absent from the events. Likewise, the proceedings were poorly attended by residents of Lampedusa, who mostly steered clear altogether. It becomes obvious in short order that the cosmopolitan performances and purposes of LampedusaInFestival are detached from the community for which it purports to speak.

Figure 8.3 Interpretive dance at opening ceremonies of LampedusaInFestival. Photo by Author.

Lampedusa attracts seekers of various kinds, primarily from Italy and elsewhere in Europe, most of whom espouse visions of a Mediterranean of peaceful coexistence and accommodation. Reference to a sampling of individuals I met and spoke with from among the attendees of the opening events of *LampedusaInFestival* should suffice to provide an impression of this. One of my first interlocutors that evening was an Englishwoman who, with apparent financial backing from Amnesty International, claimed to be on the island to negotiate the purchase of an abandoned migrant vessel for use in raising public awareness of recent events on the island by sailing from Lampedusa to London on the occasion of the 2012 Summer Olympics. I met a fine arts MA student from the Netherlands who was hoping to photograph refugees for a photography project, an Italian man who was working on his master's degree at London's School of Oriental and African Studies, a Brazilian journalist who was spending the summer on the island because she wanted to write a book on the Arab Spring, and then some German exchange students who came equipped with video cameras, hoping to produce an amateur documentary. On subsequent days I met several other activists and students, and was made aware of the presence of a Canadian human rights activist who was kayaking the world in the cause of refugee rights and had navigated a loop around Lampedusa and then stationed himself on the island briefly in the interest of "monitoring" the arrival of migrant vessels. Later that summer, this latter visitor was physically assaulted by an angry local man displeased with his activism (Gruppo EveryOne 2011).

All of these privileged outsiders conceive of Lampedusa as both a site of cosmopolitan encounter and a symbolically laden place, lying as it does at a civilizational crossroads, which renders it—or, better, ought to render it—a place of humanitarian relief and comfort, a space defined by a constitutive hybridity that resists the imposition of unifying or totalizing visions of any kind. This cosmopolitan understanding of the Mediterranean as a hybridized border zone is not new, and indeed finds resonance in several scholarly and literary formulations, such as in the writings of the Italian historical sociologist Franco Cassano (2012: 146–149) and Argentine semiotician Walter Mignolo (2000: 49–88). A complementary vision presented by David Abulafia highlights the dialectics of confrontation and coexistence between Islamic and Christian peoples in the inner sea (Abulafia 2011: 246–251; 258–270; 281–282; 340ff.); while Christian Bromberger (2007: 298) sees the Mediterranean as a sea that binds together "a system of complementary differences" conditioned by history and maintained within a field of reciprocal oppositions. Whatever the scope of past transactions among the many peoples inhabiting the shores of the Mediterranean Sea, the end result, clearly, has been the emergence of a set of "family resemblances" among all of them (see Albera and Blok 2001), recently expressed by Naor Ben-Yehoyada (2014) in terms of the metaphor of cousinage. As David Ohana (2003) points out, several Mediterranean writers over the last century have likewise espoused such a view of the region. Albert Camus, Albert Memmi, Tahar Ben-Jelloun, Jorge Semprún, Naguib Mahfouz, and Edmond Jabès all share an opposition to violence, integral nationalism, dictatorship, and ideological radicalism, an antiracism stemming from their tolerance of the other, their acceptance of the foreign and the different, a multicultural outlook that foreshadows postmodernist discourse, and their affirmation of dialogue as a form of human activity (ibid.: 59).

To what extent does this particular vision of the Mediterranean resonate with Lampedusans themselves, now and in the past? As noted above, the seafaring history of Lampedusa rendered its people mobile, economically interdependent with communities across the waters to the south, and fully enmeshed within a regional network that permitted considerable cultural exchange across linguistic and religious divides. In addition to this, the present analysis benefits by noting Lampedusa's status, within the moral geography of the Italian nation-state, as situated within the *meridione*, or South of Italy. As ethnic Sicilians, Lampedusans, like all *meridionali*, have endured economic marginalization for generations and adapted to it by way of a long-standing practice of labor migration to northern Italy. Their status as migrants within their own country since the postwar period made them subject to cultural ostracism born of a northern Italian prejudice that regarded southern Italians as backward, poor, lazy, and culturally defective overall (see Schneider 1998).

In the wake of Italian Unification, southern Italians were considered racially and morally compromised because they were close to Africa and moreover of Mediterranean rather than European "stock." Allegedly predisposed to crime and given to disorderliness, southern Italians were the apparent cultural antithesis of Europeans. As Enrica Capussotti (2010) argues, these longstanding attitudes provide the rhetorical antecedent to a much more contemporary set of inhospitable sentiments toward new arrivals from a different kind of *meridione*, namely the Global South. As such, we note a shift in conceptual frontiers: Sicilians, or indeed Lampedusans, are no longer *meridionali*, but rather guardians of the southern outpost of Europe. They are Europeans, even if only marginally.

The Anxieties of Being Marginally European

The vastly changed circumstances of the present, defined in some ways by an emergent perception that Italy is existentially threatened by immigration—a notion explicitly championed by ex-Premier Silvio Berlusconi, who claimed in 2006 that Italy must reject multiculturalism—have brought about a shift of categories of identification and a conceptual rebordering of Europe. The language of "invasion" and even a Muslim "Reverse Crusade" owes much to the writing of such figures as journalist Oriana Fallaci (2004, 2010), who has worked to render such fears respectable. The insidious form of racism that inheres in such a vision is not based explicitly on any assumption that biological differences render populations incompatible with one another, but more prosaically relies on the belief that cultural difference breeds antipathy. As Balibar (1991: 21) suggests, it is "a racism which, at first sight, does not postulate the superiority of certain groups or peoples in relation to others but 'only' the harmfulness of abolishing frontiers, the incompatibility of lifestyles and traditions." Such a vision of the apparent incommensurability of civilizations in the Italian context proceeds on the basis of an alarmism that suggests a demographic and cultural decline in the face of mass immigration from Muslim countries (Bialasiewicz 2006: 713). In this new imaginary, southern Italy is indelibly a part of a Europe that is under siege by a racialized other, and, to borrow from Jonathan Xavier Inda (2007), the repudiation of such outsiders is unquestioningly regarded as necessary to the long-term integrity of the nation-state.

Lampedusa, by an accident of geography, is the physical gate—an entry point guarded in part through a biopolitics of otherness (Fassin 2001)—that circumscribes the new arrivals at every opportunity. This is indeed the case insofar as Lampedusa is a key site for the policing of EU borders, but what does it entail for local people? Here we must take into account the larger predicament that Lampedusans find themselves in, reliant as they are on a seasonal tourist economy that is vulnerable to the disruptions caused by humanitarian emergencies (Friese 2010: 334). Once the objects, they are now the agents of what Albahari (2009: 148) calls "a disparaging moral geography" that demonizes migrants as a threat to national well-being. However, on Lampedusa this particular development is tied to the circumstances of the local economy and expectations of seasonal revenue, so it is not accidental that intolerant sentiments should come to the fore alongside expressions of resentment about Italian government's initial inaction and slow response to the crisis. More than one interlocutor in Askavusa communicated the suspicion that the Berlusconi government had let the crisis fester for several weeks for strictly political gain—specifically, that it had facilitated the creation of a media image of a small Italian locality swamped by irregular migrants for the sole purpose of fostering support for its anti-immigration policies (see Cuttitta 2012; Campesi 2011). As one woman told me, "When people see the footage of the migrants on television, they do not see Lampedusa, but rather they see Italy. And this hardens their perception of the problems that we are facing." This perspective has some resonance within the wider community, which in its entirety has time and again come forth to offer whatever relief it can to migrants during any period of crisis following a shipwreck. This includes preparation and distribution of food, collection of used clothes, and the wholesale participation of the island's small maritime crews in search and rescue and recovery operations alongside the vessels of the Italian Coast Guard. Such efforts represent the widely recognized duty of following the law of the sea, highlighting in this case a particularly clear ethical obligation inherent in local level mobilization in the absence of the requisite state resources necessary for such operations (cf. Muehlebach 2012).

One local restaurateur strongly, and somewhat flamboyantly, expressed frustration with the slowness of the government's measures to alleviate the crisis. Apparently chagrined by the loss of revenues in the summer of 2011, he posted an angry placard at the entrance of his seafood restaurant that read, in bold, uppercase letters, "Commercial enterprise nearing bankruptcy. Immigration and central government to blame. Compensate us!!!" (Attivita commerciale prossima al fallimento. Colpa del fenomeno immigrazione e del governo centrale. Risarciteci!!!). On the other hand, local musings and muted expressions of annoyance are directed toward hoteliers, whom locals widely consider to be in a position to benefit from the presence of military, police, and humanitarian personnel on the island—the very people who reside there because of the steady stream of undocumented migrants. But of course such lodgers are on Lampedusa to work, not to go on boat tours, rent cars, or spend money on dining and drinking in restaurants.

However, the most palpable frustrations were directed at the migrants themselves for their alleged role in disrupting the tranquility of local life. Public anger over the apparent disorder that accompanied the sudden influx of migrants in early 2011 spurred the mayor, Bernardino De Rubeis, to address the perceived problem of "begging and non-decorous behaviors" (*l'accattonaggio e comportamenti non decorosi*) by passing an ordinance prohibiting the use of public places as "sites of bivouac and excretion" (*siti di bivacco e deiezione*). Clearly meant to assuage local anger about an untenable situation left to fester for too long, this ordinance did little more than frame undocumented migrants as messy, unclean, disorderly Africans, and therefore as a foil to the allegedly tidy, disciplined, civic-minded Lampedusans (read: Europeans). It was symbolic in scope, and intended for local consumption. It was also illegal. De Rubeis was shortly thereafter investigated by the public prosecutor of the Region of Agrigento (Procura di Agrigento) for abuse of office and incitement to racial hatred, and was forced to rescind the ordinance (Rai GiornaleRadio 2011).

Outside the mayor's office, local anxieties were frequently expressed in more or less explicitly racialist terms. Their noteworthiness resides in how they resurrect older historical constructions of the other. One businesswoman whose livelihood depends on tourism offered me her stark perspective on the crisis that had peaked some weeks earlier: "Lampedusa was uninhabitable. We could not sleep with our doors open anymore, and even now, we're afraid. The Arabs want to reclaim this island." When probed further, she explained:

> There is a long history, don't you know? The reason Lampedusa was not settled until the nineteenth century is because of the Moorish corsairs (*corsari mori*), in sum, slave raiders from Africa, who would depopulate the island, so no one could ever live here. Even now, the Arabs will come here make themselves the bosses. We have to be vigilant, because we are a vulnerable island.

Another interlocutor—a middle-aged local man—was afraid for the safety of his daughters: "These Arabs would leer at the girls and make lewd comments. Who do they think they are! We need to protect our girls from these *delinquenti*!" One elderly resident expressed a need for vigilantism: "Lampedusa is alone. The Italian government is nowhere. They did not come to help us, and so, what do we do? The state is us! We can't just stay here and let these people run us over! These Saracens (*saraceni*)! We must protect ourselves!

It's not a new thing, this (*non è cosa nuova, questa*)." Another man declared,

> Ever since these Turks (*turchi*[6]) came everything has changed here. Tourism is blocked and nobody is coming for vacations anymore with all the mess they made. They broke into my father's house and stole food, and made themselves at home when he was away. We had to throw away the towels and sheets and even the mattresses.

Dirty, disorderly *saraceni, turchi*, a menace to women, invaders who want to "reclaim" the island: all these stereotypes of the Islamic menace hark back to antiquated sets of images that have been resurrected at a moment of crisis.[7] Furthermore, the sentiments based in these fears have found expression in concrete action. On 28 March 2011, at the height of the migration emergency, an angry protest in the main port area of Lampedusa laid bare some festering local sentiments. Fishers dragged abandoned migrant vessels onto the main quay to impede access for Italian coast guard vessels carrying rescued migrants, and the spirited shouts of protesters enjoined the migrants to go back where they came from. Participants clearly were angry about the Italian government's mismanagement of the migrant influx, but this does not constitute the entirety of the story. According to one published account, fishers blocked the port simply because, as some locals readily admitted, "they did not want migrants landing in Lampedusa" (Coddington et al. 2012: 35). This acute sense of hostility came to a head in early September 2011 on the occasion of a riot by inmates at the migrant processing center. Several local men, evidently upset by what they perceived as migrants' unreasonable demands for better food and quicker legal processing, violently attacked and assaulted the rioting inmates (Cuttitta 2012: 109). Many locals were anguished by the violent behavior of some of their compatriots, which they regarded as tarnishing the image of Lampedusa as open toward those in need (see De Pasquale and Arena 2011:104ff.). And yet the question of need, or indeed, of who justly deserves assistance from government, is at the heart of the matter. Lampedusa, after all, does not have a high school for its youth, a hospital for the sick and injured, or a birthing clinic. Islanders are forced to travel regularly to the Sicilian mainland to pursue secondary education, get treatment for injuries and illnesses, and even to give birth, creating the absurd situation in which no Lampedusan is ever born on Lampedusa. The Italian state's failure to provide these elementary services cannot but serve as an irritant to local perceptions of the refugee crisis.

The tragic events of October 2013 and April 2015—respectively, two shipwrecks that claimed a total of more than 400 lives off Lampedusa's shores, and a series of disasters that killed more than 1,500 migrants en route to Lampedusa—have attenuated some of the more inhospitable local tendencies but also affirmed the marginalization of Lampedusans themselves in national and regional debates about the role of the Italian state and the EU in addressing the ongoing refugee crisis. Meanwhile, the island remains an excellent site for the unveiling of policies devised from above, such as when on 3 October 2014, President of the European Parliament Martin Schulz, invited as part of a commemoration of the deaths of October 2013 one year after the event, affirmed a commitment to developing an entirely new set of asylum and migration policies at the EU level. This was followed by the announcement of the launch of Operation Triton, a border patrol program to manage undocumented migration on the Mediterranean Sea. While its description is couched in humanitarian language, Triton's purpose is to conduct maritime surveillance that would effectively enhance the deterrence and deflection of migrants from Italy's shores (Mountz 2011). Well attended by numerous dignitaries, including Italian federal ministers, senators, and the president of the region of Sicily and mayor of Lampedusa, the event's declared intent of commemorating the previous year's tragedy at sea was unconvincing to local people and regarded as downright hypocritical by members of Askavusa and other activists in attendance. The event was preceded by peaceful protest against various EU policies, such as support for the allegedly right-wing movement in Ukraine that ousted Russian-backed Viktor Yanukovych in February 2014, and against inaction in the face of countless migrant deaths at sea over the previous years. Within the assembly hall, Martin Schulz's speech was interrupted by intermittent applause intended to disrupt, and then by a member of Askavusa who stood up to accuse him and his entire entourage of being racists and Nazis. Amid shouting and insults, the protester was ejected from the proceedings and shortly joined by his supporters outside the event venue. In the final analysis, the entire affair was equal parts social drama and political theater, in which most of the more prominent dramatis personae were not Lampedusan at all. Yet the event served just the same as an opportunity for Lampedusans to underscore their own marginality and call attention to the need for social and economic development assistance, including better healthcare access and better funding for local schools.

Conclusion

Aware of how a swarm of television cameras, reporters, and activists could shape national perceptions of Lampedusa as an undesirable vacation destination and thus diminish the tourism revenue that is essential to the island economy, local people could only seethe at what they observed about these media workers and lend their political support to whoever could promise to address their problems. In 2011, incumbent Italian Premier Silvio Berlusconi was the answer. His visit the island in mid-2011 had been well attended. In his speech to the audience assembled outside the town hall, the Italian premier promised to restore the tranquility Lampedusa had enjoyed before the unexpected influx by promptly transporting migrants to processing centers on the Italian mainland. Further, and to great general enthusiasm, Berlusconi confessed to a love for Lampedusa and its hospitality and natural beauty, which had compelled him to begin arranging to purchase a local villa for his future summer vacations, and additionally to provide federal funds for the construction of a world-class casino and golf resort. That these were all empty promises would not matter come the 2013 general election, when Lampedusans supported Berlusconi's coalition, led by his party, *Il popolo della libertà*, with 56% of the popular vote (Ministero dell'Interno n.d.).

Local people have reacted with consternation and even outright hostility toward undocumented migrants and toward Askavusa as well, saying it holds up an image of Lampedusa as open to the world, which it cannot afford to be. One local man—a retired fisher and pensioner—expressed the matter to me in especially succinct terms, betraying a kind of subdued resentment toward Askavusa and the many seekers who visit the island when he asked, in a moment of reflection, why so many outsiders should come to the island to "look down upon us all as poor ignorant islanders who understand nothing." This unhappy sentiment is worthy of consideration, as it reflects a perspective that can be taken as a counterpoint to outside activists' engagements with local realities and local people. It also distills an element of friction between well-intentioned activists and beleaguered locals in a time of crisis. Moreover, a clear division in how refugees are perceived reflects apparently incommensurable understandings about the place of Lampedusa within the region, in both the past and the present. Here I have provided a glimpse of realities on Lampedusa that represents in microcosm a set of patterns that may reappear in varying configurations throughout southern Europe. Lampedusans are aware of their effective marginalization by a series of processes over which they have no control, to say nothing of the highly mediatized treatment of migration and the degree of militarization of their territory and surrounding waters. This has yielded a shared sense of being flotsam and jetsam, relegated amidst inexorable forces to the subaltern status of wary observers who can only hope for the best, but who frequently express their sense of precariousness through hostility toward others considerably more marginalized than them.

As to the alternatives presented by Askvusa and other activists, they are a mutation of pre-existing patterns of dispositions of openness toward the outside world that do not mesh with local visions. If history is a resource to be mobilized in response to the circumstances of the present, then it seems that there are two seemingly irreconcilable, probably inconstant interpretations of the past on Lampedusa that have nonetheless been seized on for purposes of orienting people to Lampedusa's changing place within the wider region and making sense of the transformations that have altered local life over the past decade and more. What is certain is that for much of the rest of the world, Lampedusa has come to symbolize the securitization of European Union borders and the project to halt refugee flows. In that capacity, the island will continue to remain the focus of outside attention that seldom pays heed to the view from the locality.

Acknowledgements

I wish to thank the members of Askavusa and other interlocutors on Lampedusa for their assistance and willing participation in this research. York University colleagues and graduate students offered input on an earlier version of this piece over the course of a working papers series held by the Department of Anthropology. I wish especially to thank Christopher Kyriakides and Daphne Winland for their impressions and suggestions. All shortcomings of this work remain my own.

Antonio Sorge is a political and historical anthropologist and Lecturer in the Department of Anthropology at York University in Toronto, Canada. His interests include rural change, social memory, violence, and the state. More recently, his research has engaged themes of immigration, cultural pluralism, anti-immigration politics, and the rise of neo-nationalism in Europe. He is author of *Legacies of Violence: History, Society, and the State in Sardinia* (2015).

Notes

1. The term *clandestino* is one of popular disapprobation and does not constitute a legal category in Italy. Instead, the major legal categories include *Rifugiato* or refugee, a forced migrant whose claim for asylum has been accepted; and *Richiedente asilo* or asylum seeker, a migrant who has yet to present her/his case to the authorities and be judged to be either a refugee (legitimate forced migrant) and thus possessing a right of residency in Italy, or an economic (or voluntary) migrant lacking residency rights. See Düvell (2008) for a comprehensive discussion of "clandestinity" as a politicized construct.
2. As a side note, my own existential givens may be a datum of some interest with respect to the laid-back tone and temper of social relationships I was able to foster over my stay. As a male researcher from the Global North of Italian ancestry and marked by my "whiteness" in a moment of particular anxiety throughout Italy over the presence of racialized newcomers arriving via Lampedusa, I had privileged access to a wide range of interlocutors who did not hold my presence in suspicion or question my research activities. The methodological implications of this fact are noteworthy and invite reflection on issues of access and representation.
3. This name, which translates into English as the "Barefoot Cultural Association," uses the Sicilian dialect's word for "barefoot" to symbolize an intimate, close-up engagement with the realities of the island.
4. Paolo Cuttitta (2012: 92ff.) offers an examination of the concept of border spectacle by likening the border-policing operations on Lampedusa as a performance that, in its orchestration of the processes of migrants' reception, curates an image of the role of the Italian state as simultaneously protecting its citizens from an illegal "invasion" and offering humanitarian assistance to vulnerable migrants worthy of compassion. See also Castronovo 2011.
5. See Carta di Lampedusa (n.d.). Retrieved 12 November 2015 from http://www.lacartadilampedusa.org. This document was drafted after an initial online video conference with participants from across Italy on 29 November 2013, which was followed by a conference on Lampedusa from 31 January to 2 February 2014.
6. "Turks" or *turchi* is a catch-all term, part of an older language of folk Orientalism in southern Italy that refers to the generalized other who comes from the Muslim world, and does not refer explicitly to ethnic Turks or citizens of the modern Republic of Turkey.

7. From a related perspective, these views represent a conceptual "rebordering" of Europe, here reflected in an apparent realignment of Southern Italian sympathies toward the Global North and away from a pan-Mediterranean identity shared with peoples bordering this inland sea. See Buonauito and Laforest (2011) for a discussion of this dynamic in the context of Naples, and Hettne (2002) for a broader theoretical examination. See also Loftsdóttir and Björnsdóttir in this volume.

References

Abulafia, D. 2011. *The Great Sea: A Human History of the Mediterranean.* London:
Allen Lane. Albahari, M. 2009. "Between Mediterranean Centrality and European Periphery: Migration and Heritage in Southern Italy." *International Journal of Euro-Mediterranean Studies* 1: 141–162.
Albera, D., and A. Blok. 2001. "The Mediterranean as a Field of Ethnological Study: A Retrospective," in *Anthropologie de la Méditerranée/Anthropology of the Mediterranean*, ed. D. Albera, A. Blok, and C. Bromberger, 15–37. Aix-en-Provence, France: Maisonneuve et Larose.
Balibar, E. 1991. "Is there a Neo-Racism?" in *Race, Nation, Class: Ambiguous Identities*, ed. E.Balibar and I. Wallerstein, 17–28. New York: Verso.
Ben-Yehoyada, N. 2014. "Transnational Political Cosmology: A Central Mediterranean Example." *Comparative Studies in Society and History* 56(4): 870–901.
Bialasiewicz, L. 2006. "'The Death of the West': Samuel Huntington, Oriana Fallaci and a New 'Moral' Geopolitics of Births and Bodies." *Geopolitics* 11: 701–724.
Boissevain, J. 2013. *Factions, Friends, and Feasts: Anthropological Perspectives on the Mediterranean.* New York and Oxford: Berghahn Books.
Bromberger, C. 2007. "Bridge, Wall, Mirror: Coexistence and Confrontations in the Mediterranean World." *History and Anthropology* 18(3): 291–307.
Buonauito, C., and M.-H. Laforest. 2011. "Spelling Out Exclusion in Southern Italy." *Social Identities* 17(1): 41–59.
Campesi, G. 2011. *The Arab Spring and the Crisis of the European Border Regime: Manufacturing Emergency in the Lampedusa Crisis.* European University Institute Working Paper, Robert Schuman Centre for Advanced Studies 59.
Capussotti, E. 2010. "Nordisti Contro Sudisti: Internal Migration and Racism in Turin, Italy: 1950s and 1960s." *Italian Culture* 28(2): 121–138.

Carta di Lampedusa. 2014. Retrieved 12 November 2015 from http://www.lacartadilampedusa.org.
Cassano, F. 2012. *Southern Thought and Other Essays on the Mediterranean*. New York: Fordham University Press.
Castells, M. 2012. *Networks of Outrage and Hope: Social Movements in the Internet Age*. Cambridge: Polity.
Castronovo, A. 2011. "Dalla 'Guerra dei Disperati' alle Navi Galera," in *Il Silenzio degli Altri*, ed. M. Mannoia, 83–93. Rome: Edizioni XL.
Coddington, K., et al. 2012. "Embodied Possibilities, Sovereign Geographies and Island Detention." *Shima: The International Journal of Research into Island Cultures* 6: 27–48.
Connolly, W. 2013. *The Fragility of Things: Self-Organizing Processes, Neoliberal Fantasies, and Democratic Activism*. Durham, NC: Duke University Press.
Cuttitta, P. 2012. *Lo Spettacolo del Confine: Lampedusa tra Produzione e Messa in Scena della Frontiera*. Milan: Mimesis.
De Genova, N. 2013. "Spectacles of Migrant Illegality: The Scene of Exclusion, the Obscene of Inclusion." *Ethnic and Racial Studies* 36(7). DOI:10.1080/01419870.2013.783710.
De Pasquale, E., and N. Arena. 2011. *Sullo Stesso Barcone: Lampedusa e Linosa si Raccontano*. Todi: Tau Editrice.
Digby, K. 1628. *Journal of a Voyage into the Mediterranean*. London: Camden Society.
Düvell, F. 2008. "Clandestine Migration in Europe." *Social Science Information* 47(4): 479–497.
Fallaci, O. 2004. *La Rabbia e l'Orgoglio*. Milan: Rizzoli.
———. 2010. *La Forza della Ragione*. Milan: BUR.
Fassin, D. 2001. "The Biopolitics of Otherness: Undocumented Foreigners and Racial Discrimination in French Public Debate." *Anthropology Today* 17(1): 3–7.
Fragapane, G. 1993. *Lampedusa*. Palermo: Sellerio Editore.
Friese, H. 2010. "The Limits of Hospitality: Political Philosophy, Undocumented Migration and the Local Arena." *European Journal of Social Theory* 13: 323–341.
Gruppo EveryOne. 2011. "Lampedusa. Violenze e intimidazioni contro attivista del
Gruppo EveryOne." *EveryOne: Group for International Cooperation on Human Rights Culture Official Website*. Retrieved 16 August 2015 from http://www.everyonegroup.com/it/EveryOne/MainPage/Entries/2011/9/21_Lampedusa._Violenze_e_intimidazioni_contro_attivista_del_Gruppo_EveryOne.html.
Hettne, B. 2002. "The Europeanization of Europe: Endogenous and Exogenous Dimensions." *European Integration* 24(4): 325–340.
Inda, J. X. 2007. "The Value of Immigrant Life," in *Women and Migration in the U.S.-Mexico Borderlands: A Reader*, ed. D. Segura and P. Zavella, 134–157. Durham, NC: Duke University Press.

Lindholm, C., and J. Zuquete. 2010. *The Struggle for the World: Liberation Movements for the 21st Century*. Stanford, CA: Stanford University Press.

Macdonald, S. 2012. "Presencing Europe's Pasts," in *A Companion to the Anthropology of Europe*, ed. U. Kockel, M. N. Craith, and J. Frykman, 233–252. Oxford: Blackwell.

Mignolo, W. 2000. *Local Histories/Global Designs: Coloniality, Subaltern Knowledges, and Border Thinking*. Princeton, NJ: Princeton University Press.

Ministero dell'Interno, Dipartimento per gli Affari Interni e Territoriali. n.d. "Archivio Storico delle Elezioni – Consultazione dati. Camera 24/02/2013, Area Italia, Circoscrizione Sicilia 1, Provincia Agrigento, Comune Lampedusa e Linosa." Retrieved 25 October 2015 from http://elezionistorico.interno.it/index.php?tpel=C&dtel=24/02/2013&tpa=I&tpe=C&lev0=0&levsut0=0&lev1=24&levsut1=1&lev2=1&levsut2=2&lev3=200&levsut3=3&ne1=24&ne2=1&ne3=10200&es0=S&es1=S&es2=S&es3=N&ms=S.

Mountz, A. 2011. "The Enforcement Archipelago: Detention, Haunting, and Asylum on Islands." *Political Geography* 30: 118–128.

Muehlebach, A. 2012. *The Moral Neoliberal: Welfare and Citizenship in Italy*. Chicago, IL: University of Chicago Press.

Ohana, D. 2003. "Mediterranean Humanism." *Mediterranean Historical Review* 18(1): 59–75.

Orsini, G. 2014. "Un'Isola in Mezzo al Confine: Oltre il Razzismo Istituzionale e Ritorno. Storie di Pesca e Migrazioni a Lampedusa," in *Razzismi, Discriminazioni e Confinamenti*, ed. M. Grasso, 347–358. Rome: Ediesse.

Rai GiornaleRadio. 2011. "A Lampedusa nuovi sbarchi. Indagato il sindaco De Rubeis."

Retrieved 3 December 2015 from http://www.rai.it/dl/grr/notizie/ContentItem-c8be651c-21cc-4c2b-8f06-278ee3a497a1.html?refresh_ce.

Schneider, J., ed. 1998. *Italy's 'Southern Question': Orientalism in One Country*. Oxford: Berg.

Epilogue
Declining Europe

Thomas Hylland Eriksen

A Multiplicity of Crises

Shortly after World War I, the German philosopher Oswald Spengler (1991/1922) published *Der Untergang des Abendlandes* (*The Decline of the West*, literally "The collapse of the land of the evening," or if you like, of the setting sun). Dystopian in its message about the destiny of the old continent, Spengler's analysis assumed that civilizations were like organisms with finite lives, and that European or Western civilization had now lost its momentum and exhausted the potential it had been building up since Carolingian times. Representing a teleological, cyclical philosophy of history, Spengler's perspectives were extremely influential inside and outside the German-speaking world in the interwar years but have rarely been discussed seriously since 1945. Nonetheless, the chapters in this book do resonate somewhat, however distantly, with Spenglerian ideas about aging civilizations losing their collective confidence and sense of direction. An implicit assumption of decline runs throughout this collection, with its focus on boundary-making, economic uncertainty, the enemy within, and controversies about identities and political propositions. We are currently witnessing a confluence of multiple crises in Europe. The sense of uncertainty and insecurity is almost ubiquitous, though in different ways, and partly for differing reasons, across the continent.

The most recent *economic* crisis started with the transnational financial meltdown in autumn 2007 and continued with the so-called Eurozone crisis, the Greek crisis, and economic stagnation and decline in many parts of Europe. The collapse of the Icelandic economy (Durrenberger and Pálsson 2014; Loftsdóttir and Jensen 2014) may have been the most spectacular result of the financial crisis, but the more wide-ranging "Eurozone crisis" that began when several European countries were unable to pay their debts may have deeper and more comprehensive effects. Unemployment numbers are high, especially in Southern Europe but also in northern countries like Finland, and in some regions youth unemployment is well above 50 percent. A commonly held view is that young Western Europeans alive today will be the first generation in a very long time not to improve on their parents' material standard of living—indeed, many foresee a noticeable decline in their prospects.

A perceptible crisis of *identity* can be observed at several levels of social life, from the local to the European level. With the diversification of European populations, mainly in Western Europe, discourses over national identity and its boundaries have become increasingly polarized. The looming question, raised from local communities to the level of the nation-state and beyond, simply concerns the meaning and implications of the word "we" (Eriksen 2015). Questions about whether the community should be based on a shared past or on shared locality, on ethnicity and language or citizenship and place of residence, are now far more than a mere party game indulged in by playful academics: they have become a political minefield animating practices of inclusion and exclusion, alienating people from their neighbors, inspiring anti-elite discourses, and leading to the fast growth of right-wing populist parties, from the Front National in France to the Progress Party in Norway, Jobbik in Hungary, and the True Finns in Finland. While these parties sometimes differ significantly, they all share a suspicion of the non-white stranger and of established, liberal or cosmopolitan elites as ideological fuel.

A third crisis could be labeled a crisis of *security*. A series of terrorist attacks and politically motivated violence—the Madrid and London bombings, the Norwegian terrorist attack that left seventy-seven dead, the 'Laser man' in Malmö attacking random dark-skinned people, the Bataclan massacre in Paris—has struck Europe, visibly intensifying ideological polarization around race and religion. The attack on the USA on 11 September 2001 heightened awareness that globalization and the opening of boundaries entail not just the spread of neoliberal capitalism, fancy foodstuffs, and cheap flights, but also a fundamentally changed security situation. A typical response to the perceived threat of massive political violence is increased securitization (Maguire, Frois, and Zurawski 2014), while a long-term strategy might address the underlying causes of the violence. As noted by the sociologist Frank Furedi (2005), European politicians currently tend to sell fear rather than hope in their campaigns.

Although the consequences of the *climate* crisis have been less dramatic in most of Europe than elsewhere in the world, its reality is a constant reminder of the deep contradictions of the European modern project. Fueled by coal, the industrial revolution was European at the outset, and industrial modernity is unthinkable without fossil fuels (Mitchell 2011). At the present juncture, there is a growing realization that what was the salvation of humanity for two hundred years, namely fossil fuels, is rapidly becoming our damnation. This is not a comforting thought for the continent that set fossil fuel extraction in motion, nor one that boosts collective confidence. If the end of colonialism spelled the end of European world hegemony, then the twilight of the fossil fuel era indicates that European modernity, based on the ultimately destructive practices of fossil fuel extraction, has led the world astray, with dreadful consequences that are now within view.

Related to these crises is a crisis of *legitimacy* at the level of European integration and identity. Whereas the initial engineers of what would become the European Union regarded the then European Economic Community as a recipe for growth and—perhaps mainly—peace, a later generation of leaders raised the stakes by starting a project resembling nation-building. The Maastricht Treaty, signed by most member states in 1992; the replacement of many national currencies with gradual introduction of the ECU, later the euro, in the 1990s; and the Schengen agreement facilitating internal mobility, which was implemented in the same period, all seemed to suggest that a shared European identity was feasible and imminent, and that it could be constructed from above. These optimistic visions from just a couple of decades ago suddenly seem dusty and distant. The current controversies over debt crises, immigration, and foreign policy suggest that Europe has moved a long way from the visions of unity in diversity, "Constitutional patriotism" (*Verfassungspatriotismus*), and a shared sense of Europeanness that were envisioned in the 1990s (Shore 2000). The rifts are many, and Brussels's legitimacy is faltering.

While this book was taking shape, the term crisis was used every day for months in most European media, this time to refer to the "refugee crisis." Widely understood as a consequence of the collapse of the Syrian state, the increased movement of refugees across the Mediterranean in 2015 also had other causes and components, including people fleeing drought-stricken, impoverished lands or brutal regimes in sub-Saharan Africa, or wanton violence and a general loss of hope in Iraq and Afghanistan. The lack of coordination among European countries and the contrasting views of refugees expressed by their politicians reveal not only hugely different national ideologies of inclusion and exclusion within the EU, but also the absence of a clear plan for dealing with the sudden influx of large numbers of refugees. Facing combined, mutually reinforcing crises caused by a volatile and unpredictable financial economy prone to bursting bubbles, the global ramifications of climate change, porous boundaries, and profound disagreements about collective identities, the continent is now sailing into uncharted waters.

What We Can Learn from Koselleck

The chapters of this multifaceted book capture the European crisis or "mess" from different perspectives, thematically and regionally. The book owes its coherence to a common concern with a crisis of identity due to accelerated change, latent contradictions, and politics of inclusion and exclusion. Before reflecting on the main arguments and lessons presented in this book, however, it seems appropriate to give the floor to the theorist who has explored the concept of crisis more than anyone else in European intellectual life. Although his last statement on the subject came three decades ago, Reinhardt Koselleck's analysis of crisis comes across as fresh, penetrating, and pertinent even now.

Famous for his editorship of a landmark work of intellectual genealogy, *Geschichtliche Grundbegriffe* (Basic Concepts in History"), Koselleck had earlier dealt with crisis in his monograph *Critique and Crisis* (Koselleck 1988/1959) and in several of his subsequent publications. Rather than discussing the various and, not least, changing meanings of the word, with the *Schwellenzeit* – threshold time – of the Enlightenment and Industrial Revolution as the historical turning point, I shall take the liberty of quoting Koselleck at some length. Speaking in 1985, he took a much longer perspective than is common in the social sciences, identifying three "exponential time curves" that he sees as converging in the present era. Before returning to the specifics of the European crisis and this book's approach, it may be worthwhile to listen to Koselleck's admittedly pessimistic reflections:

> Considered from the standpoint of today, the previous history of humanity can be represented by three exponential time curves. Measured with

respect to five billion years, the time that it took for the earth to be covered with a solid crust, one billion years of organic life is a short time span. But still much shorter is the time span of ten million years during which there have presumably been humanoid creatures, and only for the past two million years can artificial tools be shown to have been used.

The second exponential time curve can be drawn within the two million years during which humans distinguish themselves by using artificial tools. The first record of genuine art, so to speak, is thirty thousand years ago, the origin of agriculture and the breeding of livestock is around ten thousand years ago. And measured with respect to the two million years of self-productivity, the approximately six thousand years of urban high culture with written communication symbols is a short time span. And philosophy, poetry, and the writing of history have only taken place in an even shorter span.

The third exponential time curve begins to emerge when one proceeds from the organization of state-like high cultures that came into existence only six thousand years ago. Measured with respect to their comparatively continuous history, modern industrial society grounded in science and technology has only unfolded in the last three hundred years. The acceleration curve can be demonstrated by three series of data. The transmission of news has accelerated in a way that has practically led to the temporal convergence of the event and news of it. Transportation has also accelerated tenfold: natural means such as wind, water, and animals have been displaced by technical devices like steam engines, electric motors, and internal combustion engines. The acceleration of the means of communication has made the earth shrink to the size of a spaceship. At the same time, the increase in the population has resulted in an analogous exponential time curve: at about a half billion in the seventeenth century, the population of the world has grown, despite all mass annihilations, to 2.5 billion human beings in the middle of our century, and already approaches eight billion at the end of the twentieth century.

The three exponential time curves might be dismissed as mere number play. However, a limit obviously begins to emerge that can no longer be overstepped by technological and scientific progress. Moreover, there is the fact that in the same exponential time curve, the power for the self- destruction of autonomous humanity has multiplied. (Koselleck 2002/1985: 246–247)

For a historian, Koselleck is surprisingly inaccurate in his periodization. Life began not one billion but four billion years ago, and hominids are not known to have existed for more than 2.8 million years. Moreover, the world population stood at about six billion, not eight, in 1985. But let us consider his argument. Taking a global and admittedly grim view of acceleration and crisis, Koselleck here conceptualizes crisis as a final epoch, the period leading to collapse. This was how he saw his contemporary world. However, another meaning of the concept of crisis that deserves mention is also credible in the current European situation, possibly more so than the apocalyptic vision: namely, that of crisis as a period of transition between two situations. Whether the current era ends with a bang or with a whimper, it need not lead to the *Untergang* of humanity as we know it. One of the oldest known usages of "crisis" occurs in Hippocratic medicine, where crisis, as a medical condition, referred to a high fever with two possible outcomes: you die, or you recover. Lest we be overwhelmed by cultural pessimism, it is worthwhile to keep the latter alternative in mind.

Eight Facets of the Prism

The general focus of this book is on processes of inclusion and exclusion as responses to the contemporary crises of Europe, but it is sharpened through its emphasis on racialization, seen as a way of re-establishing boundaries and reinstating faith in the efficacy of political action at a time when crises and the vicissitudes of global forces have left European politicians humiliated by their obvious powerlessness. Yet the contributors all reveal nuance, tension, friction, and contestation in the countries they write about. No single political ontology guides any of these countries—or Europe as a whole—forward. Each of this book's chapters highlights one facet, or dimension, of the current crisis of identity. Interestingly, there seems to be little concern with the future of *European* identity in these case stories, which all discuss national borders, identities, and persons included therein.

And they do so in different ways. Let us begin with Iceland. Loftsdóttir and Björnsdóttir depict a country in which economic predictability is gone, faith in the elites has been shattered, and the formerly widespread belief in magical capitalism has been lost, at least for the time being. After the collapse of the Icelandic economy, both foreign and domestic commentators pointed out that such a crash was really unexpected for a country "of this kind"—it might have been expected in Africa, but not here. The authors show how Iceland, or rather its political and economic elites, are trying to recreate the island-state as a respectable, European, and not least white country by using feminist arguments and portraying the Icelandic woman as strong and compassionate—the savior of the country and an emblematic symbol of whiteness, given her independence. Yet they also point out how essentialist notions of gender gain currency within massive economic crisis, reflected simultaneously in nationalist discourses in Iceland and wider trends after the financial crisis in Europe in 2008 in which women's natural characteristics were seen as the solutions to the problem of capitalism. By promoting women as natural life savers, the Icelandic elites diverted attention from their own misdoings while simultaneously confirming that the country was attuned to contemporary European sensibilities.

The most striking argument in Cannedy's chapter about Ireland is perhaps one that resonates implicitly throughout the entire collection: she observes that the dichotomy of left and right has largely been lost and replaced with identity politics. She begins with the story of an African immigrant who entered Irish politics and became an elected representative of the nationalist Sinn Féin, and the subsequent discussion shows that much of the disagreement around the legitimacy of the black man's engagement in politics is centered around the notion of "deservingness." As Cannedy says, dominant "discourses tread the well-worn trope of 'true' refugees as poor, helpless individuals who, given their miserable position, should be grateful receivers (rather than demanders) of humanitarian charity," and therefore the right of non-white immigrants to take part in Irish politics and Irish society as a whole is questioned. Nobody likes a free rider, and when the world is on the move, as Bauman once put it, who is or is not a free rider becomes a contested question. When the exclusion of assumed free riders is racialized, the result is, at best, a Brazil-style color-coded hierarchy, and at worst an apartheid-style color bar.

Meanwhile, the Cameron government in neighboring Great Britain for years waved the ideological banner of "fairness," a term that targets presumed free riders and appeals to a mercantilist "common sense," which, as Garner shows, is a recipe for inequality and legitimation thereof. The main thrust of Garner's argument is that the individualization and marketization that are typical of contemporary European politics, but perhaps nowhere as stark as in the UK, drive many of the losers of the fairness ideology rightward, ideologically speaking, so that they end up blaming the victim (immigrants) for the weakening of state welfare. As one of the people quoted in Garner's study says: "Why should we have to be politically correct all the time when they are not, when they get away with it. Why should we?" The instruments in place for ensuring racial equality, it seems, apply for everybody but the white English. This is obviously because the non-whites are being excluded by the whites, not vice versa, but the situation may appear different to an unemployed white working-class Englishman, whose perception needs to be taken seriously. In a word, we need to study converts to UKIP and anti-immigration parties phenomenologically. A main reason why Douglas Holmes's *Integral Europe* (2000) remains a standard reference in theorizing about the rise of the new right, fifteen years after its publication, is arguably that Holmes took the lifeworlds of the new nativists seriously by engaging with them face to face, ethnographically.

The theme of racialized exclusion is developed in another direction in Hipfl's chapter dealing with Austria. Her study consists in a reading of an episode of the longest-running crime series in German television and its branches in the rest of the German-speaking world, namely *Tatort* (Crime Scene). The episode under scrutiny, featuring East European gangsters, prostitutes, and precarious workers (as a Scandinavian familiar with Nordic Noir, I feel pangs of recognition), addresses the porosity of the boundary between inside and outside. Unlike the Congolese-Irish Sinn Féin politician, Eastern Europeans are barely visibly different from Austrians, and they have arrived by bus, train, or car from a nearby country, not by plane from a distant tropical inferno. Yet they are harbingers of chaos, challenging boundaries and bringing filth and disorder to the otherwise sanitary, ordered Austrian society. As Hipfl summarizes the message from the *Tatort* episode, "migrants from Eastern Europe are blamed for bringing crisis into Austria's 'safe haven' by transferring not only themselves but also the problems from their country of origin." There is pressure not only on Europe's external borders, but also on its internal ones.

European countries differ in their relationship to culture, history, and ethnicity. The classic literature on nationalism commonly distinguished between a "German" (ethnocultural) and a "French" (civic, territorial) nationalism, and of the countries considered in this book, the French and the Latvian examples probably epitomize this contrast best. However, as Smith shows, the French notion of culturally neutral *citoyenneté*, open to everyone—for as de Gaulle once said, "La France n'est pas une race; c'est une idée"—is crumbling. Confronted with people who are "matter out of place" in the classic anthropological sense (Douglas 1966)—human rubbish, unproductive, unconsuming, mobile, parasitical—racial politics enters through the back door, as when then President Sarkozy ordered the removal of Roma Gypsy camps. Because race and ethnicity officially do not exist as political entities in France, the country lacks a commonly recognized vocabulary for speaking about racial and ethnic exclusion. In an era of intensified identity politics, this leads to frustration among minorities who demand to be recognized as members of named groups (notably Muslims); conversely, it makes it problematic for the authorities to bar groups from carrying out certain cultural practices, since these groups do not officially exist. The solution was thus to ban the practices without naming the group. Smith's chapter nevertheless points to a more fundamental aspect of post-Paleolithic societies, namely the structural tension between farmers and nomads. In a modern state, not having an address creates problems for the state, just as itinerant herders are a constant threat to settled farmers in African and Asian societies. As Smith puts it: "The regular association of people with specific places and placemaking practices is often key in speaking indirectly about whole populations and placing them in a hierarchical relationship to some normative standard." Is this fundamentally about place or race? Perhaps the question is unimportant. In practice, placelessness is racialized as inferior, filthy, and subversive of the social order, even as it also carries connotations of freedom and mobility. In this way itinerant Roma—stigmatized, excluded, and at the bottom of every European social ladder—may at the same time represent an alternative and a hope for disenchanted Europeans, thereby posing a double threat to the social order.

Dzenovska's two-pronged chapter about Latvia shows complementary dimensions of boundary making. It is about center and periphery, degrees of Europeanness, and ways of producing a proper European identity, and it resonates with Loftsdóttir and Björnsdóttir's chapter about Iceland: the Latvian moral community, as envisioned after independence in 1991, includes only cultural (or ethnic) Latvians, at the expense of the very significant Russian-speaking minority in the country. The latter are asked to be a national minority, which "did not mean becoming Latvian, but rather becoming a subject who understands the importance of a national way of life and strives to be a good national minority subject, that is, someone who cultivates himself or herself as a member of a particular cultural community while recognizing this community's political subordination to Latvians within a national state." This sounds somewhat like the status of the Christian Democratic party of the GDR, which could never even dream of challenging the power of the Communists. However, the majority Latvians not only distance themselves from the "less civilized" Russians but also fail to tolerate the allegedly lackadaisical and irresponsible Greeks, who have proved unable to pay their debts and taxes. If the semantic core of whiteness consists in a Protestant ethic, which seems to be the case in Latvia, then the dual distancing from Russian speakers and Greeks resembles the emphasis on feminism and individuality in Iceland.

While Italy is obviously not a Protestant country, differentiation between kinds of human lives is common there too. However, in the case discussed in Muehlebach's chapter, it is based on physical appearance and origins rather than assumptions about cultural values and practices. The contrast between a campaign for suffering Italian (white) children and campaigns to aid refugees makes the difference between their assumed needs very clear: Italian children have the right to a fulfilling life; black children merely have the right to stay alive. As Muehlebach asks: "What forms of dispossession and injustice do Italians find tolerable when they play themselves out upon black bodies? What becomes intolerable when played out in seemingly more proximate, more recognizable, worthier white lives?" This may be about race, which is certainly how it appears. But it could also, more fundamentally, be about relative wealth. The well-fed person has many desires; the hungry person has only one. In any case, the comparison between white and non-white children in need effectively shows how borders are being maintained. Nationalism and state boundaries overrule universal humanistic values.

The final chapter is not really about a country; instead it addresses the boundary of Europe as such. Sorge's chapter on Lampedusa, "an island defined by its centrality in the flux and flow of movement across the Mediterranean throughout history," concerns a place that, though technically in the same country as Muehlebach's Milan, represents something different, namely the fuzzy zone between Europe and non-Europe. Historically a crossroads, in recent years Lampedusa has been turned into a transit place for refugees dreaming of a brighter future farther north. We may reasonably ask: if Lampedusa is the external boundary of messy Europe, what does it tell us about Europe?

First of all, the cramped refugee situation in Lampedusa is a reminder that the northern and southern coasts of the Mediterranean are separated by huge inequalities in individual opportunities, material welfare, women's autonomy, and institutional accountability. The island is a bottleneck and a liminal zone where affluence meets precarity. Secondly, Lampedusa is a tangible reminder of the diversity within Europe and its main contradictions. Further north, fear, suspicion, and hatred are directed at the refugees and their helpers, but there is also sympathy, solidarity, and a desire to contribute to their well-being. Here an inclusive humanism, in other words, meets nationalism, producing the underlying issue of who the free riders are. The question for the near future is less about what or where Europe is—an issue that has been sidelined—than about a major tension running between nativist nationalism and a more cosmopolitan humanism. The concept of "deservingness" raised in Cannedy's chapter may be the most productive place to continue this exploration. Do people deserve equality merely by having been born on this planet, or do they have to earn it—and if the latter is the case, how does this come about? Are the free riders—those who want to enjoy benefits without paying the cost—refugees on welfare and unemployed Europeans, or are they instead the rich, including those Icelandic bankers?

Whiteness, hierarchy, and segmented citizenship run through this collection. The "savage slot" shifts around. It may move from Africans to Muslims, Sami to Russians, Turks to Roma, but its logic remains the same. In trying to understand and deal with these issues, neither policymakers nor researchers should focus too much on the role of Shakespeare, Christianity, or Beethoven's Ninth in the making of the European identity. A new grammar of European identities is needed, and this book offers some ideas as to how it might look.

References

Douglas. M. 1966. *Purity and Danger.* London: Routledge & Kegan Paul.
Durrenberger, E., and G. Pálsson, eds. 2014. *Gambling Debt: Iceland's Rise and Fall in the Global Economy.* Boulder, CO: University Press of Colorado.
Eriksen, T. 2015. "The Meaning of 'We,'" in *The Challenge of Minority Integration*, ed. P. Kraus and P. Kivisto, 1–21. Berlin: De Gruyter Open.
Furedi, F. 2005. *Politics of Fear: Beyond Left and Right.* London: Continuum.
Holmes, D. 2000. *Integral Europe: Fast-Capitalism, Multiculturalism, Neofascism.* Princeton, NJ: Princeton University Press.
Koselleck, R. 1988/1959. *Critique and Crisis: Enlightenment and the Pathogenesis of Modern Society.* Cambridge: MIT Press.
———. 2002/1985. "Some Questions Regarding the Conceptual History of 'Crisis,'" in *The Practice of Conceptual History: Timing History, Spacing*

Concepts, ed. R. Koselleck, 236–247. Stanford, CA: Stanford University Press.
Loftsdóttir, K., and L. Jensen, eds. 2014. *Crisis in the Nordic Countries and Beyond: At the Intersection of Environment, Finance and Multiculturalism*. Farnham: Ashgate.
Maguire, M., C. Frois, and N. Zurawski, eds. 2014. *The Anthropology of Security: Perspectives from the Frontline of Policing, Counter-Terrorism and Border Control*. London: Pluto.
Mitchell, T. 2011. *Carbon Democracy: Political Power in the Age of Oil*. London: Verso.
Shore, C. 2000. *Building Europe: The Cultural Politics of European Integration*. London: Routledge.
Spengler, O. 1991/1922. *The Decline of the West*. Oxford: Oxford University Press.

Index

ABC Children's Aid International Project, 44
Āboltiņa, Solvita, 61
Abulafia, David, 207
activists on Lampedusa, 200–203, 206, 213–215
adulthood, post-Soviet Latvia, 64–66
Afghanistan, 37, 39
Africa, aid to, 39, 44
African immigrants
asylum seekers, 110
attitudes toward, 89
in Ireland, 102, 110, 226
in politics, 102, 226
stereotypes of, 128, 211
agency, crisis of, 17, 186
agriculture, modernizing, 65
Albahari, M., 209
Algeria, 189, 199, 203
Allarme Infanzia (Childhood Alarm) campaign, 126–141, 127f
Amin, Ash, 45
Amnesty International, 163, 207
Anderson, B., 14, 16
Andrijasevic, R., 158, 159
anger as a response to crisis, 150, 164–165
anthropology, 21–22, 33, 172
Anti-Austerity Alliance, 108
Anti-Crisis (Roitman), 3
Appadurai, A., 22
Appel, H., 43
Arab Spring, 196, 207
Arendt, H., 113, 129

Argentina, 40
Associazione Culturale Askavusa, 200–203, 206, 213–215
asylum seekers. *See also* migrants
application process, 116
benefits, 90, 110–111
deservingness, 11–12, 103–105, 111, 115–121
devaluing, 163
direct provision system, 111–115, 121
discrediting, 116–117
economy and attitudes toward, 109–111
employment, 111
living conditions, 163
post-crisis attitudes toward, 110–111
processing wait-times, 103, 112
protests, 112–115
racialization of, 107, 110
racism against, 106
rights movement, 113–114
threats posed by, 16, 109
Athanasiou, A., 160, 162, 164–165
Auður Capital, 42–45
Auður Day-Work, 44
Auður I, 44
Auður's Universe, 44
aurora movements, 201
Australia, 118, 148–149
Austria
crime fiction, popularity of, 148
elections in, EU component, 5–6

precarity, normalization of, 155, 159–161
refugee crisis in, 163
sex workers in, 156, 157, 159–160
summary overview, 227

Balibar, E., 18–19, 177, 209
Baltica International Folklore Festival, 67
banking industry, 35–36, 42–45, 64
Barker, M., 120
Barth, F., 15
Basic Concepts in History (*Geschichtliche Gundbegriffe*) (Koselleck), 223
Bauman, Z., 17, 154, 161, 162–163, 186
Beck, Ulrich, 71
Benjamin, Walter, 150
Ben-Jelloun, Tahar, 208
Ben-Yehoyada, Naor, 208
Beriss, D., 177
Berlant, Lauren, 159, 165
Berlusconi, Silvio, 209, 210, 214
Besson, Louis, 182
Bhabha, H., 104
birthright citizenship, 103, 109–110, 113
Björnsdóttir, Helga, 16, 21, 31–45, 225, 228
Black and Minority Ethnic (BME) groups
public views on, UK, 88–89
vulnerability position, 95–96
black bodies, 128, 131, 229
blacks self-racialization, 178
Bloch, Ernst, 150
Bohémiens, 180
Boidi, M., 156, 157
Boissevain, Jeremy, 199
border controls, 13, 16, 117–118, 200, 213, 229
Bordoni, C., 17, 154, 162–163, 186
Bourdieu, P., 9
Brandstetter, Wolfgang, 163
Brecht, B., 150
Breivik, Anders Behring, 115

Brexit, 5–6, 8, 117
Broca, Paul, 177
Bromberger, Christian, 207–208
Brown, Gordon, 79, 82
Brunsdon, Charlotte, 151
Buchanan, Ian, 148–149
Buhl, H., 152–153
Bulgaria, 126, 154–162, 174–175
business feminism, transnational, 40, 43–44
Butler, Judith, 160–161, 164–165
Byrne, Liam, 82

Cala Madonna, 202–203, 202f
Cameron, David, 77–82, 90, 92, 94, 96, 226
Camus, Albert, 208
Cannedy, Shay, 11–12, 16, 21, 102–121, 226, 230
capitalism, 65–66
Capussotti, Enrica, 208
Carnet anthropométrique de l'identité, 181–182
Carta di Lampedusa, 200–201
Cassano, Franco, 199, 207
Castells, Manuel, 201
Catholicism, 106–107, 114, 120, 141
Celtic Tiger, 109
Chakrabarty, D., 163
Chartier, D., 40
children
aid to, 44
in poverty, 126–127, 136, 139
children, Italian
Allarme Infanzia (Childhood Alarm) campaign, 126–141, 127f
capacity to futurity, 133–135, 140–142
literacy rates, 132, 134
school completion rates, 126, 132, 136
school enrollment, 134
Chonaill, Áine Ní, 117–118
Christou, A., 8
citizenship
birthright, 103, 109–110, 113, 121n

European norms of, 110
global, 201
rights-based, 128–129, 200
Citizenship Referendum, Ireland, 113, 119–120
class-transformation reality television, 84
Clifford, James, 23
climate crisis, 222
Cold Case (tv series), 153
colonialism and the colonized
after-effects, 2, 7–10
Austria, 156
Europeanness and, 4
Iceland, 32–36, 39–40
Ireland, 104–105, 107, 119–120
color-blind policies of the state, 178
Colpani, G., 2
Commission for Racial Equality, 91
community
cultural, 57–59
moral, 57, 61–62, 228
community of rules, 69–70
compassion
collective, tv producing a, 158–159
distribution of, 54
economies of, 11, 128, 135, 165–166
reaction, 7
Connell, R., 44
Constant, Fred, 177
Corbyn, Jeremy, 95
corporate welfare, 87
cosmopolitanism, 104, 199–202
credit culture, 63–67
crime drama, televised. *See also Tatort* (tv series)
crisis, addressing and working through, 151
function of, 151
lived experience, focus on, 150–151
popularity of, 148, 150
crime fiction
affective work of, 149–150
function of, 149
pedagogical function, 149
popularity of, 148
relevance, political and cultural, 153
Scandinavian, 148

state of the nation revealed, 150
structure of feeling, 22
structures of feeling, 151, 153–154, 155, 159
crime fiction, crisis in. *See also* crisis
addressing and working through, 151
anger as a response, 150, 164–165
ethical approach, responsiveness, 164–165
expression and containment of, 150–151
gendering, 150, 158
othering and racialization of, 150, 158, 161, 165
of the police, 150, 154, 157–158, 161–164
of precarity, 150, 155, 159–161, 166
of the state/state of crisis, 149–150, 154, 161–164
of territorial sovereignty, 162–163
crisis. *See also* crime fiction, crisis in
apocalyptic vision of, 225
concept, 3–5
defined, 225
future of, 22–23
gendered embodiment of, 11
nation-states and, 17–22
race and, 2
of the state/state of crisis, 17, 171–172, 186
as structure of feeling, 22–23
term usage, 3, 225
whiteness and, 2, 12
crisis Europe, 3–7
crisis talk, 2–10, 13, 15, 17, 22–23, 179, 187
Critique and Crisis (Koselleck), 223
CSI (tv series), 152, 153

dall'Acqua, Loris, 137
D'Ancona, M., 80
Daumas, Alain, 176
debt, morality and, 56–57, 59–63, 66–67, 69
Debt: The First 5,000 Years (Graeber), 67

The Decline of the West (Der Untergang des Abendlandes) (Spengler), 220
Deegan, Sean, 116
Deleuze, G., 149
Denmark, 6, 32, 34–35, 39
Derflinger, Sabine, 154
deservingness
  asylum seekers, 11–12, 103–105, 111, 115–121
  fairness vs., 83–84, 90–91, 95–96
  question of, 226, 230
Desmond, M., 8
Dick, Hilary, 183–184
difference, construction of, 171–172, 177–179, 188–189
Digby, Kenelm, 202
direct provision system, 111–112, 121
dispossession, 164–165
Dombrovskis, Valdis, 59–60
Domínguez, Virginia, 185
The Door of Europe (La porta dell'Europa) (Paladino), 205
Douglas, Mary, 3
Dutch East Indies, 12
Dzenovska, Dace, 16, 21, 53–71, 228

economy
  asylum seekers as threat, 118–119
  emotional, 93
  England, post-crisis, 85–86
  gender and the, in Iceland, 37–45
  Iceland, 35–42
  the material, 82, 84, 86–87
  the moral, 54, 56–57, 77–78, 86–87, 95–96, 128
Eder, K., 15
educational poverty, 139
electronics shops, 63–64
Emirbayer, M., 8
emotional economy, 93
employment
  benefits spending, 84–86, 94
  crises of, 221
  moral dimension, 95
  precarity, 85, 88
  precarization of, 161
  youth, 126, 221

endurance self-narrative, 55–56, 58, 61–63, 71
England. *See also* Great Britain
  corporate welfare, 87
  economy, post-crisis, 85–86
  equality agenda, 12, 78, 87–92
  food banks, 85–86
  government, outsourcing and privatization of, 94
  migrants, public views on, 87–92
  moral economy, 77–78
  subsidy spending, 86–87, 93
  summary overview, 226–227
  taxpayer burden, 94
  welfare benefits spending, 84–86, 95
  white identities, racialization of, 77–78
England, fairness agenda
  austerity and the, 78, 87–92, 95–96
  class focus in the, 96
  equality agenda as the opposite of, 12, 78, 87–92
  momentum of the, 94
  othering in the, 95–96
  as policy, 77–78, 80–84, 86
  social and moral mission of, 96
Enlightenment, 32
entitlement, 77–79, 84, 89, 91, 95
Enza Empowering Women, 44
Epstein, Beth, 172, 177
equality agenda, 12, 78, 87–92
Equality and Human Rights Commission, 91
Eriksen, T., 14–16, 220–230
Escobar, Arturo, 2
Essed, P., 9
essentialism, 37–45
European Court of Human Rights (ECHR), 80
Europeanness
  ambiguity of, 15–16
  colonial formulations of, 10
  constructing, 15
  in context of the financial crisis, 54–56
  contours of, 55–57
  Greece, 54–55
  Iceland, 31–32, 40

Ireland, 120
Lampedusa, 208–213
Latvia, 47–48, 55–56, 70–71
moralized economic conduct in, 54
European Union
  asylum and migration policy, 206, 213
  border policy, 215
  citizenship regulations, 110
  crises in, multiplicity of, 5–6, 220–223
  expansion fears, 158
  law and population movements, 1, 171, 175
  migration/refugee crisis, 47–48
  nation-states and, 13–17
  new racism in, 120
  refugee crisis, 141–142, 222–223
  rules, abiding by, 69–70
Europism, 171
Eurozone crisis, 3, 5, 220–221
Every One campaign, 131–132, 132f

Facebook, 102–103
fairness
  deservingness and, 83–84, 90–91, 95–96
  moral obligation in, 93–94
  respectability component, 93
fairness agenda, England
  austerity and the, 78, 87–92, 95–96
  class focus in the, 96
  equality agenda as the opposite of, 12, 78, 87–92
  momentum of the, 94
  othering in the, 95–96
  as policy, 77–78, 80–84, 86
  social and moral mission of, 96
Fallaci, Oriana, 209
Fanon, Franz, 135
feeling, structures of, 22–23, 151, 153–154, 155, 159
Fehervary, Krisztina, 64
Filhol, E., 180–181
finance capitalism, 56, 65, 67
financial crisis. *See also specific countries*
  components of, 1–2

crisis narratives, 5
  global, 40, 108, 220–221
  opportunity and, 2
financial industry, women in the, 42–45
Finland, 221
food banks, 85–86
France
  anti-crime initiative, 171
  anti-racist movements, 172
  Carnet anthropométrique de l'identité, 181–182
  citizens of foreign origin, 174
  difference, construction of, 171–172, 177–179, 188–189
  discrimination in, 178
  economic crisis in, 173
  elections in, EU component, 5
  Gens du voyage in, 11, 173–174, 176, 178–179, 182–188
  livret de circulation requirement, 182, 187
  nomadic populations, regulating, 179–183
  racialization and race talk in, 176–179, 183–188
  republican universalism, 176–179, 186
  Roma, expulsion of, 11, 171, 174–176, 178–179, 186–188
  summary overview, 227–228
  titre de circulation requirement, 187
  traveling groups, regulation of, 179–181
  voluntary return program, 175
  war on crime, 173–174
Franzese, Raffaele, 137
freedom, 130–131
French High Authority against Discrimination and for Equality, 178
Front National, 221
Fuchs, C., 20
Furedi, Frank, 222

Gansel, C., 153
Garner, Steve, 11–13, 21, 77–96, 109, 115, 226

Gast, W., 153
gender ideologies, 31, 37–39, 45. See *also* women
De Genova, N., 200
Gens du voyage, 11, 173–174, 176, 178–179, 182–188
German Europe, 71
Germany
   crime fiction, popularity of, 148
   Europeanness, 54
   immigrant assimilation, 155–156
Gísladóttir, Ingibjörg Sólrún, 37
globalization, 18
Graeber, David, 67
Graham-Harrison, E., 141
Gramsci, A., 140
Great Britain. *See also* England
   anti-EU discourse, 5, 80–81
   Brexit vote, 5–6, 8, 117
   crime-based fiction in, 151
   financial crisis and the State, 79
   mugging, moral panic around, 20
   welfare reform, 81–83, 95
Great Departure, 62
Greece
   child poverty, 126
   Europeanness, 54–55
   sovereign debt crisis, 54–55, 67–69
Greek people
   characterizations of, 10
   Latvians understanding of the, 54–55, 67–69, 71
   letter from Ireland to, 108
Grosfoguel, R., 8
Guðmundsdóttir, Björk, 44
Guðmundsson, Einar Már, 44
Guillén, A., 19
Guyer, Jane, 132–133
Gypsies, 174–176, 178–181

Haarde, Geir, 42
Halawa, Mateusz, 64
Hall, Stuart, 1, 7, 20
Hill, Jane, 183–184
Hills, J., 84
Hipfl, Brigitte, 10, 11, 21, 22, 24, 148–166, 227

Hirsch, P., 152
Hollande, François, 187
Holmes, D., 7, 227
home ownership, 64, 180–181
Hortefoux, Brice, 178–179
housing
   asylum seekers, 111–112
   child refugees, 142
housing boom, 65, 108
humanitarian crisis, 129, 136, 141
humanitarianism
   deservingness and, 12–13
   racial impetus, 128–129
   racialization of, 135–136
   racial logic, 128, 130
   right-to-life ethic, 129, 131–132
   victimization discourse, 165
humanitarian reason, 127–130, 134
humanity, hierarchies of, 12, 129–131
Human Rights Act, 80–81, 175, 207
human trafficking, 154–159

Iceland
   Auður Capital, 42–45
   colonial-racism intersection, 32–33
   economic boom in, 35–38
   economic crash, 31, 39–42
   European identity, 31–32, 40
   gender, historical ideas of, 34–35
   gender ideologies, 31, 37–39, 45
   immigration to, 36–37
   imperialistic history, 32
   national identity in, 22, 34–35
   summary overview, 225–226
   whiteness in, 33–34, 105
   women in, 16, 31, 34, 37–45
Icelandic Chamber of Commerce, 42
Icelandic Peacekeeping Unit (ICRU), 37, 39
Iceland Ministry for Foreign Affairs, 37–38
identity
   crisis of, 221–223
   racial, 9
   racialized, 54
   social, 185
   whiteness and, 9, 103–107, 120

identity, national
  gender in, 22, 34–35
  whiteness and, 9, 103–105, 107, 120
Identity Ireland, 108, 115, 118
Imagined Communities (Anderson), 14
immigrants
  assimilation, 37, 155–156
  public views on, UK, 87–92
  stereotypes of, 128
Immigration Control Platform (ICP), 117–118
immigration quotas, 200
Inda, Jonathan Xavier, 209
indebted man, 56–57
infant mortality, 131
Integral Europe (Holmes), 227
International Monetary Fund (IMF), 40, 59
International Protection Act, 112
Ireland
  asylum system reforms, 117
  birthright citizenship, 103, 109–110, 113
  citizenship referendum, 113, 120
  colonization history, 104–107, 118
  economic boom in, 107–110
  Europeanness, 120
  migrants in, attitudes toward, 103, 109–111, 119
  outmigration, 108
  racism in, 102–103, 106–107
  summary overview, 226
  whiteness in national identity, 103–105, 107, 120
Ireland, asylum seekers in
  deservingness, 11–12, 103–105, 111, 115–121
  determination process, 112
  direct provision system, 111–115
  discrediting, 116–117
  economy and attitudes toward, 103, 109–111, 119
  protests, 112–115
  reception system, 111–112
Ireland, financial crisis
  austerity measures, 108
  blame assigned for, 110–111

exclusionary notions of belonging post-, 103–104
Italy
  Allarme Infanzia (Childhood Alarm) campaign, 126–141, 127*f*
  austerity measures, 126–127, 131, 138
  literacy rates, 132, 134
  North-South divide, 140–141, 208
  poverty in, 138–141
  refugee crisis in, 141–142
  rights-based citizenship, 128
  school completion rates, 126, 132
  Southern, 139–141
  summary overview, 229
  Support for Active Inclusion, 141
  welfare crisis, 134
Italy, children in
  capacity to futurity, 133–135, 140, 142
  education for, 126, 132, 134, 136, 212
  Every One campaign, 131–132, 132*f*
  in poverty, 126–127, 136
Ītis, Aigars, 61

Jabès, Edmond, 208
Jakubowicz, Alain, 176
Jansen, Stef, 61
Jensen, T., 81–82
Johannès, Franck, 179
Journey of a Voyage into the Mediterranean (Digby), 202

Knight, Daniel, 10
Koselleck, Reinhart, 3–4, 223–225
Krakauer, Siegfried, 150
Kristmundsdóttir, S., 41
Kuļikovskis, Gundars, 69

labels, 185–188, 211–212
labor markets, Iceland, 36–37
labor migrants, attitudes toward, 109–110
Lampedusa
  activists on, 200–203, 206, 213–215
  changing place of, 214–215

cosmopolitan category of people on, 199–200
Europeanness, 208–213
fishing economy, 198–199
history of, 198–199, 202–203, 208
migration film festival, 205–207
nativism, 203
Porto M museum, 203–205, 204*f*
refugee crisis in, 196–197
summary overview, 229–230
tourist industry, 197–199, 203, 205, 209, 211–212, 214
Lampedusa, migrants in
blocking, 212
deaths, 213
economics of, 210
hostility toward, 203–205, 210–212, 214
local humanitarian efforts, 210
processing center riots, 212
racialization of, 211–212
refugee detention centers, 142
shipwrecks, 213
violence against, 212
LampedusaInFestival, 205–207
language, ethnicizing, 8, 172, 176, 178–179, 185, 189, 221
Latvia
credit culture, 63–67
Europeanness, 47–48, 55–56, 70–71
financial crisis, 54, 59–63, 66
household electronics shops, 63–64
morality-nationhood intersection, post-Soviet, 57–59
outmigration, 61–62, 66
summary overview, 228–229
Latvians
endurance self-narrative, 55–56, 58, 61–63, 71
serf mentality, 70–71
understanding of the Greek people, 54–55, 67–69, 71
Lazzarato, Maurizio, 56
Lee, S., 148
Lega Nord, 139
legitimacy, crisis of, 222
Lentin, R., 106, 107
Lévêque, Stéphane, 176

Libya, 196, 199, 203
life
right to, 129, 131–132
worth living, 128–130
Lindholm, Charles, 201
Lisbon Treaty, 121n4
literacy rates, Italy, 132, 134
Lithuania, 69–70
livret de circulation, 182, 187
Loftsdóttir, Kristín, 4, 16, 21, 23–24, 31–45, 225, 228
Lorde, Audre, 164
Lorey, Isabel, 160–161

Maastricht Treaty, 222
Macaluso, Marco, 136
Mahfouz, Naguib, 208
Malkki, Liisa, 117
Manouches, 180–181
market economy, post-Soviet Latvia, 65–66
Massey, D., 7
May, Theresa, 89, 91
McVeigh, R., 106, 107
Memmi, Albert, 107, 208
mental health, asylum seekers, 112, 113
Mercille, J., 108
Michel, Antoine, 205
middle class, 65–66
Mignolo, Walter, 207
migrant crisis, 163
migrants. *See also* asylum seekers; *specific countries*
characterizations of, 159
civilizational status, 158
clandestine, 196–197
labeling of, 211–212
post-crisis attitudes toward, 110–111, 119
public views, English, 87–92
Russian-speaking Latvian residents, 58–59
sex workers, female, 154–161
stereotypical gendered images of, 165–166
threats posed by, 58–59, 105, 116–120, 156–158, 165–166, 210

vulnerability position, 95–96
  as workforce, 36–37
migration
  border controls, 13, 16, 117–118, 213
  Porto M museum of, 203–205, 204f
migration film festival, 205–207
Milano, Raffela, 137
Modan, Gabriella, 21, 184
modernity
  crime fiction and, 150
  European, 119–120
Monaghan, L., 110
morality
  economics intersection with, 54, 56–57, 59–63, 66–67, 69, 77–78, 86–87, 95–96, 128
  of fairness, 93–94
  nationhood's intersection with, 57–59
moral threat, asylum seekers as, 118–119
Moran, A., 109
Moretti, Valter, 135–136
Muehlebach, A., 10–11, 12, 21, 126–142, 229

nationalism, 8, 14, 57–59
nativism, 203
neoliberalism, 18–20, 57–59, 162, 164–165, 173
Neri, Valerio, 134
Netherlands, 5
Neville, Ted, 116
Newcomb, H., 152
Nicita, Giovanni, 137
Noiriel, Gérard, 177
nomadic populations, 174–176, 178–185
Nordic countries. *See specific countries*
Norway, 6, 34

O'Doherty, I., 116, 118
O'Flynn, M., 110
Ohana, David, 208
Omi, M., 79
Osborne, George, 80, 82, 85
Oso, L., 8

other
  the internal, 12, 106–107
  the migrant, crisis imported by, 154–159
  precariousness ascribed to the, 161
  stereotypical gendered representations of, 157
  the undeserving, 95
othering
  of crisis, 154–159, 161
  emotional, 94
  fairness project and, 96
  in the fight for fairness, 91–92
  stereotyping and, 154

Paladino, Mimmo, 205
Pandey, G., 35
patriarchal oppression and domination, migrant, 156–157
Peacock, S., 148
Pétursdóttir, Kristín, 42–45
Poe, Edgar Allan, 150
Poland, 158
Policing the Crisis (Hall et al.), 20
political correctness, 78, 89
Ponzanesi, S., 2
Pots and Pans protest, 39–40, 41
poverty
  behavior and, 83–84
  children in, 126–127, 136, 139
  cultural, 139
  economic, 139
  educational, 139
  fairness and, 83–84
  in Italy, 126–127, 136, 138–141
  racialized political geography of, 138–141
poverty porn, 81, 84, 94, 95
Power, M., 110
precarity, 150, 155, 159–161, 205, 215
Pribram, D., 153
Progress Party, 221
prostitution, 154–161

Quentin, Didier, 188
Quijano, A., 10

Race Relations (Amendment) Act, 91

race talk, 171, 176–179, 183–188
racialization
　of asylum seekers, 110
　of bodies, border controls and, 13
　covert, 11, 172, 184, 188
　of deservingness, 11
　of fairness, 88–92
　of humanitarianism, 135–136, 138–141
　of poverty, 138–141
　and race talk in France, 176–179, 183–188
　of whiteness, 9, 12–13, 77–78
racial politics of humanitarian reason, 128
racism
　cultural, 8, 158
　defined, 8
　in Ireland, 102–103, 106–107
　nationalism and, 8
　refugee crisis and, 7–8, 106
Reding, Viviane, 175
refugee crisis, 3, 53–54, 69, 141–142, 196, 212–213, 222–223
refugee crisis talk, 7
refugees
　anti-immigrant discourse, 7–8
　burden sharing scheme, 120–121
　deservingness, 103, 107
　detention centers, 141–142
　discrediting, 116–118
　genuine, 116–117
Reiris Jānis, 54, 68
Renzi, Matteo, 142
republican universalism, 176–179
responsibility, personal, 164–165
responsibilization, 164
Rice, J., 37
rights
　deservingness vs., 104
　of the stateless, 113
right-to-life ethic, 129, 131–132
Rimšēvics, Ilmārs, 69
risk, 3
Robert, A., 40, 43
Roitman, J., 3–6, 17
Rolston, B., 107

Roma, expulsion of, 11, 174–176, 178–179, 186–188
Romania, 156, 158, 174–175
Romanichels, 180–181
De Rubeis, Bernardino, 206, 211

Sabin, R., 153
sacrifice, collective, 94
Sarkozy, Nicolas, 17, 19, 97n5, 171–176, 178–179, 183, 186–187, 189, 228
Save the Children
　Allarme Infanzia (Childhood Alarm) campaign, 126–141, 127f
　Every One campaign, 131–132, 132f
Scammell, R., 141
scapegoats, 6–8, 20, 110, 118
Schengen agreement, 5, 6, 13–14, 222
Schengen Area, 36
school drop outs, 126, 132
Schulz, Martin, 213
security, crisis of, 221–222
Semprún, Jorge, 208
serf mentality, 70–71
Skeggs, B., 84
slavery, 130–131, 157–158
Šlesers, Ainārs, 65
Slovakia, 158
Smith, Andrea L., 11, 17, 20, 21, 24, 171–189, 227–228
socialism, Soviet, 57–58
social labeling theory, 185–188
Sorge, Antonio, 16, 21, 196–215, 229
South Africa, 44
sovereignty, crisis of, 17
Soviet Union in Latvia, 57–60, 63–65, 67, 70–71
Spengler, Oswald, 220
Spivak, G., 39
Sprūds, Andris, 69
State
　crisis and the, 17–22
　defined, 79
　EU and the, 13–17
stateless, rights of the, 113
State of Crisis (Bauman & Bordoni), 17, 186

Stewart, M., 188
Stoler, A. L., 32
subsidy spending, 86–87, 93
survivalism, 131–132
Sverrisdóttir, Valgerður, 37
Sweden, 32, 54
Switzerland, 6
Syrians, 120–121, 141, 163, 188

Tatort (tv series)
  cultural significance, 152
  educational intent, 152–154
  gendered embodiment of crisis, 11
  success of, 152
  summary overview, 227
Tatort (tv series), *Angezählt* episode
  crisis of police, 154, 157–158, 161–164
  crisis of precarity, 155, 159–161
  crisis of state, elucidating a, 154
  episode, 154–166
  human trafficking in prostitution, 154–159
  migrants, stereotypical gendered images of, 165–166
  othering and racialization of crisis, 161, 165
  patriarchal oppression and domination, migrant, 156–157
  the state in crisis, 161–164
  women, violence against, 154–155, 157
taxpayer burden, 94
television, class-transformation shows, 84
terrorist attacks, 221
Thailand, 40
threshold, 129
Ticktin, Miriam, 130
time curves, 223–224
tolerability, 128–129
Tómasdóttir, Halla, 42–45
trafficking, human, 17, 154–158, 165
Trienekens, S., 9
Tsiganes (Travellers), 179, 180–181
Tunisia, 196, 199, 203, 205

Ukraine, 213

UNICEF catalogue, 131
United Nations Entity for Gender Equality (UNIFEM), 38
United Nations International Children's Emergency Fund (UNICEF), 38
UN Security Council, 37–39

Vaidere, Inese, 69
Vincent, Elise, 182
voluntary return program, 175

Wacquant, L., 9
Webster, David, 86
welfare benefits spending, 84–86, 95
welfare reform, 81–83
White, Elisa, 120
White by Definition (Domínguez), 185
whiteness
  crisis intersection, 12
  helping role of, 32
  in Iceland, 33–34, 105
  Irish, 107
  national identity and, 9, 103–107, 120
  power of, 33
  racial geographies intersection, 33
  racialization of, 9, 12–13, 77–78
  researcher positionality and, 9, 33, 105, 172, 198
  shifting dynamics of, 16
  WASP identity and, 106
Wijers, Marjan, 157
Willen, Sarah, 104
Williams, Raymond, 22, 149–151, 153
Winant, H., 79
The Wire (tv series), 153
Wise Viking's Daughters, 43
Woman's Alliance, 41
women
  in banking and finance, 42–45
  and crisis, 11
  in Iceland, 16, 31, 34, 37–45
  Third World, 39
  trafficking in prostitution, 154–159
  violence against, 154–155, 157
Wood, H., 84

Wood, J., 44

Yanukovych, Viktor, 213
youth unemployment, 126, 221

Žižek, Slavoj, 7, 68–69
Zuquete, José, 201

EASA Series

Published in Association with the European Association of Social Anthropologists (EASA). Series Editor: Aleksandar Bošković, University of Belgrade

Social anthropology in Europe is growing, and the variety of work being done is expanding. This series is intended to present the best of the work produced by members of the EASA, both in monographs and in edited collections. The studies in this series describe societies, processes and institutions around the world and are intended for both scholarly and student readership.

1. LEARNING FIELDS, Vol. 1
Educational Histories of European Social Anthropology
Edited by Dorle Dracklé, Iain R. Edgar and Thomas K. Schippers

2. LEARNING FIELDS, Vol. 2
Current Policies and Practices in European Social Anthropology Education
Edited by Dorle Dracklé and Iain R. Edgar

3. GRAMMARS OF IDENTITY/ ALTERITY
A Structural Approach
Edited by Gerd Baumann and Andre Gingrich

4. MULTIPLE MEDICAL REALITIES
Patients and Healers in Biomedical, Alternative and Traditional Medicine
Edited by Helle Johannessen and Imre Lázár

5. FRACTURING RESEMBLANCES
Identity and Mimetic Conflict in Melanesia and the West
Simon Harrison

6. SKILLED VISIONS
Between Apprenticeship and Standards
Edited by Cristina Grasseni

7. GOING FIRST CLASS?
New Approaches to Privileged Travel and Movement
Edited by Vered Amit

8. EXPLORING REGIMES OF DISCIPLINE
The Dynamics of Restraint
Edited by Noel Dyck

9. KNOWING HOW TO KNOW
Fieldwork and the Ethnographic Present
Edited by Narmala Halstead, Eric Hirsch and Judith Okely

10. POSTSOCIALIST EUROPE
Anthropological Perspectives from Home
Edited by László Kürti and Peter Skalník

11. ETHNOGRAPHIC PRACTICE IN THE PRESENT
Edited by Marit Melhuus, Jon P. Mitchell and Helena Wulff

12. CULTURE WARS
Context, Models and Anthropologists' Accounts
Edited by Deborah James, Evelyn Plaice and Christina Toren

13. POWER AND MAGIC IN ITALY
Thomas Hauschild

14. POLICY WORLDS
Anthropology and the Analysis of Contemporary Power
Edited by Cris Shore, Susan Wright and Davide Però

15. HEADLINES OF NATION, SUBTEXTS OF CLASS
Working Class Populism and the Return of the Repressed in Neoliberal Europe
Edited by Don Kalb and Gábor Halmai

16. ENCOUNTERS OF BODY AND SOUL IN CONTEMPORARY RELIGIOUS PRACTICES
Anthropological Reflections
Edited by Anna Fedele and Ruy Llera Blanes

17. CARING FOR THE 'HOLY LAND'
Filipina Domestic Workers in Israel
Claudia Liebelt

18. ORDINARY LIVES AND GRAND SCHEMES
An Anthropology of Everyday Religion
Edited by Samuli Schielke and Liza Debevec

19. LANDSCAPES BEYOND LAND
Routes, Aesthetics, Narratives
Edited by Arnar Árnason, Nicolas Ellison, Jo Vergunst and Andrew Whitehouse

20. CYBERIDENTITIES AT WAR
The Moluccan Conflict on the Internet
Birgit Bräuchler

21. FAMILY UPHEAVAL
Generation, Mobility and Relatedness among Pakistani Migrants in Denmark
Mikkel Rytter

22. PERIPHERAL VISION
Politics, Technology, and Surveillance
Catarina Frois

23. BEING HUMAN, BEING MIGRANT
Senses of Self and Well-Being
Edited by Anne Sigfrid Grønseth

24. BEING A STATE AND STATES OF BEING IN HIGHLAND GEORGIA
Florian Mühlfried

25. FLEXIBLE CAPITALISM
Exchange and Ambiguity at Work
Edited by Jens Kjaerulff

26. CONTEMPORARY PAGAN AND NATIVE FAITH MOVEMENTS IN EUROPE
Colonialist and Nationalist Impulses
Edited by Kathryn Rountree

27. FIGURATION WORK
Student Participation, Democracy and University Reform in a Global Knowledge Economy
Gritt B. Nielsen

28. WORLD HERITAGE ON THE GROUND
Ethnographic Perspectives
Edited by Christoph Brumann and David Berliner

29. MOVING PLACES
Relations, Return, and Belonging
Edited by Nataša Gregorič Bon and Jaka Repič

30. THE GOOD HOLIDAY
Development, Tourism and the Politics of Benevolence in Mozambique
João Afonso Baptista

31. MANAGING AMBIGUITY
How Clientelism, Citizenship, and Power Shape Personhood in Bosnia and Herzegovina
Čarna Brković

32. MESSY EUROPE
Crisis, Race, and Nation-State in a Postcolonial World
Edited by Kristín Loftsdóttir, Andrea L. Smith, and Brigitte Hipfl

CPSIA information can be obtained
at www.ICGtesting.com
Printed in the USA
LVHW060731190921
698083LV00004BA/127